Ada

A Programmer's Guide with Microcomputer Examples

James Stanley
Donald Krantz
John Fung
Dr. Paul Stachour

Addison-Wesley Publishing Company, Inc.

Reading, Massachusetts   Menlo Park, California
Don Mills, Ontario   Wokingham, England   Amsterdam
Sydney   Singapore   Tokyo   Mexico City   Bogotá
Santiago   San Juan

Library of Congress Cataloging-in-Publication Data

Stanley, James.
    Ada, a programmer's guide with microcomputer examples.

    Includes index.
    1. Ada (Computer program language) 2. Microcomputers—Programming. I. Title.
QA76.73.A35S83   1985   005.13'3   85-15006
ISBN 0-201-16416-7

Cover design by Marshall Henrichs
Set in 10 pt. Garamond by Ampersand Publisher Services, Inc., Rutland, VT

ABCDEFGHIJ-HA-898765
First printing, October 1985

Contents

Preface

This book is designed to help you start programming in the Ada language. To get the most out of it you should know something (not necessarily very much) about programming. Some work with BASIC is a reasonable foundation; a background in a compiled language such as FORTRAN or COBOL is even better. If you are familiar with C, PL/I, or (especially) Pascal, you are halfway there because the syntax and general design of these three languages are similar to Ada's.

Though you can get to know your way around the Ada programming language by reading this book, direct access to a computer is important if you want to learn to actually write programs.

We have designed this book to help you work not only with "full" Ada compilers, which are just beginning to emerge for microcomputers, but with subset compilers, which have been around for a while and have become quite economical (one of the best currently comes in a version for less than $100). A good Ada subset can serve not only as an excellent learning tool but as a very decent single-user program development system.

Microcomputer systems that will support at least an Ada subset range from an Apple II under CP/M to an IBM-PC or compatible machine (ideally with a hard disk) running PC/MS-DOS or CP/M-86.[1]

We provide some notes on how specific Ada compilers operate in specific microcomputer environments, but it is not our intent to provide complete operating instructions. For that you will have to refer to manuals and books specific to your computer system.

We recommend that you actually key the sample programs (or your own variations of them) into your system, compile them, and store the source code. As the chapters progress, you will revise these early programs and use them as building blocks for larger programs. They can even serve as the start of a library of routines you can draw on for future programs, whether you construct them on your microcomputer or on a larger system. This sort of modularity is one of the goals of Ada design.

This book is structured to introduce a subset of Ada features generally available on microcomputers first and then move on to the more advanced features later. If terms such as "exception handling", "multitasking", "generics", "private types", "overloading", and "discriminants" mean nothing to you, don't despair. You probably will discover in this book and its examples that you already have seen many of these concepts in a more restricted context in your previous work with a computer language.

Chapter 1 covers the history and general features of Ada. A simple example program is given to provide a comparison between Ada and other microcomputer languages.

Chapters 2 and 3 cover basic syntax. There is some hard slogging here, especially in Chapter 2, and you might want to skip over some material that we included mainly for reference purposes. You can always flip back to it later. At the end of Chapter 3 we introduce you to a short program you can key in and compile. This program, which counts characters from the input stream, is worth trying because we will build on it for the next several chapters, expanding it to count words, and finally to work on a text file from disk and to give a word frequency count.

Chapter 4 covers statements and control structures. These are basic stuff, no major new concepts—although you will find that Ada incorporates some very elegant control structures that are the result of computer language research conducted in the 1970s.

Chapter 5 introduces Ada's essential program units—subprograms (which are similar to Pascal's) and packages. Here we're really moving into high country: separate compilation and user-created library packages. Data modularization and encapsulation are among the most important features of Ada.

In Chapter 6 we are back in the lowlands again, doing some necessary drudgery with I/O and exceptions.

Chapter 7 describes composite data types—arrays and records. Chapter 8 introduces real numbers and access types, Ada's brand of pointers. By the end of Chapter 8 we will have gone over all basic terrain of the language—that is, the portions of it more or less familiar to programmers who have worked with C or Pascal.

In Chapter 9 we introduce a useful example of an Ada package: a set of data types and routines that provide us with variable-length strings. Ada, like Pascal and C, has an intrinsic string which is an array. The addition of variable-length strings is typical of the way the language will be extended in a standardized fashion.

Chapter 10 brings us to the first of two major innovations in Ada: generic units. Generic units, along with packages, will enable the development of reusable—and salable—software components, off-the-shelf parts for programs.

Chapter 11 covers Ada's implementation dependencies, particularly in relation to microcomputers. Chapter 12 discusses what might be considered good Ada programming style as applied to subsets and microcomputers.

In Chapter 13 we cover multitasking, a feature of the language not interdependent with all the others, and generally one of the last to be implemented before an Ada subset becomes Ada itself.

Chapter 14 presents several topics slightly beyond the scope of a book meant for microcomputer users, at least for the moment. In this chapter we also provide some suggestions for further reading.

Finally, the appendices are meant to provide enough reference material to make this book self-sufficient. We do recommend, however, that you buy the Ada Language Reference Manual described in some detail at the end of Chapter 14.

If you are an experienced programmer you might find it convenient to work through this book by using the contents page. You will be able to pick out material that will let you work you way into the subject more quickly, depending on your previous experience. The goal, of course, is to begin keying in and compiling programs as soon as possible. There is a certain amount of necessary groundwork one must have covered, however. If you are a fairly experienced programmer, or know Pascal pretty well, you can read about data literals, types, and objects in Chapters 2 and 3, then go to the end of Chapter 3 and try out the little program that counts characters from the input stream. Doing so will get your feet in the water; you can proceed from there as you see fit.

Reading this book will not make you an Ada expert. As with any language, natural or programming, only practice and familiarity with the usage of those who are already "fluent" will do that. Good Ada programming style needs to be learned as well. Some concepts will come more easily than others depending on your previous experience. But the time you spend learning the concepts presented here will put you on the path to a good knowledge of what has been called the programming language of the future.

Acknowledgments

The authors are grateful to a number of people who took a special interest in the development of this book, helping in one way or another.

First of all, Randy Burkardt at R.R. Software and Steve Hagler at SuperSoft supplied the compilers and support necessary to develop the example programs, which in the end shaped the book. Bruce Sherman at Telesoft provided a manual for their IBM-PC XT system, under development at the time of writing.

Chase Allen devoted considerable time in the early planning phases, offering insights that only could have been provided by someone practiced not only in various standard mainframe and micro programming languages, but also in some pre-Ada tasking languages such as Jovial.

Bill McTeer not only gave pertinent advice but helped with some revisions which improved the book.

Glen Good provided some suggestions from the point of view of an Ada professional who is also at home with microcomputers.

Finally, no project like this could ever have gotten far without the professional interest and guidance of a fine publisher. At Addison-Wesley, Mark Dalton responded initially to the idea of a microcomputer Ada book, Steve Stansel sponsored it and saw it through the editorial process, and Si Goodwin made sure that it actually got into print.

1
Introduction to Ada

This chapter provides the background of Ada—where it came from, as well as where we think it's going. We include a general list of the features of the language and a simple Ada program that we compare with equivalent programs written in BASIC and in C. These comparisons help describe in general how Ada will work on your microcomputer.

History of Ada

Once upon a time (in 1974 to be exact) the United States Department of Defense (DoD) noticed that nearly 80 percent of the high costs of its computer systems involved software, not hardware. Moreover, more than half of these software costs related to the development and maintenance of embedded computer systems—that is, real-time computer systems controlling planes, ships, reactors, guided missiles, and the like. The reason for these costs were not hard to uncover.

Embedded systems need fast, compact programs. These programs were being written in assembly language or languages developed specifically for a project; therefore, they generally were not transportable. It seemed that the "wheel" was being continuously reprogrammed for embedded systems—at enormous expense.

Embedded computer programs are complex. This complexity is caused partly by the need for fail-safe error handling. For example, when a jet is coming in for a landing it is not acceptable for its computer to shut down because of arithmetic underflow. This complexity also is partly caused by the need for several real-time processes to be handled at once. For example, telephone system connections must continue to be switched even though diagnosis of errors on a faulty line is taking place.

The resulting software was not only costly to produce but hard to maintain. On small projects, when a programmer left a project the code he or she had worked on became obsolete because nobody else could figure it out. On large projects, sizable teams of development and support programmers were required. These programmers found it difficult to decipher each other's programs. When they left the project, replacements had to be trained painfully in the special language involved, disrupting the work of the team.

Seeing this chaos and remembering that COBOL and FORTRAN had been developed in the late '50s and early '60s to remedy similar problems with financial and scientific programming, the DoD created a committee—the High-Order Language Working Group, acronym HOLWG—to investigate the possibility of developing one or more standard, high-level languages for embedded systems.

Between 1974 and 1977, HOLWG issued a series of language descriptions to federal agencies, defense contractors, the academic community, and to various sectors of the military, asking for comments on high-level languages for use in embedded systems. There was surprising agreement among the returns. The features most sought after were:

- reliability
- easier maintenance
- structured constructs
- strong data typing
- relative and absolute precision specifications
- information hiding and data abstraction
- concurrent processing
- exception handling
- generic definition
- machine-dependent facilities

HOLWG concluded that no existing language met the requirements, but that a single new language for embedded systems appeared both desirable and feasible. They recommended developing such a language using Pascal, PL/I, and Algol-68 as a starting point.

Following HOLWG's recommendation, in the spring of 1977 DoD solicited proposals for language development. A total of 17 proposals were received from groups in the United States and Europe. Several rounds of evaluation and elimination of competitors followed until finally, in May 1979, a design by a multinational team under Jean Ichbiah at Honeywell Bull in France was declared the winner.

Intially the new language was nicknamed DoD-1, but by the time the design was chosen the name Ada had been suggested by the Navy Materiel Command. This name was conferred in honor of Ada, Lady Lovelace, the nineteenth century English noblewoman who worked with Charles Babbage in developing the world's first programmable computer.

Probably the most important thing about Ada's design and development process was that it was carried out in continuous consultation with a large number of experts. Because of this, the development team produced a language that satisfies a great number of needs. Besides clearing up some notorious difficulties in earlier languages, it provides some new and powerful features representing the advanced theoretical work of the 1970s.

In 1981 a language specifications manual was prepared by Ichbiah's team and was made available to compiler writers. A revised version of the manual was released in February 1983. The specifications include not only the syntax of the language but the definition of standard transportable libraries ranging from I/O handlers to commonly used routines for applications programs.

A mechanism for ensuring adherence to the specifications was set up: Until a compiler passes a grueling set of validation tests administered by the DoD, the applicant will not be *validated* and given the right to use the copyrighted name "Ada". (Note, that subset compilers are allowed to use the name for a certain period of time if they contain a clear statement that the compiler is a subset being developed toward the real thing.)

This mechanism insures an extremely important benefit for the microcomputer user: Code written in Ada and compiled on a validated microcomputer Ada compiler will compile—to the extent that it does not include the special-purpose system dependencies discussed in Chapter 11—*as is* on a VAX or a Cray 1. The same cannot be said for any other computer language.

The first validated "compiler", actually an Ada interpreter developed on a VAX at New York University, emerged in the spring of 1983. The first compilers for CP/M and MS-DOS—the two most important microcomputer operating systems—were SuperSoft and Janus, Ada subsets which, by the spring of 1984, included the important feature of separate compilation with *packages*, the primary Ada programming units.

Ada's Features

Although Ada may have started as a specialized language for embedded systems, it ended up as a general-purpose language with some features useful for embedded systems. Its syntax resembles Pascal yet its facilities range far beyond Pascal's.

Properly designed Ada programs have a distinct form and style all their own. Their main features are as follows:

Strong Data Typing—Ada partitions data types strictly, allowing conversions between different types only with an explicit conversion function. The result is more careful program design, easier debugging, and more efficient use of storage space. Unlike Pascal, however, you can legally get around the data typing when you have to. Like Pascal, PL/I, and C, Ada provides aggregate data types.

Structured Constructs—Structured programming consists of writing the program so that each part of it is broken down into modules, each of which is itself broken into modules, and so forth until the level of individual statements is reached. Language constructs that assist structured programming are iteration and selection statements allowing these functions to take place without GOTOs. Ada has three loop constructs, the simplest of which may be tailored to simulate any other loop construct. It also has IF . . . THEN . . . ELSE and the CASE statements.

Data Abstraction—Many other languages allow reasonable procedural abstraction. Ada in addition allows good data abstraction—that is, data representation that looks like something in the real world rather than a bunch of numbers. Ada's data representation combines with other language features to allow you to write programs that are not only understandable but can be changed with little impact on the other programs that use them.

Packaging—If you have written a routine that performs a mathematical conversion or handles communication with a particular device, it's a nuisance to have to type it in every time you write a program involving that function. If you discover after you've copied it a few times that it needs to be changed, it can be a real problem to find and modify all the copies. Ada lets you compile the subprogram and store it in a library. If you need it in any program from then on, you refer to it by name (*call* it) and Ada will use the already compiled subprogram from the library. This feature is an absolute necessity for handling the very large programs used in command systems; it is a convenience for anyone writing or revising programs larger than a few hundred lines. An important difference between Ada's package concept and the linkage editors available for many languages is that data typing is automatically preserved.

Data Encapsulation—Ada lets you define constants, data types, and even operators (+, −, etc.) in an enclosed package, which is then available for use by external programs. Only the features set out in a *specification* section are exportable. The internal mechanisms of the exporting are invisible and safe from meddling or damage from side effects.

Separate Compilation—Ada allows you to write your program segments in small, separate sections and to link the sections together after they have been compiled. If one section needs changing, only it must be recompiled.

Machine-Level Access—Short of assembly language routines linked into the object (execution) code file, one of the most difficult obstacles in system level programs is gaining access to information at the machine address level. Ada provides facilities for assigning data addresses down to the bit level, allowing testing of machine-dependent control flags, status words, and peripheral ports. This is most significant in the realm of real-time processing where processing of interrupts almost always involves access to the specific device involved.

Exception Handling—Since Ada was designed to produce programs for embedded systems, where they would be expected to run continuously, an important provision is for handling unexpected events—computational errors—in such a way that they don't cause the system to crash. Errors automatically "raise exceptions" and execute routines (*exception handlers*) that handle these situations.

Overloading—This is using the same name to denote different operators, enumeration type elements, variable names, or subprograms. An example of a call to an overloaded subprogram is a Get(<something>) which can be used for numbers, characters, or strings. Ada lets you overload names and symbols, then sorts things out from context, allowing you to use identical names for similar operations, yet preserving type checking.

Generic Program Units—These are molds that stamp out clones of programs on request. A matrix sort, for example, might lack only the specification for the type of data to be sorted. Provide it and Ada stamps out a customized sort routine to suit your needs. This is a feature that will allow a large market for Ada software components.

Multitasking—One of Ada's unique and attractive features is its facility to produce a program that will do more than one thing at a time. Ada's tasks are really separate processes that run simultaneously, coordinating with each other when necessary. The tasking feature is ideal for multiple-processor systems, and it allows clearer programs on single-processor systems with multiple, interrupt-driven processes. Ada is the first language to provide a basic construct that covers both the real-time (interrupt-driven) logic and concurrent processes, including multiprocessor systems.

Feature Independence—Ada is designed so that a programmer does not need to worry about the interaction between the features regularly used and those that aren't. If the programmer doesn't need to use Ada's multitasking, for example, he doesn't have to learn or to worry about it.

Ada's Future

Aside from the technical strength of its design, Ada has qualities that promise to make it attractive in the commercial marketplace for both mainframes and micros.

DoD Support—By the 1990s, command and control computers, from the big ones in aircraft carriers to the smaller, dedicated systems in jet fighters, battle tanks, and guided missiles, all will run programs written almost exclusively in Ada. This buying power ensures that Ada will be widely used, which in turn will create a pool of compilers, programmers, program support tools, and program parts.

Target Applications—Embedded systems show signs of becoming the "hot" technology item of the next decade. Talking microwave ovens are only the beginning. The developers of these commercial systems are likely to have obtained their training in the military, as did TV and logic electronics designers before them. When they develop commercial products, they will use the tools (including Ada) they learned about and used in the military. You can also expect Ada compilers for microprocessors to be heavily optimizing, since the per unit manufacturing cost of commercial embedded systems is affected by the memory and processor efficiency of the programs they run.

Standardization and Transportability—Ada is a language designed for transportability, and its strict standards will keep it that way. The last time the U.S. Department of Defense placed requirements for a language, the result was COBOL, the language now known by more programmers than any other. Transportability will insulate software developers from changes in hardware technology and assure a longer product life and a wider product base.

Package Modularity—Libraries of Ada modules, both commercial and public domain, will give you a chance to use ready-made parts for the programs you are putting together, prefabricated sorters, screen handlers, database structures, etc. Modularity will provide a new market for Ada software developers. Eventually, if you don't have the Ada subprogram you need on your shelf, your user group or computer store will.

One of the shortest programs is the classic message to the outer world. In BASIC, it can be coded:

```
10 PRINT "Hello, world."        Hello, world.
```

The words the PRINT command displays on the screen are highlighted at right.

There isn't much structure to the BASIC program; even the end statement is optional in BASIC. Contrast this to the Ada equivalent:[1]

```
with Text_IO;
procedure Greet_World is
begin
   Text_IO.Put("Hello, world.");       Hello, world.
   Text_IO.New_Line;
end Greet_World;
```

Ada's code *is* structured in a *block* named Greet_World, in the tradition of ALGOL and Pascal. This block is an independent unit, independent in ways that go far beyond anything possible in BASIC. Greet_World is an identifier, that is, a kind of name. In this case it is the name of the procedure.

If we want to change our line of BASIC into a subroutine that begins to resemble our Ada procedure, we have to add some optional elements:

1. A header identifying the subroutine;
2. A statement to print the string;
3. A footer indicating the end of the subroutine.

Here's how it might look in BASIC:

```
1000 REM GREET WORLD
1010 PRINT "Hello, world."        Hello, world.
1020 RETURN
1030 REM END GREET WORLD
```

Let's take a closer look at the layout of the Ada routine shown in Figure 1-1. Its structure will be used as a template for more elaborate programs later.

```
procedure   is        The framework is made
begin                 up of "reserved words" -
                      words you can't use
                      for anything else in
end ;                 your program.
```

Figure 1-1. Program Unit Framework

This particular structure defines a procedure. Procedures constitute one of Ada's basic program units, all of which have a general structure that matches our template.

Procedures and functions, which we will cover in greater detail in Chapter 3, are lumped together under the heading *subprogram*. This is a slightly misleading term since either of them (usually procedures) can stand alone and be compiled as programs.

The reserved words **begin** and **end** are block markers. They define the body of the procedure, where the action takes place. All statements to be executed in the program are placed between these block markers.

Notice that **Greet_World** itself calls on two subprograms: Put, which does the job of writing the character string "Hello, world.", and **New_Line**, which ends the line. **Put** and **New_Line** are standard subprograms from a *package* of related subprograms called **Text_IO**. **Text_IO** has already been compiled and is stored separately. The **with** statement at the head of **Greet_World** alerts the compiler to check **Text_IO** for subprograms called from inside the procedure block. **Text_IO** is a standard package included with every full Ada compiler. Its specifications are listed in Appendix C. Microcomputer computer subsets of Ada usually have an incomplete version of **Text_IO**.[2]

C is much closer to Ada than to BASIC. Here's a C version of **Greet_World**:

```
main( )
{
        printf( "Hello, world.\n");     Hello, world.
}
```

To output a string, the C language, like Ada, calls a procedure (**printf**) from a library.

While many languages have intrinsic I/O functions (BASIC uses the built-in command **PRINT**), Ada and C depend on standard libraries for I/O and other routines. These standard libraries are provided with the compilers and are kept available during compilation. Their advantage is that they can be added to or even changed under certain circumstances. A difference between C and Ada standard I/O libraries is that Ada libraries are really standard, and will be kept standard by the DoD. A C library usually is "standard", but nobody enforces this, and so subtle variations always exist.

Notice that the block structure of C is like Ada's, though in C the **begin** and **end** are replaced by curly brackets. Also, there is no unique identification of the program, and the source of the library function **printf** is not identified.

Pascal is very similar to Ada. Here's a Pascal version of **Greet_World**:

```
program GreetWorld;
begin
        Writeln('Hello, World.');     Hello, world.
end.
```

Ada is a free-format language, like Pascal and C, but unlike BASIC. You probably noticed that we used no line numbers in **Greet_World**. Line numbers are not allowed in

---

Ada because lines have almost no significance in Ada. The only significance of a line in Ada is that each **token** (variable names, reserved word, operator) must fit completely on one line.

If we want, we can rewrite the procedure **Greet__World** like this:

```
with Text_IO;use Text_IO;procedure Greet_World is begin Put(
"Hello, world.");New_Line;end Greet_World;
```

To the Ada compiler, this layout and the previous Ada layout are completely equivalent. The difference is to the human reader. The indentation of the first version is just by convention, to allow a human reader to quickly spot the structure of the program.

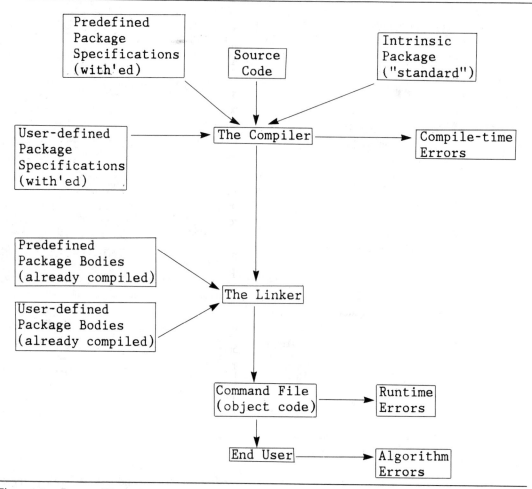

Figure 1-2.   *Program Diagram*

An Ada program consists of the code you write plus all of the library packages included. Figure 1-2 shows a flow diagram of where the source code goes into the Ada process and where the end result (the object code) comes out. We also have indicated where the three major types of errors are uncovered: The compile-time errors, where syntax errors and type-checking errors appear; the run-time errors, where "divide-by-zero" and "can't open file" types of errors appear; and the more insidious algorithmic errors, where the right statements are just in the wrong order, or vice versa.

When you write a program for Ada on a microcomputer you will be dealing with a *compiler*—a translating program that takes a text file and runs through it from top to bottom, producing *intermediate code*, which you then turn over to a linker to produce object code. The commands you must specify to cause this to take place vary from compiler to compiler.

If you have only used BASIC, you will notice more steps than you are used to. BASIC includes its own operating system and editor and usually runs *interpreted*, meaning that you can at any time use one of its commands to LOAD a program from disk, RUN it, LIST it and immediately EDIT a line in case of an error, and SAVE the corrected version. The result is the very fast correction of errors, which can spoil us for using a compiled system. Compiled systems, however, can handle a more complex language and produce programs that execute much more rapidly.

To write the original text file (program source code), chances are you will use a *screen editor*, which will allow you to move your cursor freely around the screen to edit what you have written.

Be sure that your screen editor creates an ASCII file with no embedded formatting controls. If your screen editor is a word processor you may have to take special action to avoid formatting controls. For example, to create an acceptable Ada source file in WordStar, you must choose the **N** option ("N=Create or edit a Non-document file").

When you hand over your precious program (let's call it MYPROG.PKG) to the compiler, in the Janus/Ada subset, for example, you compile it by typing:

```
A>JANUS B:MYFILE
```

Compilation can take several minutes. A fatal error can abort it at any moment, and to fix the error you would need to go back into the operating system and call up the screen editor—a time-consuming process! Linking takes more time, especially with SuperSoft. Therefore, compiling programs is not for the impatient.

It is important to read your compiler manual carefully, to determine exactly how to compile and link a program. In the Janus/Ada subset we would link our program like this:[3]

```
A>JLINK B:MYFILE
```

In this book we have used compilers that work on CP/M and MS-DOS, the two standard operating systems for 8- and 16-bit microcomputers. In developing our demonstration programs we have used Janus Ada and SuperSoft "A" on CP/M-80, and Janus on MS-DOS. Our 8-bit CP/M computers were an Osborne, a Zorba, a Morrow MicroDecision, an Apple II with a Z-80 card, a Ferguson Big Board I, and a Northstar Horizon. Most of the MS-DOS programming was done on a Sanyo 3000 using the Janus subset of Ada.

Conclusion

Whether you are looking for a single standard language to concentrate on or for a step up from FORTRAN, COBOL, or BASIC, Ada is a language with potential. If your eye is on the future of software development, Ada can't be ignored.

Ada is a language designed for professional programmers. It embodies features programmers have wanted for years but haven't been able to find in the languages available to them. These modern features provide, in a single programming language, unmatched power and flexibility. They will help you write short, reliable, and effective programs quickly.

We have shown a simple example of how these features cause Ada to differ from BASIC, C, and Pascal. We intend that you should use Ada on your own microcomputer. Check the manuals for your computer and your Ada compiler to determine the exact procedures for doing this.

2
Basic Elements

Data stored in computers must be divided into distinct types because of storage and operation formats. This is true in all languages, even if this division is done semiautomatically, as in BASIC. Ada predefines several standard data types. In this chapter we will look at how they are represented.

Character Set

For program listings, Ada uses 56 of the 95 characters in the full ASCII (American Standard Code for Information Interchange) graphic character set. This basic character set consists of the uppercase letters:

ABCDEFGHIJKLMNOPQRSTUVWXYZ

the digits:

1234567890

special characters:

"#&'( )*+,-./:;<=>-¦

and the space character.

In addition, many versions of Ada add the lowercase characters and the rest of the special symbols of the full ASCII graphic character set:

abcdefghijklmnopqrstuvwxyz

!$%?@[\]``{}˜

Even if an Ada program is written in the full graphic set with upper- and lowercase, it can always be translated into the basic 56-character set. Both upper- and lowercase can be used, and we will use them in this book for purposes of readability. But remember: The Ada programming language is case insensitive, as are most BASIC interpreters. Except when it is dealing with literal text or individual characters, which it receives in the form "abcd" or 'a', the compiler treats lowercase letters as though they were the equivalent uppercase letters so that, to the compiler:

PriMe looks like PRIME
BalanceForward looks like BALANCEFORWARD

Special Symbols

Ada uses 18 of the ASCII special graphic characters. A total of 16 of them are called *delimiters* because although they have various other uses, they also act to separate syntactic elements (such as operators or variable names) in the same way spaces and carriage returns do. They are used individually:

```
+ - * / ( ) & ' . , : ; < > = ¦
```

or as two-character compound delimiters:

```
<>   <<   >>   ..   **   :=   /=   >=   <=
```

Compound delimiters must stay welded together, with no spaces between their components. You can see a summary of Ada's delimiters and their uses in Table 2-1. Some of the examples involve constructions peculiar to the Ada programming language. They will be explained fully in later chapters.

The left and right parentheses, (and), are used in places (especially to enclose array indices) where C and Pascal use square brackets ([ ]).

The ampersand, &, is an operator for concatenation of strings and characters, not a logical "and":

```
Put( 'a' & 'b' )                 ab
Put( "be"&"gin" )                begin
```

Notice that the ampersand *delimits* the elements to the right and left of it in the last expression above, so that the use of a space is not necessary, although it is a good idea from the point of view of readability.

```
      Put( "begin" & "ing" );
and   Put("begin"&"ing");
```

Symbol	Name	Example	Read As
_	underline	long_identifier	
"	quotation	"Hi!" (used in pairs to mark strings)	
'	single quote	'A' (defines character literals)	
	(also called apostrophe, tick, or prime)		
#	sharp	16#1A# or 8#133#7	
&	ampersand	"runner"&'s'	
*	star, multiply	2 * 3	
+	plus	2 + 3	
-	hyphen, minus	3 - 2	
/	slash, divide	3 / 2	
<	less than	current < index	
=	equal	sample = model	
>	greater than	current > index	
:	colon	Scanning_Loop:	
;	semicolon	counter := counter + 1;	
,	comma	(Saturday, Sunday)	
¦	vertical bar	first ¦ second	"first or second"
(	left parenthesis		
)	right parenthesis	array(index), 5*(2+3)	

Compound Symbols

Symbol	Name		Read As
--	comment		
=>	arrow		"choose"
**	double star, exponentiate		"exponentiate"
:=	assignment		"becomes"
/=	inequality		"not equal"
>=	greater than or equal		
<=	less than or equal		
<<	left label bracket		
>>	right label bracket		
<>	box		"range coming"

Symbols Not Functional in Ada Programs

$	dollar
?	question mark
@	commercial "at"
[	left square bracket
]	right square bracket
^	circumflex
`	grave accent
{	left brace
}	right brace
~	tilde

Table 2-1. Use of ASCII Symbols in Ada

will both give "beginning", just as $A + B$ and $A+B$ have the same meaning.

A semicolon (;) is used to terminate every statement in Ada.

A vertical bar may be read "or". So, first | second is "first or second", and is not used as a logical "or" but to separate choices. The vertical bar appears both as | and as ¦ depending on your computer system.

The two-dot compound (..), read "to", appears between literals (or variables, as in Min..Max, read "Min to Max") to show a range of values.

The "equal" sign is used only for testing equality and doesn't double as an assignment operator. In Ada, as in Pascal, the unique assignment operator is := ("becomes"), the most commonly used of the compound operators.

Familiar compound comparison symbols include >= (greater than-equal to); <= (less than-equal to); and /= (does not equal).

The last of these, "does not equal" (/=), shouldn't be replaced with <>, which shows inequality in some other languages (BASIC, dBASE II).

In Ada, "box" (<>) is used as a symbol meaning a range that will be defined later, as in an array index range. The undefined index range

```
(Index range <>)
```

could be later pinned down as (Index range 1..10) or (Index range 1..1000).

The double dash symbol, --, is used to insert comments in the program text. The -- starts a comment and everything to the next carriage return is ignored by the compiler. Comments may appear anywhere a space character is legal.

Ada uses a label such as Outer__Loop: with a colon to name certain blocks in programs. (Obviously, this one would be used for a loop.) Ada provides another very special kind of label as the target of a GOTO, defined by << (left label bracket) and >> (right label bracket). Together these two label brackets define a label such as

```
<<THERE>>
```

with only one use: to serve as the target of the GOTO statement used in Ada.

```
<<THERE>>   begin
              -- do something;
              goto THERE;
            end;-- the body of an endless loop.
```

Three symbol replacements are allowed:

```
#     with     :
¦     with     !
"     with     %
```

The one most likely to be necessary for microcomputer users is the exclamation marker (!) since the vertical bar (|) is missing from some office-oriented daisy wheels.

The *Language Reference Manual* warns against using alternative symbols unless absolutely necessary.

Identifiers

Identifiers are used as names for variables, procedures, and program blocks, among other things.

In Ada an identifier is composed of letters, numerals, and the underscore (also called "underbar" or "underline") symbol, for example:

```
Radius
Text_IO
Sum
Counter_2
Final_Result
INTEGER
LONG_INTEGER
MY_OWN_INTEGER
File_Index
```

An Ada identifier must fit on a single line. It cannot be interrupted with spaces, or contain any special symbols other than the underline. It must begin with a letter, never a numeral or an underline. Furthermore, it cannot end with an underline. Finally, it cannot include two successive underlines.

Here are some illegal identifiers. Can you spot what's wrong with each of them?[1]

```
First-Index
_Buffer
23A
Last Line
Marker_
A$
```

As pointed out in the preceding chapter, you can mix upper- and lowercase letters at will. The compiler won't even notice.

Identifiers should be chosen to be meaningful—for example, "weekdays" versus "W1".

Meaningful identifiers make any Ada program more readable—especially for other people who see it for the first time.

A good identifier should not only fit what it stands for, but it should fit in with other similar names you are using in that context.

Though there is no restriction on an identifier's length except that it must fit on one line, both CP/M and MS-DOS impose an eight-character limit on filenames. Since some microcomputer Ada compilers use the names of compilation units (a procedure name, for example) as their filenames, you may have to restrict names of compilation units to eight characters.

Some microcomputer subsets of Ada only treat the first eight or ten characters of a long identifier as significant. If your are using a subset, be sure that Register__A and Register__B don't get confused. If they do, substituting A__Register and B__Register will correct the problem.[2]

Reserved Words

Certain words—a total of 63—are predefined as special-purpose identifiers called *reserved words*. The complete list, arranged alphabetically, appears in Table 2-2. You'll notice among them some template words from our sample procedure Greet__World in Chapter 1. Don't use these words as identifiers of your own or you'll get a compiler error when you compile your program.

abort	do	mod	renames
abs	else	new	return
accept	elsif	not	reverse
access	end	null	select
all	entry	of	separate
and	exception	or	subtype
array	exit	others	task
at	for	out	terminate
begin	function	package	then
body	generic	pragma	type
case	goto	private	use
constant	if	procedure	when
declare	in	raise	while
delay	is	range	with
delta	limited	record	xor
digits	loop	rem	

Table 2-2.   Ada's Reserved Words

Logical operators:

        and or xor not

Arithmetic operators:

        abs   mod   rem

Names of program units:

        package   procedure   function   task

Words used in control statements:

        if   then   elsif else   end
        for   loop   exit
        case   when   others

Table 2-3.   Commonly Used Reserved Words

Although you can't use reserved words alone as identifiers, you can (technically) use them in compound identifiers. For example, Begin__Block is okay to use because the reserved word begin is part of a longer identifier. But to avoid confusion it is a good practice to avoid embedding reserved words in identifiers[3] (one that we ignore).

Only about 60 percent of the reserved words will be used in the demonstration programs in this book. Some reserved words apply to advanced features of Ada that you aren't likely to use on your microcomputer. We have displayed the words you will be most concerned with in this book in Table 2-3.

Keywords

There is another group of predefined identifiers you can use, even though Ada already has used these names for standard identifiers within the language. These *keywords* include the names of data types such as integer and character, the names of libraries such as Text__IO, and the Names of the routines in these packages, for example, PUT, GET, NEW__LINE.

The difference between a keyword and a reserved word is that the reserved words are part of the language itself. Keywords are standard identifiers defined in terms of the language, just as you would define identifiers as type names and variable names.

A list of keywords appears in Table 2-4.

actual_delta	numeric_error
base	pred
bits	priority
BOOLEAN	real
calendar	select_error
CHARACTER	SHORT_FLOAT
clock	SHORT_INTEGER
constrained	size
constraint_error	small
controlled	standard
count	storage_error
duration	storage_size
emax	storage_unit
epsilon	STRING
failure	succ
FALSE	suppress
first	system
FLOAT	tasking_error
input_output	terminated
INTEGER	text_io
large	time
last	TRUE
length	unchecked_conversion
LONG_FLOAT	unchecked_deallocation
LONG_INTEGER	val

Table 2-4. Keywords

Program Comments

Long identifiers provide you with a fine resource for making your programs readable—if you take advantage of them. Anyone who underestimates the importance of readability has never tried to revise an uncommented program in assembly language, C, or even an early version of FORTRAN or BASIC.

Ada provides another, more traditional way of explaining what's going on: *comments*. An Ada comment is similar to a comment in BASIC. It runs from the first occurrence of a comment symbol (--) to the end of the line:

```
-- This is an Ada comment.
```

If you want to carry on to the next line you have to repeat the double dashes. Everything from the double dashes to the carriage return is ignored by the compiler:

```
if A = B then Put("Hi"); -- A comment can start
                         -- after a line of code.
```

A comment in Ada, unlike one in Pascal or C, is not constructed so that it can be wedged between the elements in a line of code:

```
if A = B  -- [COMMENT]  then put("Hi");
```

ends after **A** = **B**, as far as the compiler is concerned. Ada's comment symbol (--) acts like the REM statement in BASIC.

Literals

A *data literal* represents its face value, unlike a variable, which stands for other values. The literal representations of data in Ada generally follows conventional patterns, providing formats for characters, strings of characters, integers, and real numbers.

String Literals—A string literal is a sequence of printable ASCII characters enclosed in quotes. We have seen a string literal in our procedure Greet__World placed on the screen by the predefined procedure Put. Put was called in for the occasion from a library of standard input-output procedures, a package called Text__IO:

```
Put("This is a string.");  This is a string.
```

We can do likewise for a string of a single character:

```
Put("a");                          a
```

But when Ada wants to treat individual characters as a type in themselves, it uses single quotes ('):

```
Put('B');                          B
```

Symbols placed between single quotes must appear alone and are treated by Ada as members of the ASCII set.

Inside a string literal, the double quote signs must be doubled:

```
Put("""double quote""")      "double quote"
```

```
Put("He said ""%!#&@"".");   He said "%!#&@".
```

but a single quote as a character literal is not:

```
Put( ''' )                                    !
                                              _
```

If you try to include a character or string literal in a program without enclosing it in quotes, the compiler will confuse it with an identifier.

Can you tell what put ("begin") will produce? If you're not sure, look in the notes on this chapter in Appendix A for the answer.[4]

Numeric Literals—Ada recognizes two kinds of numeric literals, integers and real numbers. Integers are numbers without a decimal point—that is to say, without a fractional part. The following are integers:

```
3     45     7     256
```

Real numbers are equipped with a decimal point, and the Ada compiler identifies them as real from that attribute:[5]

```
4.0     21.3     0.0023
```

Even when dealing with the exact number 2, the compiler distinguishes between

```
2     and     2.0
```

as the integer and real numeric literal representation.

A digit must appear on both sides of the decimal point in a real literal.

The underscore character __ may be used within a numeric literal for readability, as it is ignored by the compiler. Thus 2__234__567 = 2234567.

Numeric literals have no sign; used in a statement, a numeric literal is taken as an expression, with a '+' sign assumed if no sign appears. Thus Ada treats 123 and −123 as simple expressions rather than literals as such. *Note:* This can cause a misunderstanding if your Ada interprets −32768 as an out-of-range positive integer before getting to the sign. A possible remedy is using INTEGER'first instead of −32768.

Ada reads and writes in base 10 (decimal) by default (i.e., unless another radix, or base, is specified). Numbers can appear in either standard notation—

```
21, 5, or 234           (for integers)
2.50, 2.0, or 345.233   (for real numbers)
```

—or in scientific notation, where the letter 'E' is an abbreviation for "times 10 to the <integer> power":

```
27E5       means 2,700,000   (integer)
52.1E-2    means .521        (real)
```

Scientific notation is especially suitable for very large or very small numbers—Jupiter's diameter in meters, or the weight of a proton in kilograms.

Literals of Other Than Base 10—The usual, or default, representation of numbers is in decimal notation, base 10. To represent numbers with other radices—the largest being 16—Ada provides a special notation using the sharp, # (pound sign). If digits greater than 9 are needed, they are represented by the capitals A through F, as needed. Besides base 10 the three other bases (radices) commonly used are binary (2), octal (8), and hexadecimal (16).

```
2#0111#   is binary for 7


8#17#     is octal for 15


16#1A#    is hexadecimal for 26
```

For microcomputer users hexadecimal notation of this kind is especially useful for referring to memory addresses and offsets, and the sizes of standard blocks of data.

Scientific notation is also available in any of the fifteen number bases Ada deals with simply by adding an E and the exponent:

```
<base> # <mantissa> # E <exponent>
```

Both the base and the exponent are in decimal, and the mantissa is in the particular number base in question.

Data Typing

Ada reads and writes data literals. Inside a program, however, data types are much more elaborate than they are in literal form. This is because in a computer each kind of data has its own storage format and its own set of operations. In terms of a program, data are often conveniently defined in structures. Ada is called a *strongly typed* language because it handles data in strictly segregated types. If you have experience with Pascal, you will find yourself on familiar ground in the following discussion.

Ada takes Pascal's typing methods as a model (or a starting point!). If your language is BASIC or FORTRAN, Ada may seem overly formal at first. Briefly, a variable has to be declared with its type at the top of a program unit, between the header and the reserved word BEGIN. Thereafter it can store data of that type only, and no other type of data can be assigned to it without an explicit provision for type conversion coded in. Exceptions to this rule are caught, at compile time or at run time, and cause an error message.

Why all the bother?

It seems strange to someone who is used to writing assignments such as

```
A = 0.75
B = 2
```

that one must remember that *A* is being assigned a real number and *B* is being assigned an integer. But the computer has to make this distinction, even though a language such as BASIC handles the matter so smoothly you're only half aware of it.

In algebra, A + B + C is a valid operation whether A and B are 1 and 2, or 1.3 and 2.5, or 1 and 2.5. Whole and fractional numbers can be mixed with no problem. But the computer's integer and real values have to be handled differently. The '+' symbol that adds 2 + 2 is not the same one that adds 2.3 + 2.3. Symbol '+' is, in fact, *overloaded*—the compiler will choose one of several different adding operations according to the data to be handled.

Ada does not have a type real as such although, as we will see, you have the option of defining one for yourself. The two predefined number types that handle real numbers in Ada are fixed and float (you may have noticed these names among the keywords). For now we will use the type float to represent real numbers. We will discuss fixed point numbers in Chapter 8 when we deal with precision. Ada's implementation of fixed-point numbers is very sophisticated, since fixed-point numbers are crucial in working with many embedded systems.

The format of data storage in terms of actual bits of memory is decided by the particular compiler and underlying hardware you use. It is one of the details that a high-level language such as Ada takes care of, and not one you need to think about unless you want to make use of some of Ada's fine tuning to save memory or for other purposes. (We'll cover these issues in Chapter 12.) In any case, numbers are stored in computer memory quite differently from the way they are written on a piece of paper. Chances are integers are stored in your micro in two successive bytes, with one of their 16 bits carrying the sign, while a floating point number, which looks on paper like an integer with a decimal point placed between its digits, is stored in the computer in a format similar to scientific notation, complete with mantissa and exponent.

This description is of logical (rather than physical) storage for microcomputers running CP/M or MS/DOS. It may give you some idea of how different written notation and storage formats for numeric data types can be.

Variables meant for different types are created in BASIC by adding special symbols to the variable name:[6]

A or A!	represents a floating point number.
A%	represents an integer
A$	represents a single character or a string of several characters.

BASIC converts numeric data freely between integer and single precision form.

In Ada, variables are assigned their type designations by *declaring* them as a certain type:

```
<variable_name> : <type_mark> ;

Int_Var  : INTEGER;
Bool_Var : BOOLEAN;
```

Ada's Data Types

You have seen instances of computer data types in literal form—real numbers, integers, characters, Booleans, and strings.

real numbers	1.414
integers	25
Booleans	TRUE
characters	'a'
strings	"This string contains 35 characters."

Integer and real number literals are instances of the Ada intrinsic (and anonymous) types types universal_integer and universal_real, respectively. Their exact representation specifications are system dependent.

The Ada compiler will assign real and integer literals to compatible types without explicit conversion by the programmer and, until they are assigned, they will retain all their digits of precision.

There are five broad classes of data in Ada (see Table 2.5):

- scalar types
- composite types
- access types
- private types
- task types

We will look at scalar types in this chapter, and one composite type, the string. Later we will cover the other composite types and access types (pointers), private types, (special-use types, which you the user define, along with their operators), and task types, which are actually concurrent subroutines with characteristics like variables.

Table 2-5 shows the relationships between all of Ada's data types; Table 2-6 shows the relationship between the scalar types we have covered in this chapter.

```
Scalar Types
      Discrete Types
            1. enumeration types
                  a. BOOLEAN
                  b. CHARACTER
                  c. user-defined
            2. INTEGER
      Real Numbers
            1. Fixed point numbers
            2. FLOATing point numbers

Composite Types
      ARRAY
      RECORD

Access Types

Private Types

Task Types
```

Table 2-5.   *Nine Predefined Types in Context*

All the data we have dealt with so far (with the exception of strings which are, as we mentioned, arrays) are *predefined scalar types*. The predefined Ada types—integer, Boolean, and character—are all scalar types, so called because their values have the quality of numbers on a scale. Think of the scale as an ordered row of values, increasing in rank from left to right. Each one has a higher rank than its predecessor and a lower rank than its successor; no two scalar values have the same rank. They are ordered, having a high end and a low end, a first value and a last value.

The values of scalar types can be mapped to one dimension. We visualize this as a line running from left to right:

```
1..2..3..4..5..6..7..8
```

For any two numbers not the same, one can be said to be larger than the other. This is true even though there might be an indefinite number of elements between any two elements on the scale. An example of this is the set of real numbers, which can have fractional parts.

Scalar types have no *components* unlike, say, the points on a two-dimensional plane which may, for example, have an angular component and a magnitude component.

Characters, Booleans, and integers are *discrete* types, meaning that their individual values are like graduations on the scale; there are no values between them. They are useful in

```
Discrete Types
   1. Enumeration types
        a. Boolean types
        b. characters
        c. user-defined types
   2. Integers

Real Numbers
   1. Fixed point numbers
   2. Floating point numbers
```

Table 2-6. Types of Scalar Data

programming for counters and indices. Discrete scalar values can be enumerated over a given range. For example, there are 8 integers in the range 1..8. Contrast them with the set of real numbers, which theoretically have an infinite number, and in practice an indefinite number, of values falling within a given range. (Fixed-point numbers are discrete but not discrete types—we'll be treating them in Chapter 8.) Ada predefines these types in a library module, an Ada package called **Standard**.

Integer type

Integers, as we have mentioned, are discrete scalar types—round numbers useful as indices and counters, among other things. In 8- and 16-bit microcomputers they usually are stored in two bytes of memory, which give the possible values a range of −32768 to 32767. The type integer is defined in the Ada library package **Standard** and is available at all times for use in your program.

A range of 64K (65,536) is usually sufficient for indexing but, to provide a programmer with the tools for working with large numbers, most compilers supply a type **LONG_INTEGER** with storage of four bytes—32 bits—for a range of −2_147_483_648.. +2_147_483_647.

Character type

Ada's type character is predefined to include the ASCII symbols from NUL to DEL, plus the alphabetic, numeric, and special characters.[7] Don't confuse Ada's character type, whose literals are set off with single quotes ('), with strings, which are arrays whose literal representation uses double quotes ("):

      '**A**'   character literal
      "**A**"   one-element string literal

The Boolean type is defined in the Ada library package **Standard** as

```
type BOOLEAN is (FALSE, TRUE);
```

Its two literal values are enumerated between the parentheses in an Ada type declaration. If you look at the standard library package in Appendix D you will see the declaration listed just like this. It is a predefined enumeration type.

Boolean types are useful as flags; it is good style to give them identifiers which describe *conditions*, for example:

```
Light_On : BOOLEAN;
```

The Boolean variable **Light_On** can then be used in a clearly described test for a conditional branch:

```
if Light_On then
    Check_Water_Level;
end if;
```

Check_Water_Level is a procedure (like **Put**) defined elsewhere in the program that will be performed if **Light_On** is true. The statement

```
if Light_On = TRUE then
    Check_Water_Level;
 end if;
```

would work, but it would be redundant and bad Ada style. In many cases where the compiler doesn't optimize code well it would generate extra code and run slower. Code optimization is not currently the long suit of microcomputer Ada compilers.

Boolean variables are declared the same way integer variables are:

```
 Light_On          :        BOOLEAN         ;
<variable name>  <colon>  <type name> <semi-colon>
```

They can be given a value in an assignment statement:

```
Light_On := TRUE;
```

There is no predefined type "real" in Ada; real numbers are classified as either floating point or fixed point and assigned a suitable name (called a **type_mark**), **FLOAT** or **FIXED**, for example. We will discuss real number types in detail in Chapter 8. They have some special attributes having to do with machine representation and accuracy.

String Types

So far we have treated Ada's scalar types—integers, real numbers (float and fixed), and enumeration types, including Boolean and character types. There is one nonscalar type we will mention here: the string, which in Ada is an array.

The string type is defined in the **Standard** package thus:

```
type STRING is ARRAY (POSITIVE range <>) of CHARACTER;
```

The box (<>) is a kind of wild-card symbol meaning that a precise value for the range, or dimension, will be supplied at the time a specific string type is declared. The declaration for a variable of the string type can be:

```
Screen_Line : STRING(1..80);
```

where 80 is the number of characters in the one-dimensional array, that is, the length of the string.

Custom Data Types: User-defined Enumeration Types

One reason for Ada's specifically named and constrained types, with everything spelled out in such detail, is to provide for storage allocation. But detailed type specifications do more: They give you the tools you need to create your own data types. Consider the possibilities of just one of these customizing techniques: user-defined enumeration types.

Recall how type BOOLEAN was defined—or predefined—in the library package **Standard**. Using the same format

```
type <type name> is ( <list of values> );
```

you can create your own enumeration types. For example:

```
type GENDERS is (MALE, FEMALE);
type TANK_LEVELS is (LOW, MEDIUM, HIGH);
type SEASONS is (SPRING, SUMMER, AUTUMN, WINTER);
```

Enumeration types allow us to *abstract data*, that is, move the representation away from machine reality and toward real-world reality. We will see how these types are created in Chapter 3.

Attributes

Attributes describe characteristics of language elements, for example, types, variables, and program units. They are actually functions that return information about these characteristics and are sometimes called "environmental inquiry functions".

Attributes are environmental characteristics of an element of the language, like a type, variable, or a program unit. Ada provides a convenient mechanism for finding the attributes of all discrete types. The general form is

```
<name of type> <apostrophe> <attribute desired>
```

The attributes usually available on subset compilers (on Janus, anyway) are first and last, which refer to the first and last values of the type.[8] For the three discrete types we have just covered, with the ASCII set on microcomputers, they are:

```
INTEGER'first      =      -32786
INTEGER'last       =      32787


BOOLEAN'first      =      FALSE
BOOLEAN'last       =      TRUE


CHARACTER'first    =      NUL
CHARACTER'last     =      DEL
```

They are especially useful in providing the values you need to interface with the system.

We could assign, for example, the maximum value of the type INTEGER for any system compiling our Ada program to a variable by writing:

```
MAXINT := INTEGER'last;
```

There are many attribute functions defined for full Ada. Appendix G lists predefined attribute functions and your compiler may have additional functions available. We'll be looking at attribute functions in the context in which they are used later in the book, so don't go charging off to Appendix G just yet.

Conclusion

Ada's basic components are pretty familiar, after all. As we go along you will notice that Ada's new features have their roots in earlier programming languages, especially Algol and Pascal.

In the next chapter we will discuss operators, expressions, and data objects of the types we have just seen. We will elaborate on the functions Ada provides for deriving attributes of types and their objects, and for converting data from one type to another. We will show how you can create subtypes and entirely new types, and how to use these features for microcomputer programming.

3
Basic Types and Expressions

In this chapter we examine data objects, operators, and expressions, and we take another look at data types—a rich and complex subject in Ada. We first have a look at packages, specifically packages that are predefined for the language.

If you are a fairly experienced programmer we suggest that you read this chapter selectively at first. To start writing programs, learning to declare integer and character type variables and constants might be enough. This foundation should let you begin actually coding. Later you can come back to this material to learn the fine points of enumeration types and subtypes. Of course you'll also need to be able to write expressions but, except for operator precedence, you'll find Ada's expressions familiar.

Expressions

Expressions are the nuts and bolts of any computer program. What exactly is an expression? The *Language Reference Manual* (*LRM*) states that an expression is a formula used to compute a value. Expressions are composed of literals, constants and variables (objects), and function calls, all joined by operations.[1]

Ada has its own small peculiarities about writing expressions, as any language does. Most of them relate to operator precedence. Also, because Ada is such a large language, there are several "subtypes" of expressions. They all look about the same, even though there are subtle distinctions. We will present the different types of expressions here and define some of the terms used later in the chapter. Expressions are usually used in the body of a program unit—in assignment statements, or to compute a value for a decision. Here are some examples:

```
5
Sine( Theta ) * 50.0
A + 5 * C
```

The first is the integer literal "5", really an abbreviation of "+5". The second is the result of a call to function **Sine**, which might compute the sine of the value contained in variable **Theta**. The result of **Sine** is multiplied by the real literal "50.0". The third expression is evaluated as the value of the variable **A** added to (5 times the value of variable **C**), according to the rules of operator precedence.

A *simple expression* is made up of scalar variables, constants, literals, and operators. The basic criterion for a simple expression is that it can't have function calls. A simple expression always has a scalar result. Here are some examples:

```
5
PI * 3.3
A + 5 * C
```

A *static expression* is made up of constants that have fixed values, literals, and operators. A static expression always evaluates to the same result, and the result is something that the compiler can figure out by looking at the text of your program. All nonliteral values used in a static expression must be computable at compile time.

A *universal expression* has a result of either universal__real or universal__integer. Basically this means that any component of the expression must be a numeric literal. As we'll see later, certain attribute functions return universal values, too, and can be used either in, or as, universal expressions. Universal expressions are always *simple static* expressions.

A *qualified expression* is used to explicitly state the type or subtype of an operand. In a case where we aren't sure the compiler can determine the type of an expression by looking at it, we can explicitly state the type by enclosing an expression in parentheses, and preceeding it with a type__mark and apostrophe:

```
INTEGER'( 25 + 17 )
```

It is not a good idea to write long expressions without parentheses where there is any sort of possible confusion about operator precedence, either by the compiler or by a human reader.

Extra parentheses never hurt an expression. They don't add to execution time, and they can save weeks of debugging, especially if you are used to the precedence rules of other languages.

Operators

The operators that manipulate data in Ada are defined separately for each type. An expression such as

```
A + B
```

is evaluated by the compiler, and the proper + function (in Ada, operators are functions) is applied at execution time to return a single value. The operator + used for **INTEGER** is not the same as the one used for **FLOAT**, so in the expression above **A** and **B** must be of the same data type.

When dealing with nonliteral data objects, except in a few cases, only objects of the same type can appear as operands to a given operator, in the same expression.

Literals, which are of the anonymous type **UNIVERSAL_INTEGER** or **UNIVERSAL_REAL**, can be used interchangeably with operands of compatible types within expressions because all numeric types are considered subtypes of one or the other of these two anonymous types.

Operator precedence

Ada's scheme of precedence for arithmetic operators is similar to that used in algebra. Everything else being equal, Ada handles operators within an expression from left to right and in this order:

Exponentiation: **
Multiplying: * / mod rem
Unary adding: + — abs
Binary adding: + — * /

Notice that unary operators have a lower precedence than multiplying operators; this is different from the usage in many languages, particularly C, but similar to algebra. Operators on the same level of precedence are evaluated from left to right; operators of higher precedence override the right-to-left rule:

2 + 3 * 5	gives	2 + 15	gives	17
13 - 2 ** 2	gives	13 - 4	gives	9

As in algebra, precedence rules can be manipulated by using parentheses:

(2+3)*5	gives	5*5	gives	25
(13-2)**2	gives	11**2	gives	121

Ada doesn't have ternary (three operand) operators or conditional expressions as found in C and Algol.

Integer operators

There are ten arithmetic operators defined for the integer type:

```
+   -   *   /   **   mod   rem   abs
```

Three of these operators act as unary operators—they accept a single value and return a single value:

+   unary plus or identity
−   unary minus or negation
abs   returns the absolute value (no sign)

Note: In Ada, abs is considered an operator, not a function call as it is in many other languages, and so it can be written into expressions with or without parentheses. It is syntactically identical to the unary plus or minus operators.

If for demonstration purposes we make the following declarations:

```
a : INTEGER :=  1;
n : INTEGER := -1;
```

then:

+a   returns the value 1
n   returns the value −1
−a   returns the value −1
abs n returns the value 1

If you look into **Standard** package, you'll see the unary operators declared for integers as if they were regular function calls, for example:

```
function "+" (Right: INTEGER) return INTEGER;
```

Inside the parenthesis is the parameter handled by the unary operator +, which is an object of type **integer** to its right. An integer is returned. All of the predefined operators have similar declarations in **Standard**.

The other seven arithmetic operators for integer types are binary (require two operands):

```
+   -   *   /   mod   rem   **
```

These operate on the operands to both the right and the left of them. A look into **Standard** would reveal the following specification for the binary '+' operator:

```
function "+" (Left, Right: INTEGER) return INTEGER;
```

The addition, subtraction, and multiplication functions are familiar enough:

```
+   addition          2 + 3 gives 5
-   subtraction       3 - 2 gives 1
*   multiplication    2 * 3 gives 6
```

Division with integers has a twist: Because only an integer value may be returned (Ada's strong typing at work again), the quotient of a division expression can only be an integer—it can't have a fraction attached. So:

```
12/3        gives        4
```

which is just fine, but the expression

```
13/3        gives        4
```

not the real number 4.33. How can we get a remainder in an integer operation like this?
Ada defines two functions named with the reserved words

```
mod     and     rem
```

which return *only* the remainder. There are two functions because programmers and mathemeticians disagree on what exactly a "remainder" is.

For expressions with operands of the same sign, they return a positive remainder. If the signs of the divisor and dividend are different, MOD has the sign of the divisor and REM has the sign of the dividend. Additionally REM produces a remainder whose absolute value is the same as if the absolute values of the operands were used, and subsequently changes behavior as it passes through zero.

```
(X/Y) * Y + X rem Y = X
X mod Y = X - (X/Y) * Y + Y
```

Usually you will be using the MOD operator, as it produces results consistent with modulo arithmetic.

The final operator for integers is the exponentiation operator, one of those compound symbols:

```
**          exponentiation        C**2 means "C squared"
```

Used with integers, this operator has a restriction: the exponent (right-hand value) cannot be negative.

Expressions with floating-point values use the same kinds of operators as expressions with integers, with two differences. First, floating-point operators are separately defined in the **Standard** package, as the operators for all distinct types must be distinctly defined. They work only with data of type **float** to their left and right, and they return only data of type **float**. Second, they resemble algebraic operators even more than integer operators do because some of the restrictions applying to integers do not apply to floating point numbers.

The floating point operators are:

```
unary:  + − abs
binary: + − * / **
```

There are no **mod** and **rem** operators because floating-point division can return a fractional quotient:

```
3.0 / 2.0 = 1.5
```

An exponent in floating-point arithmetic may be signed; it *must be an integer.*

The precedence of floating-point operators is the same as for the equivalent integer operators.

Besides arithmetic operators, which return numeric values, Ada provides three kinds of operators that return Boolean values (type **BOOLEAN - TRUE** or **FALSE**). They are the logical operators, relational operators, and the membership operators.

Relational operators

These operators are defined for all predefined types. They are:

```
=    equals
/=   not equal to
>    greater than
>=   greater than or equal to
<    less than
<=   less than or equal to
```

```
1 = 1 gives TRUE
2 = 3 gives FALSE
2 < 3 gives TRUE
```

Logical operators

Ada provides four operators that act on Boolean variables and return Boolean results. These are **and**, **or**, **Xor**, and **not**. All high-level languages include these operators in some form or another, and low-level languages usually can simulate them using bitwise logical operations.

and			or		
Operand 1	Operand 2	Result	Operand 1	Operand 2	Result
true	true	true	true	true	true
true	false	false	true	false	true
false	true	false	false	true	true
false	false	false	false	false	false

xor			not	
Operand 1	Operand 2	Result		
true	true	false	Operand	Result
true	false	true		
false	true	true	true	false
false	false	false	false	true

Table 3-1.   Truth Tables of Boolean Operators

In Ada **not** has the higher precedence of the four Boolean operators, while the other three operators **and**, **or**, and **xor**, share a lower level of precedence. The numeric relational operators fall between these two groups, making it possible to write many expressions without parentheses:

```
5 > 4  or  TRUE = FALSE  or  not TRUE = FALSE
```

In the above example **not** has the highest precedence and is evaluated first. The relational operators have an intermediate precedence, and are evaluated left to right. The **or** operators are the lowest precedence in this example, and are evaluated last, left to right:

```
(5 > 4) or (TRUE = FALSE) or ((not TRUE) = FALSE)
```

Ada doesn't allow you to directly associate unlike logical operators of the same level of precedence; that is to say, to use them in an expression without parentheses.
The expression

```
A and B and C     is acceptable, while
A or B and C
```

**	not	abs				highest-order
*	/	mod	rem			multiplying
+	-					unary adding
+	-	&				binary adding
=	/=	<	<=	>	>=	relational
and	or	xor				logical

Table 3-2. Ada's Six Classes of Operators in Order of Decreasing Precedence

is not acceptable and must have clarifying parenthesis to determine order of evaluation:

```
(A or B) and C        -or-
A or (B and C)
```

Notice that the comparison operators have greater precedence than the logical operators, allowing short expressions such as

```
Line_Length > 80   or   Line_Number > 66
```

to be written without parentheses. But since the logical operator **not** is on the highest priority level along with the multiplying operators, take care not to confuse

```
not EOL or NUL        which is the same as
(not EOL) or (NUL)    with
not (EOL or NUL)      which is logically identical with
(not EOL) and (not NUL)
```

Moreover the expression **not 1 > 2** will be unraveled as $(not\ 1) > 2$, and, since **not** cannot be applied to numeric values, an error message will pop up when you compile.

Membership operators

Ada provides two operators that return Boolean results, to determine whether or not a given value falls within a range of discrete values (integer values or enumerated values). The range is specified in standard Ada form, a lower boundary and a higher boundary separated by two periods, or by giving the type__mark (name) of a subtype. The operators are:

```
in
not in
```

Some examples of using these operators as parts of Boolean expressions:

Operation	Left Operand	Symbol	Right Operand	Result Type
Exponentiation:	Numeric Type	**	Integer	Same Numeric Type
Commutative:				
multiplication	integer	*	integer	same integer
	fixed	*	integer	same fixed type
	integer	*	fixed	same fixed type
	fixed	*	fixed	universal fixed
	float	*	float	same float
division	integer	/	integer	same integer
	fixed	/	integer	same fixed
	fixed	/	fixed	universal fixed
	float	/	float	same float
		mod		
		rem		
Unary Operators:				
identity		+	numeric	numeric
negation		-	numeric	numeric
absolute value		abs	numeric	numeric
logical negation		not	Boolean, one dimensional Boolean array	Boolean
Associative:				
addition	numeric	+	numeric	same numeric
subtraction	numeric	-	numeric	same numeric
Relational:				
equality	note 1	=	note 1	Boolean
inequality	note 1	/=	note 1	Boolean
less than	note 2	<	note 2	Boolean
less than or equal	note 2	<=	note 2	Boolean
greater than	note 2	>	note 2	Boolean
greater than or equal	note 2	>=	note 2	Boolean
Membership:				
in discrete range		in		Boolean
not in discrete range		not in		Boolean

```
Logical:
  conjunction    Boolean        and   Boolean       same
  inclusive or   Boolean        or    Boolean       same
  exclusive or   Boolean        xor   Boolean       same
```

Note 1: any type except limited private
Note 2: any scalar type or one dimensional discrete array

Table 3-3. Ada's Operators

```
WEDNESDAY in MONDAY..FRIDAY
Age in 1..4
Char in UPPER_CASE
User_Input in NATURAL
```

Each of these expressions test whether the value of a discrete object is part of a discrete range. Each would have a value of **TRUE** or **FALSE** and could be used in if statements or other places where a Boolean value is needed.

in and not in have the same precedence as the relational operators. Table 3-3 shows Ada's operator's grouped according to precedence along with the types of their operands and results.

Objects

A major use of data types is to define the format of storage slots in computer memory. The individual slots themselves are called *objects*. Each object stores a data value (or, in the case of composite types, a cluster of data values) and each object has a name or *identifier*, for example, **A**, **Sum**, **Counter**.

Ada has two fundamental kinds of objects: *variables* and *constants*. The value of a constant is set the moment it is *elaborated* (each time the program unit declaring the constant is invoked) in its declaration, and cannot be changed. A variable may assume different values at different times during a given program unit's execution.

Every piece of data in Ada must be associated with an explicit type. Ada's rules about this specify that a data object (a variable or constant):

- Must have a unique type;
- can only be assigned data of that type; and
- can be used only with the operators defined for that type.

We specify the type of an object by *declaring* the object in our program. Where in BASIC a variable can be implicitly declared anywhere in a program, in Ada (as in Pascal and other structured languages) an object must be declared in the *declaration part* (*declaration section*) of the program unit—between the heading of the unit and the reserved word **begin**.

Variables

Once a variable is declared, values consistent with its type may be freely assigned to it in the body of the program. A new value assigned to a variable simply replaces whatever value was there before.

A variable is declared like this:

```
<name> : <type_mark> ;
```

<name> is an identifier, which we will use from that point on to refer to the variable; <type_mark> is the type that the variable will have, for example:

```
Ducks_Available : INTEGER;
```

After we declare a variable in the declaration section of a program unit, we can use it freely in the body of the program, either as a part of an expression or to hold values derived from expressions. To *assign* a value to a variable we use an *assignment statement:*

```
<variable> := <expression>;
```

The := symbol is used for all assignments in Ada. The value of an expression is assigned to variable of a suitable type:

```
Int_Var := 100;
Bool_Val := TRUE;
Float_Var := 5.0 * Sin( Theta );
```

Assignments are statements in and of themselves. Only one variable may be assigned to in an assignment statement, and assignments can't be nested inside expressions as they can in some other languages.

Variable initialization

Ada, unlike Pascal, allows assignment of a value to an object at the time of declaration. This is done by extending the whole declaration with an initial assignment, like this:

```
Index              : INTEGER    := 3;
Mean               : FLOAT      := 2.3;
Current_Character  : CHARACTER  := 'm';
Light_On           : BOOLEAN    := TRUE;
```

A group of objects (constants or variables) may be assigned a type and initialized with a value, all in one shot:

```
Counter_1, Counter_2, Counter_3 : INTEGER:= 0;
```

Note that while we may *initialize* more than one object per assignment in the declaration part of a program, we still can't *assign* to more than one object per statement in the body of a program unit.

The expression used to initialize an object (either variable or constant) must be a simple expression. Just about anything can be used in the initialization expression, even other objects, as long as they have been previously elaborated (we'll define this shortly). The compiler may perform a default initialization; if not, an uninitialized variable contains random data (a.k.a. "garbage").

Constants

A constant is a value which can't be changed during execution of the program unit where it is declared.

A constant declaration looks just like a variable declaration with an initializer, with the addition of the reserved word **constant** inserted just before the type—mark:

```
Line_Length : constant INTEGER:= 80;
```

Once a value has been assigned to a constant, that value cannot be changed until the next time the unit where the constant is declared is reexecuted.

An attempt to assign a value to a constant in the body of a program will cause an error message in the compilation.

In describing Ada's data types, we referred to the typing of data objects. Constants are considered objects just as variables are, and even require storage space, because each time the declaration is processed (elaborated) during program execution a new value could be assigned to the constant. Constants need not be numeric.

There is a difference between Ada constants and constants in other languages. What in other languages may be called "constants", a number which is always the same every time the program executes, is called a *named number* in Ada.

A named number, or declared number, is a special sort of constant. Other constants are changeable in the sense that they can represent values derived from expressions that include variable values. Their restriction is that they cannot be changed during the execution of the particular unit in which they are declared. A named number can only be the value of a number and that number must be completely computable by the compiler at the same time the program is compiled.

A named number can only be assigned the value of a *static expression*:

```
Named_Number := <static expression>
```

Named numbers are declared like other constants in the declaration section of a program unit, except no type—mark (INTEGER, FLOAT, CHARACTER) is used. The compiler can figure out the type by examining the assigned value, since that value is explicit. So:

```
Pi : constant :=   3.1416;
```

is a proper declaration of a named number.

```
Number : constant :=   23/5;
```

is legal because the expression in the assignment is static. But

```
Number : constant :=  A/5;
```

might not be legal as a named number because the value of the variable *A* may be ambiguous at compile time. This would be a legal named number if *A* was also a named number.

```
procedure Three_Assignments is          } Heading

     A_Variable : INTEGER;              { Declaration

begin

     A_Variable := 3;
     A_Variable := 5;                   } Body
     A_Variable := 7;

end Three_Assignments;                   } End
```

In the display above we see a sample procedure blocked out with heading, declaration section, body, and end (note that the end is optionally tagged with the procedure name). As you will see in Chapter 5, this structure applies to all Ada's program units: subprograms (procedures and functions), packages, and tasks.

When a program unit like the one above is executed, the declarations in the declaration section are said to be *elaborated*, a process that includes reserving space in memory.

Elaboration is an Ada term which means (in the words of the Reference Manual) "the process by which the declaration of an object achieves its effect". Every time a subprogram is called, new memory locations are reserved for whatever variables and constants are declared. The values of constants are also computed at this point, and if the variables are to be initialized, the initial values are placed into the variables at this time.

Elaboration is a complex and important concept in Ada, one we will see in other contexts later on. For now keep in mind that an object doesn't exist before the program unit in which it is declared is executed, and that an object vanishes when execution of the program unit is done.

Just for reference (in case you look this up under "elaboration" in the index): Objects declared in a package's declaration part are elaborated when the program starts executing, and the space reserved remains static during execution. Variables declared in a package specification take the place of the "static" storage class variables of other languages.

Examples of Objects

We can write a procedure to initialize its variable in the declaration section like this:[2]

```
with Text_IO;
Procedure A_Char is
   Area : FLOAT := 3.1416 * 7 ** 2
begin
   Text_IO.Put(Char);                              A
end A_Var;
```

The literal expression above reads "3.1416 times seven squared" and matches the pattern of the formula for the area of a circle. In line with Ada's effort toward the abstraction of data, we can generalize it thus:

```
PI * Radius ** 2;
```

so that

```
Area := PI * Radius ** 2;
```

serves as a statement that will give us the area of any circle in the variable **Area**. We must supply the value of the variable **Radius**. We will assume that the named number **PI** has been declared and assigned its value in the parent procedure which calls this procedure.[3]

```
with Text_IO;
procedure Print_Circle_Area is
   Radius : FLOAT := 7.0;
   Area    : FLOAT;
begin
   Area := = PI * Radius ** 2;
   Text_IO.Put( Area );
END Print_Circle_Area;
```

By the way, though the above procedure is compilable on both the SuperSoft "A" and the Janus Ada subset compilers, it lacks a feature required in full Ada, the setting up (*instantiating*) for the output of numeric data. **Put** can be used with a string without a problem, but the setting-up must be done for numeric data. You will see an example of the instantiation of integer I/O at the end of this chapter. The subject will be taken up in detail in Chapter 6.

Custom Data Types

Ada allows you to create your own data types to be used along with the predefined data types we mentioned earlier (**INTEGER, BOOLEAN, FLOAT,** etc.).

Custom types make debugging easier. They also allow creating types of data that actually reflect the real world, a large improvement on mathematical languages like FORTRAN.

Two varieties of Ada types that help reflect real-world conditions are user-defined *enumeration types* and *subtypes*.

User-defined enumeration types[4]

You will recall the declaration of the predefined type **BOOLEAN** from the library package **Standard**:

```
type BOOLEAN is ( FALSE, TRUE );
```

Using the same format, we can create our own enumeration types, using the template in Figure 3-1. You can create your own enumeration types with sets of discrete values like (RED, YELLOW, BLUE), (HIGH, LOW), (NORTH, SOUTH, EAST, WEST):

```
         type <          > is ( <list_of_values> );

-- <type_name        ; the new type_mark, and is
   any legal        er
-- <list_of_v       s a list of either identifiers or
   character        delimited by commas
```

Figure 3-1.   Enumeration Type Declaration Template

```
type COLORS is (RED, YELLOW, BLUE);
type HEIGHT is (HIGH, LOW);
type DIRECTION is (NORTH, SOUTH, EAST, WEST);
```

When declaring enumeration types as per the template in Figure 3-1, <type_name> is replaced with a legal identifier, which becomes from that point onward a type_mark, and can be used just as you would use the type_marks INTEGER, CHARACTER, etc.

<list_of_values> is a list of either identifiers or character literals delimited by commas. The leftmost item in the list has the lowest value, and the rightmost item has the highest value.

Enumeration types are discrete types, and so are handy for loop counters and array indices.

An element appearing in one enumerated type may also appear in another. For example, a character type which included all the vowels would have elements from a type that included all letters. Elements which appear in more than one type are said to be *overloaded*. Examples are

```
type FLAG_COLOR is (RED, WHITE, BLUE);
type TRAFFIC_LIGHT_COLOR is (RED, YELLOW, GREEN);
```

where RED is overloaded.[5]

Usually the compiler can determine from context the type of an overloaded element (by checking the type of the receiving variable in an assignment, for example). In other cases the type may be ambiguous. In that event we can *qualify* the element, or specify for the compiler which type the element belongs to, by using a *qualified expression*.

Using the letters-vowels example above, we could qualify the character literal 'A' as being an element of type VOWEL like this:

```
VOWEL'( 'A' )
```

Table 3-4 lists some user-defined enumeration types.

```
type SUIT is (CLUBS, DIAMONDS, HEARTS, SPADES);
type GENDER is ( 'M', 'F' );
type LEVEL is (LOW, MEDIUM, HIGH);
type TRAFFIC_LIGHT is (RED, YELLOW, GREEN);
type PRIMARY_COLOR is (RED, YELLOW, BLUE);
type SPECTRUM is (INFRA_RED, RED, ORANGE, YELLOW,
                  GREEN, BLUE, VIOLET, ULTRA_VIOLET);
type OIL_PAINT is (
 THALO_RED_ROSE, GRUMBACHER_RED_PRIMARY,
 CADMIUM_VERMILIUM, CADMIUM_ORANGE,
 CADMIUM_YELLOW_ORANGE, YELLOW_PRIMARY,
 THALO_YELLOW_GREEN, LIGHT_PERMANENT_GREEN,
 MANGANESE_BLUE, COBALT_BLUE, FRENCH_ULTRAMARINE_BLUE,
 COBALT_VIOLET    );
```

Table 3-4. Some User-defined Enumeration Types

Subtypes

A *subtype* is a constrained form of a parent type. "What does this mean?" you might ask. Let's look at another type of data abstraction.

If we declare the variable Room__108 as an integer to account for the number of students in one section of grade one at the Keewaydin School:

```
Room_108 : INTEGER;
```

we know that we can store any number of students up to the maximum system integer size (usually 32,767 in microcomputers) in it, or an equally large negative number. We could remind ourselves of that by using a comment:

```
Room_108 : INTEGER; -- range -32,768 to 32,767
```

It would be much more realistic if we could limit the range of integers to the number of students a classroom can be expected to hold, eliminating negative numbers altogether.

We can *constrain* the type **INTEGER** to being able to hold only the number 0 to 30 by creating a subtype:

```
subtype ROOM_CAPACITY is INTEGER range 1..30;
```

Then we can declare variables:

```
Room_108 : ROOM_CAPACITY;
```

Variables of type **ROOM__CAPACITY** are said to be *constrained*, or restricted, to the integers 1 through 30 inclusive. Attempting to assign an integer outside this range to a variable of type room__quantity will generate an error when the program is executing.

A subtype declaration takes the following form:

```
subtype <name> is <subtype_indication> ;
```

where <name> is the new type__mark for the subtype, and <subtype__indication> is the parent type's type__mark, optionally followed by a *range constraint*. A range constraint is defined by the reserved word **range** followed by a range, which is a lower limit and an upper limit separated by two dots ("dot-dot" notation). Here are some sample declarations:

```
subtype INT is INTEGER;
subtype UPPER_CASE is CHARACTER range 'A'..'Z';
subtype TEMPERATURE is INTEGER range -30..100;
```

Subtypes can be declared from enumeration types like this:

```
type WEEK is (
     MONDAY, TUESDAY, WEDNESDAY, THURSDAY, FRIDAY,
     SATURDAY, SUNDAY);
--
subtype WEEKEND is WEEK range SATURDAY..SUNDAY;
subtype WORK_WEEK is DAYS range MONDAY..FRIDAY;
subtype BAD_DAYS is WEEK;
```

Ada predefines two important subtypes of **INTEGER**. The first is subtype **NATURAL**, which includes the numbers from zero to **INTEGER'last**, the largest integer supported by your compiler. The second is **POSITIVE**, which includes the numbers from 1 to **INTEGER'last**. These subtypes are extensively used in Ada's predefined types and subprograms. They are especially useful for array indices and ranges.[6]

Numeric Type Conversion

Since we usually can't mix objects of different types in an expression, we need a mechanism for converting values of one type to values of another type.

Subtypes are considered the same as their parents except for specific constraints. *Implicit conversion* is done between any numeric type and its subtypes. After the actual conversion (conversion to the parent type) the value is checked for the constraints of the target type and if it doesn't fit, an error occurs.

Data of different types, as opposed to different subtypes, can be made compatible with each other with an explicit conversion function, represented in the Ada manual as:

```
type_mark( )
```

where **type_mark** represents a type specifier such as **INTEGER** or **FLOAT**. Conversions performed using these type conversion functions are called *explicit conversions*, because we explicitly state what the conversion will be.

The conversion function **Integer(Float_Value)** converts the floating point value represented by **Float_Value** to an integer.

Assuming the declarations

```
Fractional_Number : FLOAT := 2.3;
Whole_Number : INTEGER;
```

then the assignment

```
Whole_Number := INTEGER( Fractional_Number );
```

will accomplish the same thing that

```
20 F = 2.3
30 W% = F
```

does in BASIC—with one difference: Where BASIC *truncates*, Ada *rounds* by adding 0.5 to the floating-point value, and then truncating. For example:

```
real                    integer
10.8      becomes        10       -- in BASIC
10.8      becomes        11       -- in Ada
```

Type conversion functions are automatically provided when you declare numeric types. Conversion is only allowed between *comformable* types, or types that have a logical conversion possible. It wouldn't be possible to convert a string type to a Boolean, for example, because there is no logical mapping between character arrays and Boolean scalars. There is no obvious conversion of the Boolean **TRUE** to integer, for example, while an obvious conversion from our earlier subtype **ROOM_CAPACITY** to **INTEGER** or **FLOAT** exists.

Attributes of Discrete Objects

In Chapter 2 we mentioned that *types* may have characteristics that we can examine using the environmental inquiry attribute functions. Just as *types* have attribute functions that return

Attribute Function	Parameter Type	Return Type
first		same
last		same
succ	any*	same
pred	any*	same
pos	any*	integer
val	integer	any*

* Any discrete type

Table 3-5. Attribute Functions

characteristics of the type, such as **first** and **last**, *objects* have attributes and attribute functions.

We can ask about characteristics of an object by using certain attribute functions. For example, to find the positional order of an element in the enumerated type **CHARACTER** we write:

```
CHARACTER'pos('A')
```

which evaluates to 65 because capital "A" is the 65th element of enumeration type **CHARACTER**.

Attribute functions can give us information about objects we are unsure of. Besides using them to convert between integer and enumerated types, we can also use these functions when dealing with objects passed as parameters to subprograms, where we don't have a lot of information about the object.

A complete list of attributes and their return types is provided in Appendix G. We include informal descriptions of some of the common attribute functions herein.

An enumeration type can serve as a good example of the attribute functions for discrete objects and types:

```
type DAYS is (SUN, MON, TUE, WED, THUR, FRI, SAT );
```

As you may remember, the format of an attribute inquiry is:

```
<prefix> ' <attribute_name>
```

<prefix> is a **type_mark** for a discrete data type.

The **first** function returns the minimum, or leftmost, value of the specified type. **DAYS'first** returns **SUN**.

```
<discrete_type> ' <function> ( <parameter> )

-- <discrete_type> is a defined discrete data type_mark
-- <function> is an attribute function name
-- <parameter> varies with <function>, may not be neeeded.
```

Figure 3-2. Attribute Template

The **last** function returns the maximum, or rightmost, value of the specified type. DAYS'**last** returns **SAT**.

The **succ** function returns the value to the right of the parameter in the specified type, and the **pred** returns the value to the left of the parameter. These are said to be *successors* and *predecessors* of the parameter. **type__mark'first** has no defined predecessor, and **type__mark'last** has no defined successor. DAYS'**pred(TUE) = MON**, and DAYS'**succ(TUE) = WED**.

pos is the inverse of **val**. Each element of a discrete type has a unique *position number*. The position value of type **INTEGER** (or its subtypes) is equal to itself. The position of an enumerated type is defined by the order it appears in the definition. The positions are numbered starting at zero, and range to (number of elements) − 1. **pos** returns the positional value of an element: DAYS'**pos(MON) = 1**. The **val** function returns the element of a type whose position is specified as the parameter: DAYS'**val(2) = TUE** The following identity is true for **pos** and **val**:

```
type_mark'val( type_mark'pos( <element> ) ) = <element>
```

One of the major advantages of the attribute functions is that we can manipulate abstracted data. For example, it would be hard to increment a variable of type **DAYS**, as **TUE + 1** doesn't make any sense to a computer. However, **Weekday := succ(TUE)** does make sense.

Pragmas

When you look over the **Standard** package you will notice the keyword **pragma** cropping up in what look like functions. These are *compiler directives*, perhaps better described as suggestions to the compiler about the way the program should be compiled. They apply only during compilation, not later on during execution. They are not (strictly speaking) part of the program itself.

Pragmas are somewhat implementation dependent, and may vary from compiler to compiler. Ada has predefined pragmas, as is required of all compilers; these are listed in Appendix G.[7]

The spirit of pragmas is to use them so that a program can still run correctly even if the pragmas are all removed. The following are some examples of pragmas:

```
pragma pack( string );     -- reduces storage
pragma optimize( time );   -- try for fast code
pragma list( off );        -- don't list source code
```

Predefined Packages

Like the C language, Ada has few statements and provision at all for I/O. I/O is provided in the standardized packages that came with your compiler: **Text__IO**, **Sequential__IO**, **Direct__IO**, and **Low__Level__IO**.

The data types **INTEGER**, **FLOAT**, etc. are not intrinsic to Ada—they are types created by an additional package supplied with all Ada compilers called **Standard**, the predefined language environment, or Standard Package. It is listed in its entirety in Appendix D.

The package **Standard** contains most of the predefined identifiers (*keywords*) in Ada. The Ada manual has a listing of **Standard**'s specification section, and all validated Ada compilers must include it.

Standard's body is implementation defined. Typically it is embedded in the compiler. The initial versions of Janus/Ada and SuperSoft Ada have standard packages that are incomplete for one reason or another (some reasons are listed in the notes on this chapter).

Ada compilers automatically include package **Standard** at the beginning of each unit compiled. You don't need to take any action to include it.

A Simple Program

To try and pull together some of the information in this chapter and to show you a few of the details of an Ada program, we'll examine line-by-line a simple Ada procedure to count printable characters typed in by the operator. In later chapters we'll enlarge this procedure to do something more useful. The entire program is presented as Figure 3-3.[8]

The first portion of our file is a comment block explaining what it is we have. It's a good idea to put a comment at the head of each file you write. Although this isn't dictated by the language, it's simply good practice.

```
-- Character Count version 1: Counts printable (non-control)

-- ASCII characters from the keyboard. Use Control-Z to

-- terminate.
```

```
with Text_IO;
procedure Count1 is
   package Int_IO is new Text_IO.Integer_IO( INTEGER );
   Input_Char  : CHARACTER;                -- used to get input
   Counter     : INTEGER := 0;             -- keeps track of count
   Control_Z   : constant CHARACTER := character'val( 26 );
begin
<<START>>                                  -- goto loop label
   Text_IO.Get( Input_Char );             -- obtain input from user
   if Input_Char in ' '..'~' then         -- test for being non-control char
      Counter := Counter + 1;             -- if so, increment count
   end if;
   if Input_Char /= Control_Z then        -- are we done?
      goto START;                         -- no, get another character
   end if;
   Int_IO.Put( Counter );                 -- print result
end Count1;
```

Figure 3-3. Character Count Version 1: Counts Printable (non-control) ASCII Characters from the Keyboard. Use Control-Z to Terminate.

As you can see, the comment describes the general process, the version number, and usage information, enough to figure out what the procedure does without looking at the code.

Next comes what is called the *context clause*, which we will see more of in Chapter 5. Basically this line says that the procedure will be using parts of a library package called **Text__IO**. **Text__IO** contains most of the commonly used input/output subprograms in Ada.

```
with Text_IO;
```

Note that the context clause is the first line of code besides comments in the file.

After the context comes the *subprogram declaration*, which declares the type of subprogram (procedure as opposed to function) and names it:

```
procedure Count1 is
```

If this procedure needed parameters, they also would be declared here. Chapter 5 explores this subject in greater detail.

The declaration part of the procedure follows the heading. We declare all objects, types, subtypes, supporting subprograms, etc. here:

```
package Int_IO is new Text_IO.Integer_IO( INTEGER );
Input_Char  : CHARACTER;            -- used to get input
Counter     : INTEGER := 0;         -- keeps track of count
Control_Z   : constant CHARACTER := CHARACTER'val( 26 );
```

The first item is called an *instantiation*. This is required in all Ada compilers that support generics, which excludes most of the microcomputer subsets. The instantiation creates a new package of I/O routines designed for type **INTEGER**, using as template a generic package called **Integer__IO** contained in the package **Text__IO**. We can tell that **Integer__IO** is in **Text__IO** because of the special notation form mentioned in the context clause explanation:

```
Text_IO.Integer_IO
```

This notation, with the dot between the parent (**Text__IO**) and the contained element (**Integer__IO**), is called *selected component* or *named component* or *dot* notation.

Chapter 6 contains more detailed information on I/O and instantiation.

After the instantiation we declare three objects, a character variable (**Input__Char**) to hold characters as the user types them in, an integer variable (**Counter**) initialized to zero to use as a character counter, and a constant (**Control__Z**) to serve as a flag for end of input. Note that a named number couldn't be used in place of the constant because the value of the constant is a character, an enumeration type that is not a legal value for a named number.

This concludes the declaration part of the procedure. Next we can write the body, where executable code is placed. The body begins with the reserved word **begin**:

```
begin
```

The body of this procedure will accept characters typed in by the user, counting all of the noncontrol characters, until it receives a Control-Z, at which point it will print a total. We'll need to set up a loop to execute this properly; we'll use the **goto** to implement the loop. Ordinarily we wouldn't use the **goto**, but let's keep things close to BASIC until next chapter. The **goto** requires a target label to jump to; the label is declared simply by writing it into the program:

```
<<START>>                      -- goto loop label
```

Now we can accept a character from the keyboard and place this character into our variable **Input__Char**, using an input procedure (**Get**) from the package **Text__IO**:

```
Text_IO.Get( Char );           -- obtain input from user
```

Once we have the character we can test it using the membership operator in. We have chosen to use a discrete range, and if the character isn't a control character we increment the counter:

```
if Char in ' '..'~' then      -- test for being non-control char
   Counter := Counter + 1;    -- if so, increment count
end if;
```

We could have done this test several other ways, for example by using two tests in a logical expression:

```
if Char > ' ' and Char < '~' then
```

We also could have declared a subtype of character in the declaration section:

```
subtype VISIBLE_CHARACTER is CHARACTER range ' '..'~';
```

and then used the membership operator:

```
if Char in VISIBLE_CHARACTER then
```

which probably provides superior abstracting. All in all, however, the discrete range is a reasonable method. Once we test the character we also need to see if we have reached the termination character Control-Z, to see if we're done and can print the result. If we aren't, we'll loop using the goto statement; otherwise, we'll fall through the end of the if statement:

```
if Char /= Control_Z then     -- are we done?
   goto START;                 -- no, get another character
end if;
```

After we fall through, all that remains to be done is to print the result:

```
Int_IO.Put( Counter );        -- print result
```

using the procedure put, which is contained in the new package we instantiated as Int__IO, and then to end the procedure:

```
end Count1;
```

This chapter contains assorted basic information about types, expressions, and operators. It by no means provides you with the complete story, but it should give you a good, sound foundation. After reading the next three chapters you'll be well on your way to writing more complicated programs in Ada.

4
Control Structures

One of the essential features of any computer programming language is the ability to perform tests on conditions and choose one of several alternate actions according to the results.

Consider this BASIC program segment:

```
100 T% = 1 * 2 * 3 * 4 * 5
200 PRINT "THE PRODUCT OF CONSECUTIVE NUMBERS FROM 1 TO 5";
300 PRINT " IS: ";T%
400 END
```

This segment computes the product of consecutive numbers from 1 to 5, prints two strings telling you the result, and ends. It performs these actions in a series of four *statements*, performed one after the other without deviation. This is an example of *straight-line code*.

A program made up of straight-line code makes for dull reading. Its dullness is misleading; the longer such a program gets, the harder it is to write. What a job it would be to write, say, 9,000 lines of code executing from start to finish without deviation!

That's not to say that straight-line coding doesn't have its place. In time-critical routines—a disk-drive control program, for example, where disk sector reads are timed by software—straight-line code may be necessary for speed.

We can write a generalized program that gives the factorial of any integer from $N = 1$ to $N = 7$ ($N = 8$ will produce a number larger than MAXINT) using the formula:

$$N! = N * (N-1) * (N-2)... * 3 * 2 * 1$$

We will get erroneous results if N is outside the range $1 < N < 7$, but we can screen out this possibility by introducing input testing and elementary conditional branches, as shown in Figure 4-1.

First we test to make sure the number N is within the acceptable range. If not, we go to line 650, print a message to the user, then go back to line 100 and try again (lines 100–250).

```
100 PRINT "TYPE A NUMBER FROM 1 TO 7: ";
150 INPUT N%
200 IF N% < 1 OR N% > 7 THEN 650
250 REM end of input error testing

300 T% = 1
350 FOR X% = N% TO 1 STEP -1
400 T% = T% * X%
450 NEXT X%
500 REM end of computation loop

550 PRINT "THE FACTORIAL OF ";N%;" IS ";T%
600 GOTO 800

650 PRINT "THE NUMBER ";N%;" IS OUT OF RANGE."
700 PRINT "          - TRY AGAIN - "
750 GOTO 100
800 END
```

Figure 4-1. BASIC Factorial

Second we use a *control structure*, the FOR-NEXT loop (with a negative increment), to supply us with successive values for X% ranging from N down to 1. Within the control structure the factorial result is accumulated.

Finally we print our result. We have performed tests to determine our next course of action, and have branched to different parts of our program according to their outcome. We have set up a *loop* structure in lines 300 through 500. The loop continues until an *exit condition* is met: X% becomes less than 1.

Testing

The simplest form of testing has the following format:

```
IF <condition> THEN <action>
```

In BASIC, <action> can be a statement (an assignment, for example) or a series of statements; it is frequently a GOTO (implicit or explicit) or GOSUB statement that moves control to another line number somewhere else in the program.

In most other languages the same format applies. So, for example, in C the statement in line 200 would appear with only slightly altered syntax:

```
if( (n < 1) || (n > 7) )
        goto L650;
```

> "||" means "or"

Where L650 represent line number 650.

In Ada, the format of the IF statement is very similar:

```
if <condition> then
  < action(s) >;
end if;
```

Notice the **end if;**—it sets the action apart as a distinct and self-contained unit, able to encapsulate a series of statements without ambiguity.

The condition tested for is a Boolean expression, usually made up of one or more comparisons. In line 200 of our BASIC factorial program the tests determining whether the input is within range produces an answer of either true or false, and on true, control moves to the THEN branch to handle an input error (lines 650–750). Otherwise, control "falls through" to line 300 and computes the answer.

Any expression yielding Boolean results may be used as a test in a conditional statement:

```
A > B              -- arithmetic
L and M            -- logical
A not in 1..10     -- membership
A > B and C = D    -- mixed
```

Ada also provides Boolean variables that can hold a value of either **TRUE** or **FALSE** and can be used as flags to signal the result of a test. A flag can be tested in a conditional statement and the branch made according to the value it holds. For example:

```
if Flag_Up then
    Put("Flag is up.");
end if;
```

We can set a Boolean flag in Ada by assigning a Boolean value directly to it, or by assigning the result of a Boolean expression to it:

```
Flag_One, Flag_Two : BOOLEAN;
   .          .

   .          .
Flag_One := True;        -- direct assignment
Flag_Two := One > Two;   -- result of compare
```

As we mentioned earlier, the test condition can be the result of compound (multiple) comparisons. For example, the two tests in line 200 of FACTORIAL.BAS together determine the condition.

We may use the compound or multiple relations as long as the result evaluates to either **TRUE** or **FALSE**. There is no limit to the number of relations that can be used in a test statement, though care must be taken to observe the rules of precedence.

Recall the general format of the test statement:

```
IF condition(s) THEN action(s)
```

We have illustrated a program branching to a single action according to the result of a test. But a test can result in a *sequence* of actions in a *compound statement*. In many languages compound statements must be delimited with special symbols or reserved words: The **BEGIN** and **END** of Pascal, for example.

Ada's format is similar except that the **then** and **end if;** of the Ada **if** statement do the job of defining the compound statement:

```
Number,Counter:      INTEGER;
Flag:                BOOLEAN;
.                    .
.                    .
if Number < 1 or Number > 7 then
    Put("Number is out of range.");
    New_Line;
    Counter := Counter + 1;
    Flag := TRUE;
end if;
.                    .
```

The important point here is that there is no syntactic difference in Ada between a single statement and a compound statement controlled by the **if** structure.

Frequently the result of a test determines which of two or more alternative actions must be performed before continuing the program. Our factorial program includes a good example. The error handler reads:

```
650 PRINT "THE NUMBER ";N%;" IS OUT OF RANGE."
655 PRINT "          - TRY AGAIN - "
750 GOTO 100
800 END
```

It tells us only that N% is out of range. If we want to establish whether N% is out of range because it is too small or because it is too large, we need to make two separate tests:

```
650 IF N% < 1 THEN PRINT "THE NUMBER IS TOO SMALL"
700 IF N% > 7 THEN PRINT "THE NUMBER IS TOO LARGE"
750 PRINT "        - TRY AGAIN -"
755 GOTO 100
800 END
```

Here we have to decide between two minor alternative actions before we continue. Both tests are always made, even though only one can be true.

We can combine both of these tests into a single Ada control structure:

```
if Number < 1 THEN
      Put( "The Number is too small" );
else
      Put( "The Number is too large" );
end if;
```

The statement or statements executed by a **TRUE** evaluation are now delimited by the reserved words **then** and **else**, and the statements executed by a **FALSE** evaluation are now delimited by the reserved words **else** and **end if**.

Should we need more than two alternatives in this sort of decision structure, we could use multiple **if** statements in the manner of Pascal; see Figure 4-2.

```
IF <condition 1> THEN
     <action 1>;
ELSE IF <condition 2> THEN
     <action 2>;
     ELSE IF <condition 3> THEN
          <action 3>;
             .            .
             .            .
          ELSE IF <condition n> THEN
             <action n>;
               ELSE
                   <action for all other conditions>;
               END IF;
          END IF;
      END IF;
  END IF;
```

Figure 4-2.   IF ELSE IF Construction (Pascal)

```
    if <condition 1> then
         <action 1>;
    elsif <condition 2> then
         <action 2>;
    elsif <condition 3> then
         <action 3>;

              .        .
              .        .
              .        .

    elsif <condition n> then
         <action n>;
    else
         <action for all other conditions>;
    end if;

-- <condition x> is a Boolean expression
-- <action> blocks are one or more statements, and are
    delimited by then and either elsif, else, or
    end if
```

Figure 4-3. if elsif else *Template (Ada)*

Ada, however, provides us with a much more efficient construct: elsif. elsif is not just an else and an if stuck together; it is a distinct construct. The advantage to the elsif is that we don't create a new if block each time. No nesting of if statements is generated, and we don't need all those end if's. All of the evaluations are performed at the same logical level of the program, as outlined in Figure 4-3.

Using these forms our Ada factorial program can be rewritten as Figure 4-4.[1]

```
with Text_IO;
procedure Factorial is
     Int_IO is new Text_IO.Integer_IO( INTEGER );
     Number, Result : INTEGER;
begin
<<TOP>>                           -- A label used as a goto target
     Text_IO.Put( "Type a number from 1 to 7: " );
     Text_IO.Get( Number );   -- Gets our number from user
     if Number < 1 then
          Text_IO.Put( "The number is too small - " );
          goto TOP;
```

Figure 4-4. Factorial in Ada   *(continued)*

```
        elsif Number > 7 then
             Text_IO.Put( "The number is too large - " );
             goto TOP;
        else
             Text_IO.Put( "The number is acceptable" );
        endif;

-- Here we compute the factorial and assign the answer
-- to the variable result, and then print the answer

end Factorial;
```

Figure 4-4. continued

Note that by using the **if..then..elsif..else** structures we have clarified the flow of the program considerably and we have avoided making several additional tests. Though we are using GOTO's (Ada-style), there is nothing like the mish-mosh we come up with when we use a batch of GOTO's in BASIC. As a matter of fact, we can avoid the use of GOTO's entirely—in Ada (see Figure 4-5).

```
begin
  Text_IO.Get( Input_Char );
  if Input_Char = CHARACTER'val( 10 ) then
    Cursor_Down;
  elsif Input_Char = CHARACTER'val( 13 ) then
    Cursor_Left_Edge;
  elsif Input_Char = CHARACTER'val( 8 ) then
    Cursor_Left_One;
    Erase_At_Cursor;
  elsif Input_Char in 'A'..'H' then
    Do_Menu;
  else
    Text_IO.Put( Input_Char );
  end if;
end;
```

Figure 4-5. if elsif Example

We have seen multiple comparisons combined in a test using the logical operators or and and to produce a Boolean result. The order of the test is from left to right, except when rules of precedence or parentheses dictate otherwise. Here is an example of multiple comparisons that will not produce the expected result:

```
Divisor, Dividend : INTEGER;
  .                    .
  .                    .
if Divisor = 0 or Dividend / Divisor < 1 then ...
```

When the condition **Divisor = 0** is met, the result of the test is **TRUE**. The second half of the test, **Dividend/Divisor** < 1, is unnecessary and will produce an error if evaluated. In some language compilers, however, the second part of the test is always performed nonetheless, creating a "divide by zero" error.

In Ada a special language feature, the *short-circuit form*, provides logical operators that can bypass the second part of a test depending on the results of the first part. Ada's two short-circuit logical operators are **and then** and **or else**.

```
if <condition> and then <condition> then
if <condition> or else <condition> then
```

In the first case with the **and then** operator, the second condition is tested only if the first is TRUE; otherwise it is bypassed. In the second case with **or else**, the second condition is tested only if the first is **FALSE**. We can rewrite our example with the short-circuit form thus:

```
if (Divisor = 0) or else ((Dividend / Divisor) < 1) then
```

Notice that we use parentheses even though they are not necessary. Even with the parentheses, the second part of the test

```
(Dividend / Divisor) < 1
```

will not be carried out when the divisor is zero. Later on in the book we will see how Ada can handle divide-by-zero and other errors with another efficient construction called an *exception handler*.

We can choose one of several sets of actions according to the result of a test in a **if** statement. The **elsif** branch inside an **if** statement is used to avoid the overhead involved with nested **if** statements.

There are situations where another structure—the case statement—is more efficient and more readable.

In a **case** statement, the decision branch is chosen by testing the result of a discrete expression (usually, the discrete expression is a variable) against a series of simple static expressions or ranges of the same type as the expression. The test is for *equality* or *membership*. See Figure 4-6 for the template of the structure of the **case** statement.

Except for **others**, the choices must all be instances or ranges of the type value produced by the **case** expression. One and only one choice may evaluate to **TRUE**, and the actions described by the statements following the => symbol for the branch will be executed. When those statements are finished, control passes to the first statement following the **end case;**.

The => symbol (spoken: "choose") is an Ada special symbol. You can think of the case statement as a kind of multiple choice selector. **others** is a default that catches cases that don't fit the supplied alternatives.

A situation where a case statement might be suitable is when deciding what to do based on keyboard input:

```
case <expression> is
    when <choice 1>   =>   <action 1>;
    when <choice 2>   =>   <action 2>;
    when <choice 3>   =>   <action 3>;
       .                       .
       .                       .
    when others       =>   <default action>;
end case;

--<expression> evaluates to a discrete type.
--<choice> is static expressions or static ranges,
  separated by vertical bar "or" symbols.
--<action> is one or more statements.
```

Figure 4-6. **case** *Template*

Is the character:
Line feed? Eject a line.
Return? Move the cursor left.
Backspace? erase the previous character.
An uppercase letter? Do a menu choice

.
.
.

Others? Must be printable, so print it.

The **case** statement is terminated with an **end case;**, which makes it resemble the **if** structure. In the analogy above, this would be something like "end of question". Hence, using the **case** statement, we can rewrite the analogy above as shown in Figure 4-7.

A complex multiple **if** statement frequently can be transformed into much simpler and more readable code by using the **case** statement. In fact this should probably be done wherever possible.

Remember the restriction on the use of **case** statements: The expression in a **case** statement that determines or matches the choices in the various branches must evaluate to a discrete type. Therefore, the following will not work:

```
Decimal_Number : FLOAT;
.                        .
.                        .
.                        .
case Decimal_Number is  ...
```

as **Decimal_Number** represents a real number, not a discrete value.

```
Text_IO.Get( Input_Char );
case input_char is
   when CHARACTER'val( 10 ) =>
      Cursor_Down;
   when CHARACTER'val( 13 ) =>
      Cursor_Left_Edge;
   when CHARACTER'val( 8 )  =>
      Cursor_Left_One;
      Erase_At_Cursor;
   when 'A'..'H'            =>
      Do_Menu;
   when others             =>
      Text_IO.Put( Input_Char );
end case;
```

Figure 4-7. **case** Example

Note that in Figure 4-7 the various choices that belong to the same group and take on the same set of actions are put in the same **when** statement, separated by the vertical bar "or" symbol. One therefore can read the **when** statement as "When it is choice #1, or 2, or 3, then do this . . .".

We could have put each choice in a separate **when** statement—at the expense of clarity and efficiency.

If the **others** clause is given, it must be the last alternative listed. **others** is not required if all possible other alternatives are explicitly listed as choices, but it's always a good idea, just in case (no pun intended!).

Since every possibility must be exhausted in a **case** statement, the **others** branch is frequently a convenient way of dropping through the structure without generating an error. Filtering an input for the letters **A**, **B**, and **C**, for example, we might write

```
case Input_Value of
    when 'A' ¦ 'a' => Action_A;
    when 'B' ¦ 'b' => Action_B;
    when 'C' ¦ 'c' => Action_C;
    when others => null;
end case;
```

The **null;** in the **others** branch is called a *null statement* and does nothing at all. If that branch is selected, control falls through to the end of the **case** structure.

Programmers who have despaired over Pascal's or C's empty null statement (indicated by a hanging semicolon) will find Ada's **null** spares them a lot of debugging time (have you ever accidentally put a semicolon at the end of a **while** condition?).

Loops

One of the features that makes a computer a useful tool is its ability to repeat a set of instructions indefinitely. It will tirelessly do mundane, repetitive tasks over and over again because a computer is a big, dumb, fast adding/machine typewriter that doesn't know any better.

Computer languages usually have one or more control structures that make our adding machine/typewriter repeat a task. In BASIC, for example, there is the FOR loop, and usually the WHILE-WEND loop. In Pascal there is the FOR loop, WHILE loop, and the REPEAT..UNTIL loop. Similarly, in C we have the FOR loop, WHILE loop, and the DO..WHILE loop.

In Ada the simplest of the three control structures for repetition is the **loop** structure, which has the format shown in Figure 4-8. The loop structure is consistent with Ada's other structures in that it has an **end** statement to terminate it.

```
loop
      <statement>;
end loop;
```

-- <statement> is one or more statements.

Figure 4-8. loop *Template*

The loop structure, as its name implies, performs the actions within its boundaries repeatedly. Notice there is no implicit termination of the loop in its simplest form. Indeed, a simple loop structure without explicit termination becomes an infinite loop—a loop with no exit:

```
loop
      Put("This is an infinite loop.");
      New_Line;
end loop;
```

An infinite loop may or may not be desirable, depending on the application. Normally, it is not. Certain conditions, such as arithmetic errors, inside the loop structure may provide us with an unscheduled exit even from an infinite loop. A condition of this kind is known as an *exception* in Ada. We will discuss *exception handling* in Chapter 6. For now we'll content ourselves with the language features provided in Ada that allow us to exit the loop control structure in a normal manner.

The most obvious way to transfer control from one place to another in an Ada program (as in *almost* any other language; there always are exceptions—like Modula-2) is to use the goto statement. As you may recall the label associated with Ada's goto statement is marked with double arrows: < <label> >. The infinite loop above can be broken by inserting a goto statment in the loop control structure:

```
            loop
                  Put("This is no longer an infinite loop.");
                  New_Line;
                  goto OUTSIDE;
            end loop;
      <<OUTSIDE>>
                  .                    .
```

In Ada, the goto is rarely used to get out of a loop. Instead, we use the exit statement.

exit causes immediate control transfer from inside the loop structure to the statement immediately following the loop. Here it is, in its simplest form:

```
exit;
```

Again, as in the case of a simple GOTO statement, the transfer of control is unconditional, that is, the loop is exited immediately. Compare the example above with its GOTO with the one below using EXIT:

```
loop
    Put("This is also not an infinite loop.");
    New_Line;
    Put("In fact, it could be called a one-shot loop.");
    exit;
end loop;
-- We continue here after the
-- exit statement is encountered.
```

Since the whole point of a loop is repetition, the simple **exit** statement is always combined with a test which determines whether it is to be skipped over (to continue the loop) or executed:

```
loop
    Put("Looping...");
    New_Line;
    Counter := Counter + 1;
    if Counter >= Loop_Limit then
        exit;
    end if;
end loop;
Put("Counter exceeds Loop_Limit");
New_Line;
```

Using an **if** statement with the **exit** statement is relatively clumsy—

```
if <condition> then
    exit;
end if;
```

especially since Ada provides a very nice extension to the exit statement that accomplishes the same thing:

```
exit when <condition> ;
```

The rules for <condition> are the same as for the **if** statement <condition>. This language feature is both more natural and more readable than the corresponding **if** statement. We can transform our loop example into:

```
loop
    Put("Looping...");
    New_Line;
    Counter := Counter + 1;
    exit when Counter >= Loop_Limit;
end loop;
Put("Counter exceeds loop_limit");
New_Line;
```

Loops may be nested, in which case the exit statement will cause an exit from the immediate enclosing loop only.

In multiple nested loop structures, however, we often want to exit several loop levels at the same time. We could use the **goto** statement, but Ada provides a much better facility to achieve the same result. This is known as a 'named' loop, and has the general format illustrated in Figure 4-9.

By naming loops we can use the **exit** statement to exit from more than one loop at a time:

```
Name_1:    loop                            -- loop #1 starts here
Name_2:        loop                        -- loop #2 starts here
               --
               exit Name_1 when <condition>;
               --
           end loop Name_2;                -- loop #2 ends here
       end loop Name_1;                    -- loop #1 ends here
       -- Control structure ends up here.
```

The complete form of the exit statement is shown in Figure 4-10.

```
<loop label>:  loop
                   <statements>;
               end loop <loop label>;

-- <loop label> is any legal identifier.
-- <statement> is one or more statements.
```

Figure 4-9. Named loop *Template*

```
        exit <loop label> when <condition>;

-- <loop label> is the name of an enclosing loop, and is
   optional. If omitted, exit is from the innermost
   enclosing loop.
-- when is optional.
-- Condition is a Boolean expression, and is present if
   when is present.
```

Figure 4-10. **exit** *Statement Template*

The loop name is optional; the **when** and its associated condition also are optional. The ability to break out of an inner loop is an extremely powerful feature of the Ada language, as is the ability to arbitrarily position the exit point within the body of the loop:

```
-- example (1)
loop
    exit when not this_is_true;
    -- statements
    --
end loop;

-- example (2)
loop
    -- statements
    --
    exit when this_is_true;
end loop;

        for <control variable> in <discrete range> loop
            <statement>;
        end loop;

-- <control variable> is any legal identifer. It is
   implicitly declared by the loop, is local to the loop,
   and cannot be modified.
-- <discrete range> is a range of discrete values in the
   form Low_Limit..High_Limit.
-- <statement> is one or more statements.
```

Figure 4-11. **for** *Statement Template*

Notice how in example (1) putting the **exit when** at the top of the loop amounts to a **while** loop, and putting the **exit when** at the bottom as in (2) amounts to a **repeat-until** loop.

for Loop

Ada provides a Pascal-like **for** loop, useful in iteration when the termination point is known ahead of time (see template in Figure 4-11).

```
--    Factorial Program
--    Compute the factorial of N, where N is less than 7

with Text_IO;
procedure Factorial is
    package Int_IO is new Text_IO.Integer_IO( INTEGER );
    Max_Number : constant INTEGER := 7;
    Min_Number : constant INTEGER := 1;
    Result, N  : INTEGER := 1;
begin
        -- ask for input, loop until acceptable.
    loop
        Text_IO.Put( "Type a number between 1 and 7: " );
        Int_IO.Get( N );
        exit when N <= Max_Number and N >= Min_Number;
        Text_IO.Put( "That number is not acceptable - " );
    end loop;
    Text_IO.New_Line;
        -- compute factorial
    for Index in 2..N loop
        Result := Result * Index;
    end loop;
        -- print results
    Text_IO.Put( "The factorial of " );
    Int_IO.Put( N );
    Text_IO.Put( " is " );
    Text_IO.Put( Result );
    Text_IO.New_Line;
end Factorial;
```

Figure 4-12. Factorial Program in Ada

```
for <Control Variable> in reverse <Discrete Range> loop
    <Statement>;
end loop;

-- <Control Variable> is any legal identifer. It is
   implicitly declared by the loop, is local to the loop,
   and cannot be assigned to.
-- <Discrete Range> is a range of discrete values in the
   form low_limit..high_limit.
-- <Statement> is one or more statements.
```

Figure 4-13. **for** *Template—Reverse Indexed*

The loop control variable is automatically declared as a discrete type. Unlike other Ada variables it does not have to be predeclared. The contol variable is *local* to the loop (more on this in the chapter on *scope*), and the variable may not be assigned to or otherwise altered.

The control variable may be of any discrete type, including enumerated types. The type of the control variable is implied by the specified range.

Figure 4-12 presents the factorial program again, using a **for** loop.[2]

Notice in this program that we have made use of the short-circuit form when testing the input, and that we have made use of the fact that factorial of 1 is equal to 1.

A variation of the **for** loop in Ada, which allows for the decrement or countdown of the control variable where the initial value of the control variable is the maximum value of the range, and the final value of the control variable is the minimum value of the range, is shown in Figure 4-13.

We could have written the **for** loop in our last version of the factorial program like this:

```
Result := 1;
for Index in reverse 2..n loop
    Result := Result * Index;
end loop;
```

Notice the only difference between the first and second **for** loops is the insertion of the reserved word **reverse**.

The exit statement may be used inside the **for** loop if you so desire, and **for** loops may also be named.

while Loop

Ada's third loop construct is the **while**, depicted in Figure 4-14.

Ada

```
          while <Condition> loop
               <Statement>;
          end loop;


-- <Condition> is a Boolean expression.
-- <Statement> is one or more statements.
```

Figure 4-14. **while** *Template*

As long as <Condition> is true, the loop is executed. When the condition becomes false the loop is exited, with control transferred to the statement immediately after the **end** loop. Note that since the condition is tested at the very top of the loop, if <Condition> is initially false, the statements within the loop's body will never be executed at all.

As an example suppose we have a Boolean variable **Port_Ready** that is set by another routine when a hardware port is ready. The following illustrates the use of the **while** loop:

```
Port_Ready      : BOOLEAN;
.                        .
.                        .
while not Port_Ready loop
     Put("Port is not ready...");
     New_Line;
     -- test port again
end loop;
Put("Port is ready.");
```

As with the **for** and simple loops, the **while** loop may be named and the **exit** statement may be used.

The simple loop structure can be easily used in place of the **while** loop, and less easily in place of the **for** loop. Which construction you choose in any situation should depend on which gives the clearest and simplest picture of what you're trying to accomplish.

A Sample Program

As a last example to illustrate the use of some features covered in this chapter, Figure 4-15 presents a short, looping program that takes input typed by the user and counts the number of words and characters typed. (For simplicity, a word is any set of adjacent visible characters.[3]) The program gives a report and terminates when a Control-Z is encountered in the input stream. For practice you might want to type this program in and run it to acquaint yourself with the various loop structures, and then rewrite parts of the code using different ones.

```ada
-- Counts words from input stream until  Z is encountered.
with Text_IO;
procedure Wc4 is
     package INT_IO is new Text_IO.Integer_IO(INTEGER);
     subtype VISIBLE_CHARACTERS is CHARACTER range '!'..'~';
     Input_Char              : CHARACTER;
     Word_Count, Char_Count : INTEGER   := 0;
     Control_Z               : CHARACTER := CHARACTER'val( 26 );
     In_A_Word               : BOOLEAN := FALSE;
begin
        -- prompt user for input
     Text_IO.Put( "Enter text, end with ^Z: " );
        -- get CHARACTERs until ^Z encountered
     loop
         Text_IO.Get( Input_Char );
         exit when Input_Char = Control_Z;
         -- add one to CHARACTER count
         Char_Count := Char_Count + 1;
         if  -- test for transition into a word
             not In_A_Word and Input_Char in VISIBLE_CHARACTERS
         then
             In_A_Word := TRUE;
             Word_Count := Word_Count + 1;
         elsif -- test for transition to white space
             In_A_Word and Input_Char not in VISIBLE_CHARACTERS
         then
             In_A_Word := FALSE;
         end if;
     end loop;
        -- display results
     Text_IO.New_Line;
     Text_IO.Put( "Words counted: " ); Text_IO.Put( Word_Count );
     Text_IO.New_Line;
     Text_IO.Put( "Chars counted: " ); Text_IO.Put( Char_Count );
     Text_IO.New_Line;
end Wc4;
```

Figure 4-15.   Word Count

```
   SIMPLE          ................COMPOUND................

          .               .                                        .
    .             .                                          .
    .             .                                          .
    .             .
    .         BRANCH-ON-TEST  LOOP-ON-TEST  SIMPLE-LOOP   BLOCK
          --------------   ------------   -----------   -----
Assignment   if               for            loop       begin/end
goto         case             while
exit         and then
Call         or else
null
return
raise


(This chart does not include tasking statements.)
```

Figure 4-16.   Statements and Control Structures

By the time you have gone over Ada's I/O in Chapter 6, you should be able to modify this program to operate on text files, turning it into a useful utility.

Conclusion

In this chapter we covered all of Ada's statements and structures, except for the *block statement* (which is covered in the next chapter), *exception* statements (covered in Chapter 6), and *tasking* statements (covered in Chapter 13).

With these statements and control structures, all of which are summarized in Figure 4-16, you are ready for packages and subprograms, which we'll tackle next.

5

Program Units: Subprograms and Packages

In this chapter we will look at some of Ada's *program units* and how these modules fit together to make programs. We'll discuss program unit structure, ways to pass parameters to subprograms, scope and visibility rules, packages, and performing separate compilations.

A program unit is a self-contained structure defining data and operations on data. It can be compiled into a working program or program segment that will probably do something useful, such as display "Hello, world" on the screen, return the square root of three, or beat you at chess.

Ada programs can be made up of three basic kinds of programs units (and several kinds of subunits). The basic program units are:

- subprograms
- packages
- generic units

Subprograms are the procedures and functions we have already used in some of our examples in earlier chapters. The procedure and function subprograms introduced in earlier chapters included some unexplained details, however. We will cover them in this chapter and go on to explain packages, which are collections of logically related types, objects, other packages, and subprograms that can be exported to separate subprograms or packages the way Text_IO exports Put and Get.

Generic units are not "programs" in themselves but are templates from which new program units can be produced. They will be covered in Chapter 11 as an advanced feature of the language (a feature frequently unavailable on microcomputer subsets). Subunits are the basic units split into two or more modules.

Tasks are special program units used in parallel processing that run simultaneously and in coordination with one another and the main program. We'll cover them in Chapter 12.

All of Ada's program units have a similar, modular structure. Modularity allows for separate compilation of program fragments and also for implementation independence and for replaceability of software components.

Each Ada program is a set of modules that the compiler and linker merge into a single executable program. A big advantage of this system is that it enables several people to work on a program at once. It facilitates the development of libraries of useful subprograms, types, and systems constants, as well as packages defining both types and operations on those types.

Modularity also has an interesting side effect: Any unit may have any other unit enclosed within it. For example, a subprogram can contain a package, which can in turn contain other packages or subprograms, which in turn could each contain still other packages or subprograms!

Subprograms

Ada, like other structured languages, allows us to extend the language by writing small chunks of reusable code known as *subprograms*. In addition, Ada allows us to collect these subprograms into a library unit and call them from other programs.

Recall that our program **Greet_World** used a predefined subprogram **Put** in the line

```
Text_IO.Put( "Hello, world." );
```

calling it in from a library package called **Text_IO**. Ada has two types of subprograms: *functions* and *procedures*.

The most obvious difference between the two is that a function always returns a value, just as an expression does, while a procedure never explicitly does so. **Put** in the above example is a procedure. We wouldn't expect a subprogram that outputs something to return a value to us (unless we were writing in C). Conversely, you wouldn't expect a function that computes a square root to do anything but return to you the square root of the argument, for you to use as part of an expression.

The following are simple examples of functions and procedures:

```
-- A procedure
with Text_IO;
procedure Press_Any_Key_To_Continue is
    Char : CHARACTER; -- A scratch object
begin
    Text_IO.Put( "Press any key to continue..." );
```

```
        Text_IO.Get( Char );
    end Press_Any_Key_To_Continue;

    -- A function
    function Nor( Item_One, Item_Two : BOOLEAN ) return
BOOLEAN is
    begin
            return not( Item_One or Item_Two );
    end Nor;
```

Since a function returns a value it must be used as part of an expression. Conversely, since a procedure can't return a value, it can't be used as part of an expression but must be used as a statement. So we write procedures when we want to perform an action of some sort, and we write functions when we want to compute a value.

Declaring Subprograms

The first line of a subprogram (ignoring any **with** or **use** clause) is the *subprogram declaration*. This tells us three important things about the subprogram:

- Whether it is a procedure or a function;
- what name it goes by; and
- what additional values (*parameters*) are required to operate the subprogram.

Figure 5-1 shows templates for our two types of subprograms. Note the structural differences between the subprogram declarations of procedures and functions, specifically the use of the reserved word **return** at the end of the function (but not the procedure) declaration.

Because of Ada's strong typing, the compiler has to know what type of value a function will return so it can correctly evaluate an expression where the function appears.

As we mentioned in Chapter 1, a *return* is implied at the end of procedures. We can return from a procedure or function earlier than the very end if we want, simply by placing a **return** statement anywhere in our subprogram:

```
--
if Name = "" then
    Put( "Bad name" );
    return;
end if;
--
```

```
procedure <Identifier>(<Formal Parameters>) is
<Declarative_Part>
begin
<Body>
end <Identifier>;

function <Identifier>(<Formal Parameters>) return <Type_Mark> is
<Declarative_Part>
begin
<Body>
end <Identifier>;

-- The <Identifier>, at beginning and end, names the
   subprogram.
-- The <Formal Parameters> defines the data objects (or
   literals) that will be passed to the subprogram. (See
   Figure 5-4). These are optional.
-- <Declarative Part> is where variables local to the
   subprogram are declared. This is optional.
-- <Body> is the executable portion of the subprogram.
```

Figure 5-1. *Subprogram Template: Procedures and Functions*

In the case of a function, we also need to specify what value to return to the caller. We do this by placing a value after the **return** statement:

```
return Pi * Radius**2;
return A_Local_Variable_or_Expression;
```

Since it is the point of a function to compute and return a value, it is an error to run off the end of a function without specifying a return value; functions have no implied return at the end. It is also an error to return a value different from that specified by the function declaration:

```
function Random_Real_Number return FLOAT is
--
--
```

In the above function it would be an error to return a value of any type other than **FLOAT**.

A return statement can be used anywhere in the body of a procedure, and no value may be returned with it:

```
procedure Demo_Return( A : INTEGER ) is
begin
  case A > 0 is
    when TRUE  => Do_Something;
    when FALSE => return; -- no value is returned
  end case;
end Demo_Return;
```

Subprograms operate on three kinds of objects when performing their assigned job. The first kind are *local* objects that are declared in the subprogram's *declaration part* (the part between the reserved words **is** and **begin**). These local objects are used only within the subprogram that declares them.

The second kind of objects are *global variables*, variables declared outside the subprogram and in existence when the subprogram is called. If you have changed a variable with a GOSUB subroutine in BASIC, you have worked on a global variable. Global variables are easy to abuse and we generally avoid using them in a language like Ada, as Quiche Eating Structured Programmers scorn us when we do.

The third kind are *parameters*—objects that relay values to and from the entity calling the subprogram and the subprogram itself. Subprogram parameters define the specific task for the subprogram.

Subprogram Parameters

Subprogram parameters are declared as *formal parameters*. In the declaration of a subprogram we specify the name (for internal use by the subprogram only), type, and mode of each parameter the subprogram will use. When a call is made to a subprogram the actual values specified by the calling program (called, oddly enough, "actual parameters") replace the "dummy" formal parameters specified in the subprogram declaration.

In effect, and usually in fact, the value of the actual parameter is copied to the formal parameter. The formal parameter is an object for internal use by the subprogram.

Ada has three parameter modes available: **in**, **in out**, and **out**.

An **in** parameter is a value passed to the subprogram to help the subprogram do its job. As an example the **put** procedure uses an **in** parameter to tell **put** what to display. An **in** parameter may not be modified by the body of the subprogram. **in** parameters are treated exactly the same as constants within a subprogram.

Functions may only have parameters of mode **in**, because the designers of Ada felt that would be more natural, and also would help reduce side effects (unexpected results caused by hard-to-spot assignments and modifications). You wouldn't expect, say, a sine function to modify the angle used to compute the sine or to cause any effects in the program other than to supply the sine of the supplied angle. If side effects are desirable you can still modify global or static variables inside a function.

```
( <Identifier(s)> : <Mode> <Type_Mark> {; repeat } )

-- <Identifier(s)> - one or more variable names of the same
   type, separated by commas.

-- <Mode> is used only in procedures, and defaults to in if
   not specified. Possibilities are in, in out, and out.

-- <Type_Mark> is the identifier of a predeclared data type.

-- {; repeat} We separate formal parameters with a
   semicolon.

-- A parameter list is optional, but it may have any number
   of parameters.
```

Figure 5-2.   Formal Parameter List Template

Out parameters are allowed for procedures. An **out** parameter can't deliver any value to the procedure; it can only bring a value back from a procedure. The actual parameter used when calling a procedure is filled with a value inside the procedure, by an assignment to the formal parameter. We use **out** parameters to retrieve values for us, as with the **Get** procedure, which fetches a value from outside the program, and brings that value to us in an **out** parameter.

in out parameters are a combination of **in** and **out** parameters. We can deliver a value to the subprogram and we can bring back a new value from the subprogram. An example is our **Bump** procedure (on page 83), where we need to know the current value of a counter in order to increment it. You may want to use parameters of mode in **out** exclusively at first.

There are three basic rules for beginners to remember about parameter modes:

First, if a parameter is specified as **out** or **in out**, you may not use a literal value as an actual parameter.

Second, if a mode isn't specified for a procedure parameter, it is assumed to be mode **in**.

Third, a formal parameter of type **in** may not be assigned to, as we said above. This precludes passing **in** formal parameters as **out** or **in out** inside the subprogram. Here is an example:

```
function Next( First : INTEGER ) return INTEGER is
begin
     Get( First );      -- illegal
     return First;
end Next;
```

Since the formal parameter **First** is an **in** parameter (remember—all function parameters are type **in**) it can't be passed to **Get**, which asks for an **out** parameter. Figure 5-2 gives a template for formal parameters.

Ada allows passing parameters by position, the method used in most computer languages.[1] In positional parameter passing we place an actual parameter in the calling list in place of each of the formal parameters in the subprogram declaration, associating the actual parameters with the formal parameters, that is, allowing them to copy values from each other:

```
-- the function declaration
function Larger( Left,Right : INTEGER) return INTEGER is

-- calling Max with positional notation
Put( Larger( Value_One, Value_Two ) );
```

In the above example actual parameter **Value__One** would associate with formal parameter **Left**, and **value__Two** with **Right**.

Ada has another method of parameter passing, called *named parameter association*. In named parameter association we name the formal parameters with the actual parameters, indicating association with the "choose" symbol, =>. We could write the above call like this (note that the order of parameters in named association is unimportant):

```
Put( Larger( Right => Value_One, Left => Value_Two ) );
```

This is a much clearer association, and is especially useful if a subprogram has a lot of parameters, or if expressions are used as parameters, or with *default parameters* (discussed below).[2]

We can mix named parameter association with positional parameter association to a limited extent:

```
Put( Larger( Value_One, Right => Value_Two ) );
```

The rule when mixing association methods is that on a left-to-right scan of the parameter list, when you start using named associations you have to stick with using a named association. This is because once you stop using positional association the compiler loses track of where it is in the parameter list, and needs the names of the formal parameters to keep the list straight. Actually there isn't any compelling reason to mix named and positional associations within a single call to a subprogram, so you probably should avoid doing it.

A powerful feature in Ada is the use of *default parameters*. We can assign a default value to a formal parameter in the same way we initialize a variable:

```
-- declaration of New_Line
Procedure New_Line( Number_Of_Spaces : NATURAL := 1 );
```

will assign the value 1 to the parameter **Number_Of_Spaces** if we fail to provide an actual parameter, so that

```
-- calling New_Line using the default
New_Line;
```

will cause a spacing of one line, and

```
-- calling New_Line with explict actual parameter
New_Line( 10 );
```

will cause a spacing of ten lines. This example is similar to how the predefined subprogram **New_Line** is actually declared in package **Text_IO**.

When default parameters are used, the compiler will use a default value whenever we don't give an actual parameter with a subprogram call.

When using a combination of default parameters and named parameter association we can write very powerful and flexible subprograms that are easy to use. The I/O subprograms in the next chapter have formatting options we usually don't need to use. We have been using the **Put** procedure throughout the early part of this book by specifying a single parameter, the item to be output. As you will see in Chapter 6, **Put** has extensive formatting capabilities, which may ignored until needed, because the formatting in **Put** is specified by parameters that have default values.

Note that only parameters of mode **in** can have default parameter assignments. If you think about it you'll see why it doesn't make sense to have a default parameter value for an **in out** or **out** parameter.

A Subprogram Example

We now have more than enough information to start writing subprograms. Let's look at the process involved in generating a subprogram.

Whenever we do something more than once in a program, we have a reason to create a subprogram to do the job, especially if the same subprogram may be useful in other programs. Let's see how this applies to the character counting program from the end of Chapter 3, shown again in Figure 5-3.

We have highlighted the portion of the program that increments the character counter. In the case of this program we'll cook up a subprogram that increments a counter for us—an illustrative example rather than a useful one.

We could write this subprogram (let's call it **Bump**) either as a procedure or as a function. Either way we'll have to supply it with the present value of a counter in order for it to compute the next value, much as we supplied the string "Hello, world." for **Put** to output.

```
--- Character Count version 1: Counts printable (non-control)
--- ASCII characters from the keyboard. Use Control-Z to
--- terminate.

with Text_IO;
procedure Count1 is
   package INT_IO is new Text_IO.Integer_IO( INTEGER );
   Input_Char  : CHARACTER;          -- used to get input
   Counter     : INTEGER := 0;    -- keeps track of count
   Control_Z   : constant CHARACTER := CHARACTER'val( 26 );
begin
<<START>>                            -- goto loop label
   Text_IO.Get( Input_Char );        -- obtain input from user
   if Input_Char in ' '..'~' then -- test for being non-control char
      Counter := Counter + 1;        -- if so, increment count
   end if;
   if Input_Char /= Control_Z then-- are we done?
      goto START;                     -- no, get another CHARACTER
   end if;
   INT_IO.Put( Counter );           -- print result
end Count1;
```

Figure 5-3.   Character Count, Version 1

If we write our subprogram as a function we will have to use the function (which is, as you recall, used in or as an expression) as part of an assignment statement:

```
Counter := Bump( Counter );
```

This does the job, but it offers no clear improvement over the original:

```
Counter := Counter + 1;
```

Written as a procedure, however, **Bump** itself acts as a statement. The variable **Counter** goes in with a value and comes out with the original value + 1:

```
Bump( Counter );
```

The procedure form looks a little better; it reads better; it's more to the point.

Now that we have decided what form the subprogram should take, we need to write it out:

```
procedure Bump( Int_Counter : in out INTEGER ) is

begin
      Int_Counter := Int_Counter + 1;
end Bump;
```

Now that we have developed this nice module, where do we put it so that Count1 can use it? There are several places that it could go, so let's look at the simplest one first.

To make Bump available for use in Count1, the simplest approach is to place Bump in the declaration part of Count1, *after all the variables and types have been declared*. The new version (Count2) appears as Figure 5-4.

Where else could we have put Bump? One other place is in a *package*. We would put Bump in a package if we wanted to make it available to other programs the way Text_IO.Put is.

Packages

There is an interesting interchangeability about the elements of Ada. By rewriting the specification line of Count1 we can turn it into a *package body*, another one of Ada's program units. Figure 5-5 shows how to do this.

Packages are the fundamental building blocks for programs in Ada. They can include data types, constants, variables, and subprograms just as subprograms can, yet packages are designed so that some or all of these elements can be made available to other programs.

Package specifications

Imagine that you can construct a paper mask to fit over our Count program with slots to show the data types and objects and the subprograms you want to make available for export to other programs.

```
--- Character Count version 2: Counts printable (non-control)
--- ASCII characters from the keyboard. Use Control-Z to
--- terminate. GOTO removed and replaced with LOOP.

with Text_IO;
procedure Count2 is
    package INT_IO is new Text_IO.Integer_IO( INTEGER );
    Input_Char  : CHARACTER;
    Counter     : INTEGER := 0;
    Control_Z   : constant CHARACTER := CHARACTER'val( 26 );


-- procedure Bump increments a counter for us
--
    procedure Bump( Int_Counter : in out INTEGER ) is
    begin
        Int_Counter := Int_Counter + 1;
    end Bump;

begin
    loop
        Text_IO.Get( Input_Char );
        exit when Input_Char = Control_Z;
        if Input_Char in ' '..'~' then
            Bump( Counter );
        end if;
    end loop;
    INT_IO.Put( Counter );
end Count2;
```

Figure 5-4. Character Count, Version 2

```
with Text_IO;
procedure Count3 is

  →  package INT_IO is new Text_IO.Integer_IO( INTEGER );
     Input_Char  : CHARACTER;
  →  Counter     : INTEGER := 0;
     Control_Z   : constant CHARACTER := CHARACTER'val( 26 );


  →  procedure Bump( Int_Counter : in out INTEGER ) is
     begin
         Int_Counter := Int_Counter + 1;
     end Bump;

begin
    loop
        Text_IO.Get( Input_Char );
        exit when Input_Char = Control_Z;
        if Input_Char in ' '..'˜' then
            Bump( Counter );
        end if;
    end loop;
    INT_IO.Put( Counter );
end Count3;
```

Figure 5-5. Count *Procedure with Nested* Bump

In Count3 (Figure 5-5) we want to export the three items highlighted: the package Int_IO, the variable Counter, and the subprogram Bump.

We do this by converting our procedure into the two parts of a package called Countpack (Figure 5-6). The top part, from

```
package Countpak is
```

to

```
end Countpak;
```

is the *specification* and includes the exportable items.

```
with Text_IO;
package Countpak is

    ──▸ package INT_IO is new Text_IO.Integer_IO( INTEGER );
    ──▸ Counter : INTEGER := 0;

    ──▸ procedure Bump( Int_Counter : in out INTEGER );
        procedure Debump(Int_Counter : in out INTEGER );

end Countpak;

package body Countpak is

    procedure Bump( Int_Counter : in out INTEGER ) is
    begin
        Int_Counter := Int_Counter + 1;
    end Bump;

    procedure Debump( Int_Counter : in out INTEGER ) is
    begin
        Int_Counter := Int_Counter - 1;
    end Debump;


end Countpak;


-------------------------------------------------------------------

with Text_IO, Countpak;
procedure Count4 is

    Input_Char  : CHARACTER;
    Control_Z   : constant CHARACTER := CHARACTER'val( 26 );
```

(continued)

Figure 5-6. Count *Procedure Calling* Bump *from Package*

```
begin
    loop
        Text_IO.Get( Input_Char );
        exit when Input_Char = Countpak\Control_Z;
        if Input_Char in  ' '..'~' then
            Countpak.Bump( Countpak.Counter );
        end if;
    end loop;
    Countpak.Int_IO.Put( Countpak.Counter );
end Count4;
```

Figure 5-6 continued.

When writing a package specification, include only those items other programs will use when **with**ing this package. If types are created for export, the entire type declaration must be written out in the specification. If variables are declared, the entire declaration is written out. If functions or procedures are to be exported, we write the declarations only up to the reserved word **is**, which is replaced by a semicolon.[3]

Keeping the unnecessary details of the package out of sight is part of what's called *information hiding*. We do this to keep the user of the package from making unwarranted assumptions about the package. In effect you are saying, "What you see is what you get." If the user can see the whole package, he or she may assume things that may no longer be true if you make changes.

In our package **Countpak**, we make only the three items we picked out available to other programs. Everything else is hidden.

We keep the specification and the body of a library package in separate source files, and compile them separately. This makes maintenance much easier, as we know we only have to recompile programs depending on this package if we change the specification. As long as we are only going to change the body and not the specification, all we need to do is relink programs that depend on this package (programs that **with** this package) to incorporate the new code into them.

When it comes to using a package or its components, the specification for that package is all the programmer needs to know. The specification is the contract between the package implementation and anyone else who uses that package. How the body is implemented is a matter of detail not required by the user of the package.

```
-- Specification

package <Name> is
     -- type declarations
     -- object declarations
     -- subprogram specifications
end <Name>;

-- Body

package body <Name> is
     -- local type and object declarations
     -- subprogram bodies
begin
     -- initialization code
end <Name>;
```

Figure 5-7. Package Specification and Body Template

Types, constants, and variables set out in a specification are available to the body associated with the specification, and can't be duplicated in that body's specification section. Subprogram declarations in the specification must be repeated in full in the declaration part of the body (along with the body code for the subprogram), and the declarations must match exactly.[4] Additional types, variables, constants, and subprograms may be declared in the body for private use as well. Figure 5-7 contains a template for specifications and bodies.

Note the section of Figure 5-7 that is marked "initialization code." This is an optional section at the end of the package where any code required to initialize the package is placed. This corresponds to the actual **Count1** program in Figure 5-3.

This initialization code is executed during the elaboration of the package, as it starts to execute. In the case of a library unit (like **Text_IO**) this occurs at the start of the whole program. Generally this section of a package is used to initialize the package before any of the components is called. For example, **Text_IO** will have an initialization section that opens the default input and output files.

Recall that we can place packages anywhere a subprogram can appear. A package can be placed inside another package's declaration part or in a subprogram's declaration part. If we place a package in another declaration, the package initialization code is executed each time the declaration part of the host program unit is elaborated. To use an extreme example, if the **Put** procedure had a package embedded in its declaration part, the package initialization code, if any, would be executed each time we called **Put**.[5]

Withing and Using packages

In Ada, programs are written and compiled in a certain *context*. The context of a program determines what external elements are available to the program for its use.

To specify a context for an Ada program we use (what else?) a *context specification* or *context clause*. The context clause is the **with** clause you have seen at the beginning of our examples, and sometimes a **use** clause. The **with** clause names all the other library units (usually packages, although naked procedures and functions can also be library units) required for the current package to operate.

A **with** clause appears at the very beginning of a compilation unit, before the declaration of the program unit, before the declaration of the program unit. In most cases this will be at the beginning of the source file, excluding any comments.

We can name any number of library units in a **with** clause. The rules of Ada state that if a package is **with**ed in a package specification it is also **with**ed in the body, whether or not the body also **with**s the same package (the body can, however, **with** additional packages). The rules also state that the effect of **with**ing a package more than once is the same as **with**ing it once, even if it's done twice in the same **with** clause.

The **use** clause also may be part of the context. It can be placed immediately after the **with** clause, or it can be placed inside a declaration part somewhere. The purpose of the **use** clause is to make the names of items in a **with**ed package visible to the compiler. If a package is **with**ed but not **use**d, we have to use named component, or dot, notation to refer to a component of the package:[6]

```
with Text_IO;
--
Text_IO.Put( "Hello, World" );
```

If we also **use** a package, the names of the components in that package become **directly visible**, so we can drop the dot notation:[7]

```
with Text_IO; use Text_IO;
--
Put( "Hello, World" );
```

There are pros and cons to the **use** clause. On the one hand, it saves an awful lot of typing. On the other hand, dot notation makes it very clear where stuff is coming from and makes it easier to change the modules of large programs.

Dot notation is still required to resolve ambiguity, as when two different **with**ed and **use**d packages export similar objects.

A **use** clause is effective only in the block where it has *scope*; it is scope that we discuss next.

Scope and Visibility

Ada was designed for use in large projects, where many programmers work on different parts of a program. As a consequence its design incorporates many features to enable compilation of separate units, and to avoid conflicts between one programmer's handiwork and another's. These include the rules about when a given object or subprogram may be referenced (scope), how the object or subprogram is referenced (visibility), as well as the details of separate compilation and the order in which units must be compiled or recompiled.

Scope refers to the region of the program where an entity may be referenced. The general rule is that an object or subprogram (entity) will be declared in the declaration part of a program unit, and then is available to the end of that unit. After the end of the unit where an entity is declared, that entity in effect ceases to exist.

As an example, we have been declaring low-level procedures and functions, such as **Bump**, in the declaration part of package bodies, our executable units.

In our program **Count2** we declared a subprogram **Bump**, which was available from the point where we declared it until the end of the package body. **Bump** would not be available to a subprogram that was declared prior to **Bump** in **Count2**'s declaration part, but would be available to any part of the program that appeared after it, either in the declaration part of **Count2** or in the body of **Count2**.

Looking closer at this example, consider the formal parameter to **Bump**, **Int_Counter**. Formal parameters are available from the point where they appear (the heading line of the subprogram) to the end of the subprogram.

If we had declared variables or types in the declaration part of **Bump**, they would be available to all of **Bump**, and also to any subprograms declared in the declaration part of **Bump**, because of the rule that subprograms must appear as the last items in a declaration part.

Loop index variables are limited in scope to the loop which they control.

Loop labels and **goto** labels are declared by implication (they are declared because they are there) and are local (their scope is restricted) to the subprogram in which they are declared. Therefore the range of a **goto** is restricted to the subprogram in which it is declared. Labels are considered to be declared in the enclosing declaration part, and therefore a forward reference to a **goto** label is possible within a subprogram.

We can restrict scope even farther by using *block statements* inside a subprogram. The simplest form of a block statement is:

```
begin
    -- any number of statements
end;
```

A block statement can be named the same way a loop is:

```
Block_Label:
begin
    -- any number of statements
end Block_Label;
```

Finally, by using the reserved word **declare**, we can declare items local to the block statement:

```
declare
      -- declarations
begin
      -- any number of statements
end;
```

A block statement has the same form as all of Ada's other blocks:

```
<label>:                          -- optional
     declare                      -- optional
         <declaration part>
     begin
         <code or body>
     exception                    -- optional
         <exception handler>
     end <label>;
```

Entities declared in a block statement are local to the block and can't be referenced outside the block. Taking modularity to the limit, we can place subprograms and packages in the declaration part of a declare block, although in practice this isn't done much.

Blocks are used almost entirely for restricting scope, either of variables, or more commonly, exceptions. We'll see the block used for restricting the scope of exceptions in the next chapter.

Aside from avoiding name conflicts, one of the purposes of scope is saving memory space. In BASIC, where all variables are *global*, or available to all parts of the program, a variable must be kept around forever in case another part of the program needs to use it. In Ada a variable ceases to exist when execution passes outside its scope, and its storage may be reclaimed.

Whether by design or accident, a program can have one or more identifiers of the same name, and perhaps of the same type. In BASIC this could be (and often is) a disaster. Ada provides *visibility rules* to resolve name conflicts.

If a name is unique then it is directly visible throughout its entire scope. If a name is not unique then conflicts between different entities with the same name may sometimes be resolved by context. For example, suppose both an integer variable and a float variable were named **Var1**. The context would clearly define which type of variable is intended.

If context can't be used to resolve name conflicts, then the entity declared in the innermost enclosing program unit is the only one that is visible. Consider the following:

```
procedure XYZ is
     Temp : INTEGER;
begin
     --
     --
     INNER:
     declare
          Temp : INTEGER;
     begin
     --
     end INNER;
     --
end XYZ;
```

Within the block statement **INNER**, any reference to the variable **Temp** will be assumed to be to the **Temp** declared in the declare block **INNER**. The **Temp** declared in the procedure declaration is said to be **Hidden** by the declaration in **INNER**, within the scope of the block statement.

If we need to refer to the outer **Temp** while in **INNER**, we can use named component (dot) notation:

```
XYZ.Temp
```

It's a good idea to think twice before hiding names like this. While the compiler can figure things out, it's harder for human readers.

To summarize visibility and scope:

- Any number of entities of the same name and type can overlap scope.
- Only one entity of a given name and type is visible at any one time, the one with the innermost scope.
- Only one entity of a given name and type may have a given scope. Others must be enclosed or must enclose.
- Access to variables that are hidden is by named component notation (dot notation).

- Hidden variables are harder for humans to deal with than for compilers.
- Visibility rules ensure that no inadvertant access to identically named entities occurs.

Part of the visibility rules govern access to components of **with**ed packages. We have been making package components, whether they be subprograms, objects, or types, directly visible to the **use** clause:

```
with Text_IO; use Text_IO;
--
Put( "Hello" );
```

We also have used named component (dot) notation:

```
with Text_IO;
--
Text_IO.Put( "Hello" );
```

There is an alternative: We can rename entities. We might do this for several reasons, the most common one being in order to save keystrokes when using components of another package. We can re-write the last example like this:

```
with Text_IO;
procedure Put_String( S : STRING ) renames Text_IO.Put;
--
Put_String( "Hello" );
```

Any entity can be renamed. We could rename these:

```
type VISIBLE_CHARACTERS is ( CHARACTER range ' '..'~' );
Name_Array   : array( 1..100 ) of STRING;
Data_Error   : exception;
```

     renamed to

```
type VIS_CHAR renames VISIBLE_CHARACTERS;
NA            : ARRAY renames Name_Array;
Name          : STRING renames Name_Array( 10 );
Clumsy_User : EXCEPTION renames Data_Error;
procedure Put(Item : in CHARACTER) renames Text_IO.Put;
```

One benefit of renaming subprograms is that we can supply new default parameters when renaming them.[8]

A danger of renaming is that we can refer to the same object by different names (a practice known as *aliasing*).

Subprogram Overloading

A subject related to visibility is overloading. (In Chapter 6 we present many examples of overloaded I/O subprograms.) An overloaded subprogram is one whose name is identical to the name of another subprogram. Any number of subprograms can share the same name. In fact, *all* subprograms in a program may have the same name (oh, boy, what fun!).

Overloading allows us to give a common name to related subprograms that perform similar tasks. The I/O procedure Put is overloaded 12 times, not counting generic instantiations, which increase the number of Puts by six for each instantiation.

Ada figures out which version of an overloaded subprogram you want to use by examining the number, type, and positions of parameters and, in the case of functions, by the return type. The correct version then is loaded for that particular call.

A problem can arise when literals are used as parameters. All integer types have literals of type *universal__integer*; string literals are universal to character arrays; all float literals are *Universal__Real*; etc. There are two methods of resolving any ambiguity: either by named parameter passing, or by using a qualified expression for the literal:

```
-- two derived types to resolve parameter types:
      type RADIANS is new FLOAT;   -- a derived type
      type DEGREES is new FLOAT;   -- a derived type

-- two different sine functions:
      function Sine( R : RADIANS ) return FLOAT;
      function Sine( D : DEGREES ) return FLOAT;

-- two different variables of differing types:
      Value_Radians : RADIANS;
      Value_Degrees : DEGREES;

-- unambiguous calls:
      Put( Sine( Value_Radians ) );
      Put( Sine( Value_Degrees ) );

-- ambiguous literal call:
      Put( Sine( 90.0 ) );

-- unambiguous literal calls:
      Put( Sine( RADIANS'( 3.14) ) );     -- qualified expression
```

```
Put( Sine( DEGREES'( 180.0)));    --qualified expression
Put( Sine( R => 3.14 ));          --named association
Put( Sine( D => 180.0 ));         --named association
```

Operators may be overloaded as well as subprograms.[9] Any Ada operator may be overloaded, with the exception of the membership operators and the short-circuit logical operators **or else** and **and then**, which actually are control structures.

Operators are overloaded by writing a function that has the operator enclosed in quotes as its name, in the function declaration line:

```
type MATRIX is ARRAY( range 1..5 ) of FLOAT;
function "+"(Left, Right : MATRIX ) return MATRIX is
begin
---
```

When a operator is overloaded it can be used just like the predefined operators. Its precedence is the same as the equivalent predefined operator.

Unary operators must take exactly one parameter, and binary operators must take exactly two parameters. Also, default parameters are not allowed.

When overloading operators that take differing types as operands it's usually a good idea to overload for the commutative case, too (as the concatenation operator, &, is overloaded to accept either **char & string** or **string & char**).

Separate Compilation

As we saw in the section on scope, an entity must be declared before it can be used. This is why all of the supporting subprograms for our example programs have been placed in the declaration section of the programs.

This method works, but is confusing to someone new to Ada. Most professional programmers like to write the main procedure first in the source file, and then work toward the least-generalized procedures at the end of the source file (a "top–down" approach). Our Ada programs up to this point have been just the opposite.

We can use separate compilation to get around this. In separate compilation we can declare a *stub* in our main source file. A stub is basically the subprogram declaration with the reserved word **separate** replacing the body from the reserved word **is** to the end of the subprogram.[10]

```
procedure Bump( Counter : in out INTEGER ) is separate;
```

This stub declares the procedure **Bump** and its formal parameters. The complete procedure is in a separate file:

```
separate( <name> )
procedure Bump( Counter : in out INTEGER ) is
begin
     Counter := Counter + 1;
end Bump;
```

The <name> in this example is the name of the parent unit. Since the name of the parent is required, separate procedures can only be used with that parent.

The body of a separate **subunit** may be recompiled without recompiling the main program unit. Package bodies and tasks may also be separately compiled:

```
-- main program unit
--
package Trig is
  type RADIANS is new FLOAT;
  function Sine( R : RADIANS );
  function Cosine( R : RADIANS );
end Trig;
package body Trig is separate;

task Type_Ahead_Buffer is
  entry Key_Status( Flag : out BOOLEAN );
  entry Get_Key( Keystroke : out CHARACTER );
end Type_Ahead_Buffer;
task body Type_Ahead_Buffer is separate;
--
--


-- another file:

separate( Main )
package body Trig is
-- implementation of "Trig"

-- a third file:

separate( Main )
task body Type_Ahead_Buffer is
-- implementation of "Type_Ahead_Buffer"
```

Separate compilation works well for top-down programming, or for teams of programmers, because we can write the required specifications of a separate unit as we write the high-level code and then add the low level code as we get the time or inclination. (Or—even better—we can make one of the technicians write that stuff!)

Compilation Order

Ada was designed for separate compilation. This means that unless we want to, we don't have to compile an entire program at one time. (We usually don't want to.)

Each time we compile, we can compile one or more of the following *compilation units*:

- subprogram body
- subprogram declaration
- package body
- package specification
- subunit
- generic declaration
- generic instantiation

Tasks are not compilation units.

Each compilation unit in a particular program system belongs to a *program library* and is called a *library unit*. Every library unit requires a unique name.

The main unit in a program must be a parameterless procedure. There are varying ways of indicating to the compiler which unit is the main unit, as this is not defined by the language. Consult your compiler reference for this information.[11]

Each time we compile the library unit is treated as if it were in the declaration part of package **Standard**, so all of **Standard**'s resources are available to any library unit.

It makes a difference what order library units and subunits are compiled in. Ada requires that type checking be carried out for all parts of a program; the compiler can only check if the supporting routines are already compiled. This also ensures that the syntax of the supporting routines is correct.

The following are the basics of compilation order:

1. Anything that is **with**ed must be compiled before the unit that **with**s it is compiled.
2. Specifications are always compiled before their associated bodies.
3. The body associated with a specification can only be compiled after the specification. The body may be modified and recompiled without recompiling the specification if the specification is unchanged.
4. In separate compilation, the parent must be compiled first, and then the subunit. The subunit may be changed and recompiled without recompiling the parent.
5. If a package specification is recompiled, all programs that **with** that package also must be recompiled.

We can create our own packages, compile them, and have them ready on disk along with the predefined packages that come with the compiler. In general, useful packages can be divided into three kinds:

1. Collections of system constants (similar to stdio.h in C) plus generally useful data types. These can all be collected in a package specification and compiled without a body, since no subprogram bodies need elaborating.
2. Collections of logically related subprograms like **Text_IO**. Packages of this sort list subprogram specifications in a specifications section and have the subprogram bodies in a package body.
3. Coordinated collections of abstracted data types and their operators. (Package **Standard** is an example of this variety). This kind of package can be "encapsulated"—made relatively impervious to user meddling—by using private types. The whole process will be discussed in Chapter 11.

Conclusion

Ada's packages and separate compilation are part of an overall language structure that allows modular development and maintenance of large-scale programs. Packages are not exactly new in concept, even on micros. Apple II users have been taking advantage of UCSD Pascal's "unit" for several years; but the unit is an extension of standard Pascal. This useful feature, like many others, has been adopted and standardized in Ada.

One feature not discussed in this chapter is *exceptions*. An optional section of error handlers, or *exception handlers*, can be placed at the end of a program unit. We will postpone our treatment of exceptions to the next chapter, where we can give useful examples.

6
Input/Output

We frequently overlook how essential input/output (I/O) is to any computer program. Since a program is virtually useless if it can't display its results, or is limited to operating on the data already stored in the program, I/O is a critical feature of any programming language. Many people don't realize that over half of an applications or embedded system programmer's time can be spent on I/O of one sort or another.

I/O is very system dependent. Every computer is configured differently, with different physical devices (disks, printers, keyboards, displays) and different ways of logically addressing those devices. Identical computers using different operating systems can have widely divergent means of accomplishing the same I/O procedure.

These dependencies make if extremely difficult to implement I/O in a language specification. The designers of Ada took the same approach that the designers of C took: They simply didn't put any I/O *statements* into the language.

All of Ada's I/O is written, and written *in Ada*, as *subprograms* rather than as *statements* or language features. It is the responsibility of the designer of a compiler library to make sure that the I/O appears to be subprograms rather than language extensions or new statements.

The Ada specification includes standard packages of required I/O routines. An Ada *subset* may not have these packages, or their subprograms may be spread around in packages with names other than the standard ones. Chances are they are similar enough to the standard ones so that you'll be able to use them after reading this chapter. Note that a full Ada compiler is required to have all of the I/O subprograms discussed here.

I/O for Beginners

Ada has many standard I/O procedures, most of which the average microcomputer user will never need. But you will without doubt need at least some of them and, since which ones you need will depend on your applications, you probably should familiarize yourself with the terrain.[1] A map of how to proceed might read like this:

1. First read about the I/O concept and handling exceptions. Then read about the file management subprograms:

   ```
   Create     Open      Close     Delete
   ```

2. Next, read about the default file subprograms:

   ```
   Set_Input     Set_Output
   ```

3. Last, read about the simple forms of **Put** and **Get** for characters, strings, and integers. Also look at:

   ```
   Put_Line      Get_Line      New_Line      Skip_Line
   ```

These steps are plenty for the beginning programmer or first-time Ada user. Later on you probably will want to look at I/O for real types, enumeration types, and then at the **Direct__IO** and **Sequential__IO** packages. Finally, look over the formatting features in **Text__IO**.

Because Ada's required I/O is so comprehensive this chapter barely has room to be an I/O reference, let alone give numerous examples in a tutorial fashion. We suggest you begin with simple I/O features and ignore the finer points of I/O until later, instead of trying to absorb all of the hundred or so variations of the I/O subprograms all at once.

The I/O Concept

Ada treats all I/O as *stream files*. This means that all input and output, including that to devices such as a console, are considered to be to or from data streams. There are two key concepts here: First, that any I/O is file I/O, and uses file oriented subprograms; second, that these files are streams of identically typed data objects.

Picture an interactive environment (such as a microcomputer) where the keyboard supplies an input stream of objects of type character and the monitor displays an output stream of the same type. These devices may not be considered files in other environments; yet they are in Ada. Other I/O streams may move to and from the disk drives; a printer might display an output stream; and a modem may supply an input stream and then transmit an output stream. The *devices* are considered *external files*, as opposed to the internal representation of *files*. *Streams* connect an external file to the internal file representation as a file object.

Think of the input stream as the end of a pipe, dispensing one unit of information at a time. As each unit is removed from the end of the pipe, another takes its place until the stream is exhausted. Output is similar; units are placed in the output stream pipe one at a time. Again, all objects in any given stream must be of the same type.[2]

In the specification for **Text__IO** (listed in Appendix D) you will find the following standard procedure **Open**.[3] It is the procedure you will use to establish a connection between your program's file object and an *external* text file:

```
type FILE_TYPE is limited private;
type FILE_MODE is ( IN_FILE, OUT_FILE );

procedure Open( File : in out FILE_TYPE;
                Mode : in      FILE_MODE;
                Name : in      STRING := "";
                Form : in      STRING := "" );
```

Note the two type declarations. The first—**FILE__TYPE**— is *limited private*. We cover limited private types in Chapter 10. In a nutshell, by using a limited private type the author of the package hides the details of this type and restricts the amount of fooling around you can do with an object of this type. You can create objects of type **FILE__TYPE**, and you can pass these objects to the subprograms in **Text__IO**, but you can't do much else with them.

An object declared as **FILE__TYPE** becomes a *file*. When we link the file to an *external file* with the **Open** procedure, we specify which direction the stream is heading by using one of the two elements of the enumeration type **FILE__MODE**, also defined above. A text stream may be either an input stream or an output stream, but not both.

We have not had to deal with these file objects and concepts yet because **with**ing the **Text__IO** package automatically creates a *default input* and a *default output* file (remember the initialization code at the end of package bodies?) which are linked to external files and opened for use. We expect the default input to be linked to the keyboard (the *standard input*), and the default output to be linked to the display (the *standard output*) in a microcomputer environment.

The package **Text__IO** contains, among others, the familiar procedures **Get** and **Put**. They default to input from the *standard input* and output to *standard output*.

The FILE__TYPE

As defined by the *Language Reference Manual*, an object of type **FILE__TYPE** is an unbounded sequence of identical components. This means that a file has no size limit, and that every component of the file is of the same type, whether it be CHARACTER, INTEGER, FLOAT, a particular record type, an array, or a user-defined type. Everything contained in a file must have the same *type__mark*. In the case of the default input and default output files, the component type is **CHARACTER**.

The file object is considered by Ada to be the *file*, not the external representation. When we refer to a "file", what we mean is the file object, of type **FILE__TYPE**, declared in our program.

In practical terms, to use files we must declare an object of type **FILE__TYPE** (a file), which will link our program to the external file (modem, printer, display, disk, etc.). The object declared is similar to the *file number* in BASIC, or the *file pointer* in C, or the *File Control Block* in CP/M or MS-DOS. The file object created somehow contains enough information for the computer to access the external file, although the details of how this is accomplished are hidden by **Text_IO**. One of the strengths of Ada is that it is unimportant to the programmer how these sorts of thing are accomplished.[4]

Once the file is declared it is linked to the external file by the **Open** procedure. We pass the file (**FILE__TYPE** object) to an I/O procedure when we access the external file, so that the I/O procedure can identify the correct external file. When we are finished with the file we use a **Close** procedure to sever the link to the external file, at which point we may reuse the file (**FILE__TYPE** object) to link to another external file.[5]

Here's an example of a declaration of a text file:

```
with Text_IO; -- FILE_TYPE for text is declared in Text_IO
procedure Main is
    --
    Output_File : Text_IO.FILE_TYPE;
    --
```

Output__File is the file object—actually, the file our program deals with. We link it with an external file (such as a disk file) with the **Open** procedure, which will specify the disk file's name and mode; but it is **Output__File**, not the disk file, that our program deals with directly.

The I/O Packages

The three I/O packages specified in the Ada manual are **Text__IO**, **Direct__IO**, and **Sequential__IO**. **Text__IO** is used for the input/output of text (ASCII character data) and includes provisions for formatting text. **Direct__IO** and **Sequential__IO** include subprograms for random and sequential I/O, respectively, and can handle any data type by *instantiation* (a flashy term you have seen before but are probably still hazy about) for that type. **Text__IO** may be expressed entirely in terms of **Sequential__IO**.

We will ignore a fourth I/O package, **Low__Level__IO**, because it is extremely implementation dependent and is not very useful to the average microcomputer user.

Text__IO is not a generic package, although it has generic packages embedded in it along with nongeneric subprograms. The other two packages are generic and therefore must be *instantiated* for each type of data to be output.

Instantiation

Ada's strong typing requires I/O subprograms to know exactly what kind of data they will be handling. In order to input or output any data type we would have to have an overloaded subprogram for every conceivable type of data, including all possible user-defined enumeration types.

Obviously this is impossible. To get around this requirement we use the Ada feature *generics*, covered fully in Chapter 10. Briefly, generic units are similar to assembly language macros, although more complicated. In the case of I/O you could think of an instantiation process taking a "template" I/O subprogram or package and substituting a type name you've specified for a dummy type name in the template unit, and then compiling the template. In other words if you need I/O for a special enumeration type, you instantiate I/O by substituting the name of your enumeration type into a template package. The instantiation process creates a new distinct package customized for a particular data type. The instantiation process is fairly simple and involves providing a new name for the customized unit, and giving the generic unit instructions on how to customize itself.[6]

You already may have been puzzled by the **Put** package we had to instantiate in our character count programs before we could output integers. We instantiated the generic package **Integer__IO** (embedded in **Text__IO**), which is equipped for integer types (long, short, and normal), including integer subtypes and integer derived types, as a new package called **Int__IO**, which could output **INTEGER** types.

Here is another example, the instantiation of the generic package **Direct__IO** for the type **INTEGER**:

```
with Direct_IO;
--
package Integer_Direct_IO is new Direct_IO( INTEGER );
use Integer_Direct_IO;
```

This instantiation creates a new instance of **Direct__IO**, a package called **Integer__Direct__IO**. The new package is automatically **with**ed and we may, as we have in the example, **use** it to make the components directly visible. If not **use**d, all references to the subprograms and the package-defined *type__marks* must be in named-component (dot) notation:

```
Integer_Direct_IO.Put( 127 );
```

With the exception of CHARACTER and STRING I/O in package **Text__IO**, *all data types to be input or output must be instantiated.* To put it another way, any time you want to do I/O on a numeric type you have to instantiate a package to handle that type. While this may seem to be an inconvenience, the payback is increased generalization of the library subprograms, and a substantial reduction in the amount of code the compiler needs to link to the final program.

Remember, however, that each instantiation potentially creates some new code that will be linked to your final object program (a well-optimized system will have generics share code). Don't instantiate packages unless you're actually going to use them.

A trick you can use sometimes in a full Ada system to avoid instantiation is the use of the image attribute. If, for instance, you only need to output one integer in a program, you could use the following form:

```
Text_IO.Put( INTEGER'Image( 128 ) );
```

The image attribute returns a string image of the input parameter, and so can use the string type Put already present in Text_IO. The image attribute works with any discrete type.

I/O Errors and Exception Handling

A major design goal for any program should be to make the program bomb-proof. There are ways in nearly every language to make a program *robust* (a computer science buzzword for bomb-proof); in Ada these methods are particularly elegant.

Consider the problem of opening a file from a user-input filename. In BASIC we write something like this:

```
----
1010 ON ERROR GOTO 2000
1020 INPUT "Please enter the filename"; A$
1030 OPEN "R", 1, A$
----
----
2000 PRINT "Error - Can't open file."
2099 RESUME 1020
```

This works okay, but we need to set up the ON ERROR branch before each condition that could cause an error. If we forget, or if an unplanned-for error occurs before the next ON ERROR, we have a mess. If we don't have ON ERROR statements the program just stops, and any data held in memory are lost.

In C, which never stops for any reason, we have to make other provisions. We try to open a file and then test to be sure the file was successfully opened. This is a fairly common approach to error handling in procedural languages: You attempt an operation and then test for successful completion. Ada, however, has a different approach, called *exception handling*. In Ada we can write our code as if everything always works fine, and leave errors to be handled by *exception handlers*. An exception is *raised* when certain predefined errors occur (these are declared in Standard, and are fairly self-evident), the library I/O programs can raise certain exceptions, and you can also define exceptions of your own.[7]

Exceptions have names, just like subprograms and variables. We place code at the end of blocks, subprograms, packages, and other program units to handle exceptions raised within those units. Let's look at an exception handler for the file opening example:

```
with Text_IO;
function File_Opener return FILE_TYPE is
     File_Object : Text_IO.FILE_TYPE;
     Filename : STRING( 1..20 );
     Lastchar : INTEGER;
begin
     Text_IO.Put( "Please enter filename: " );
     Text_IO.Get_Line( File_Name, Last => Lastchar );
     Text_IO.Open( File_Object, Filename( 1..Lastchar ), IN_FILE );
             -- an array slice, see ch. 7
     return File_Object;
exception
     when NAME_ERROR =>    -- raised by "open"
         Text_IO.Put( "Error - Can't find that file" );
         Text_IO.New_Line;
         return File_Opener;       -- recursive call, try again
end File_Opener;
```

Notice that we have added a new part to the subprogram body: the *exception block*. We write the main portion of the code as if it will always work, and then we use the reserved word **exception** to mark the end of the normal code and the beginning of the error handler.

The form of the error handler is similar to the **case** control structure. We have the selection process, where we name one or more exceptions (if more than one exception is to be handled by exception-handling code, we use the vertical bar symbol to delimit the exception name, and a "choose" symbol (=>) just as we do in the **case** statement. We can use all the same statements in each alternative selection branch that we use in any other part of a body.

The **Open** procedure in Ada raises an exception called **NAME_ERROR** if a file does not exist.

It can also generate other exceptions:

- **STATUS_ERROR** (This is covered later, for it can't occur in this sub-program.)
- **USE_ERROR** if the file can't be opened in the manner requested. (Example: opening a video display for input.)

We can write a separate handler for each exception that could be raised by the **Open** procedure:

```
with Text_IO; use Text_IO;
function File_Opener return FILE_TYPE is
     File_Object : FILE_TYPE;
```

```
      Filename : STRING( 1..20 );
      Lastchar : INTEGER;
begin
      Put( "Please enter filename: " );
      Get_Line( File_Name, Last => Lastchar );
      Open( File_Object, Filename( 1..Lastchar), IN_FILE );
      return File_Object;
exception
      when NAME_ERROR =>
            Put( "Error - Can't find that file" );
            New_Line;
            return File_Opener;        -- recursive call
      when USE_ERROR =>
            Put( "Error - Can't use that file that way" );
            New_Line;
            return File_Opener;        -- recursive call
      when others =>
            Put( "Unexpected error in file_opener" );
            New_Line;
end file_opener;
```

We included an **others** clause in the last example; such a clause would actually be a poor choice here because it appears to the computer that the error has been handled when actually nothing has been done. A better choice would be to leave the other exceptions unhandled, to handle them explicitly, or to terminate the program by raising your own exception or reraising the exception. An additional problem is that the **Put** and **Get** procedures in **File_Opener** can also raise exceptions, which may require other handlers.

The exceptions handled by name in the above example print an error message and then call **File_Opener** again. This sort of *recursive* call is allowed in Ada. If the recursive call were not included, control would resume at the point where **File_Opener** was called. A program unit is terminated when an exception is raised, whether or not the exception is handled—and an exception would be raised at that point because the program expects **File_Opener** to return a valid **FILE_TYPE** (a function that doesn't return a value raises the predefined exception **PROGRAM_ERROR**).

When an exception is raised, the unit where the exception occurs stops executing and looks for a handler at the end of the unit. What happens if an exception is raised for which we don't have an exception handler?

Unhandled exception are *propagated* back up the calling sequence that led to the error. If we had, for example, a procedure **Re_Direct** which called **File_Opener**, an exception not handled in the **File_Opener** would be propagated back to **Re_Direct**, and the same exception would be reraised at the point where **Re_Direct** called **File_Opener**.

If Re__Direct doesn't have a handler for the reraised exception, the exception would be propagated back to whoever called Re__Direct, and reraised again at the point where Re__Direct was called. This propagation continues until we either find a handler for the exception or the exception is propagated to the main subprogram. If no exception handler is found in the main subprogram, the program stops.

Note that when an exception is raised, even if the error is handled, we never resume execution in the unit where the error occurred. For this reason, when you expect that an exception will happen as a matter of course, either write a subprogram that is as small as possible, like the File__Opener example, or enclose the code that could cause the exception in a block statement. Near the end of this chapter we include an example of block-enclosed exceptions in a procedure called Dialogue.

In some cases we might want to handle an exception, yet still let it be propagated. The poor example above, File__Opener, where we printed a message about the unexpected error, can be fixed and made into a good example. We can still print the error message, but we also can propagate the exception to the calling program for handling by reraising the exception in the exception handler. We do this by using the statement raise, which can occur in its simplest form only in an exception handler:

```
exception
    when NAME_ERROR =>
         Put( "Error - Can't find that file" );
         New_Line;
         return File_Opener;        -- recursive call
    when USE_ERROR =>
         Put( "Error - Can't use that file that way" );
         New_Line;
         return File_Opener;        -- recursive call
    when others =>
         Put( "Unexpected error in file_opener" );
         New_Line;
         raise;                      -- propagate exception
end File_Opener;
```

The simple raise statement reraises the exception that caused the exception handler to be invoked.

While we're on the subject of exceptions, let's look at how your can raise your own. It's pretty easy, actually. All you have to do is declare the name of the exception in the declaration part of the subprogram which contains the raise statement or, if the subprogram is enclosed in a package, in the specification of the package. Then, at the point where you have determined an error condition, you just raise it:

```
-- Mostly pseudo code!
procedure Ask_For_Filename( Name : out STRING ) is
```

```
      CLUMSY_USER : exception;
begin
   -- prompt for a file name
   -- get response
   -- examine response for validity
   if <response is stupid> then
      raise CLUMSY_USER;
   end if;
end Ask_For_Filename;
```

An exception raised in a program unit either can be handled by that same unit or, more commonly, propagated back to the caller. A **raise** statement that names an exception can occur anywhere, as opposed to the simple raise, which can only occur in an exception handler.

A final point about exceptions: The rules for visibility of exception names are the same as for any other identifiers. If you plan on handling exceptions raised by a library package, you either have to use that library package, as we have done in these examples, or use dot notation to indicate to the compiler where the exceptions are defined.

We will list the exceptions raised with each I/O subprogram in a table; those that require more explanation will be listed with each subprogram description.

The I/O exceptions are contained in a standard package called **IO_Exceptions**, which is automatically loaded when one of the three standard I/O packages are **with**ed. The standard I/O packages *rename* the exceptions so that they appear to be defined in the three packages (see Appendix D). The possible I/O exceptions are:

STATUS_ERROR—raised when trying any operations except **Create**, **Open**, or **Is_Open** on a file that is not open. **Create** and **Open** will raise this exception when attempting to open a file that already is open. (Note: This refers to the internal file object being open, not to the device or external file). *Example:* trying to **Put** to a file that hasn't been opened.

MODE_ERROR—raised when trying to read from a write-only file, write to a read-only file, or trying to assign files of the wrong read-only or write-only mode as the default input or output file. *Example:* Opening a file for reading, and then trying to assign it as the standard output file.

NAME_ERROR—raised when using an improper external file or device name in **Open** or **Create**, or when a file does not exist for **Open**, or if a external file's access attributes don't allow access in the mode attempted. *Example:* Trying to open a file with *operating system* read-only attributes as an output file.

USE_ERROR—raised when an operation is attempted which is not possible due to characteristics of the external file, or if the FORM parameter is improper for the device or external file specified. *Example:* Trying to open a printer for input.

DEVICE_ERROR—raised when the underlying physical device malfunctions. *Example:* A bad sector on a disk file.

END_ERROR—raised when trying to read or skip past the end-of-file mark. *Example:* Trying to read a character from a text file after all the data have been read from it.

DATA_ERROR—raised when attempting to input data of a type not compatible with the requested operation. *Example:* Trying to read an integer number as a fixed-point number.

LAYOUT_ERROR—raised when trying to output data when the constraints of the output device, such as page and line boundaries, are exceeded. See the descriptions of the individual subprograms for more details.

File Management

Five procedures control the link to the external file: **Create, Open, Close, Delete,** and **Reset**. There are also four functions that return file status: **Mode, Name, Form,** and **Is_Open**. These are common to all three I/O packages, with a minor difference in the declaration of the type **FILE_MODE**. The header of the specification for each package is listed with the package description.

We present these nine subprograms here because the file management is uniform for the three types of files (text, sequential, direct). The specifications for all three packages read like this:

```
procedure Create( File : in out FILE_TYPE;
                  Mode : in      FILE_MODE := OUT_FILE;
                  Name : in      STRING    := "";
                  Form : in      STRING    := ""; );

procedure Open  ( File : in out FILE_TYPE;
                  Mode : in      FILE_MODE := OUT_FILE;
                  Name : in      STRING    := "";
                  Form : in      STRING    := ""; );

procedure Close ( File : in out FILE_TYPE );

procedure Delete( File : in out FILE_TYPE );

procedure Reset ( File : in out FILE_TYPE );
procedure Reset ( File : in out FILE_TYPE;
                  Mode : in      FILE_MODE );

function Mode   ( File : in FILE_TYPE ) return FILE_MODE;

function Name   ( File : in FILE_TYPE ) return STRING;
```

```
function Form   ( File : in FILE_TYPE ) return STRING;

function Is_Open( File : in FILE_TYPE ) return BOOLEAN;
```

For all the subprograms the following descriptions of the formal parameters apply:

File is an object of type **FILE__TYPE**.

Name is a string that represents the system name of the file, which will be system dependent. An Ada compiler for a microcomputer most likely will use system names for nondisk files—e.g., in CP/M, **LST:** as the printer; perhaps **PUN:** and **RDR:** for a modem; **CON:** or **TTY:** for console devices.

Mode is an enumeration type defining the access mode of the file. **IN__FILE** and **OUT__FILE** are the two options for **Text__IO** and **Sequential__IO**; **Direct__IO** ("random access" I/O in BASIC) has a third option of **INOUT__FILE**.

Form is implementation dependent; it carries other information which may be required to open a file (access rights, passwords, search pathways, etc.). Notice that there are default null strings for the **Name** and **Form** parameters in the file management procedures.[8]

Also keep in mind that while all three packages have the same procedures for file management, and all act in a similar manner, you must use the subprogram that is intended for the package and file type. For example, you can't open a text I/O file with an **Open** from **Direct__IO**, or a sequential file with the **Open** from **Text__IO**.

In fact, none of the subprograms in **Direct__IO** or **Sequential__IO** even exist until they are instantiated for a particular type.

File Management Descriptions

Create—establishes a new external file and links the external file to the file object **File**. When a file is created it is automatically opened, so a subsequent **Open** operation is unnecessary (and is an error). The default mode for files is **OUT__FILE** for text and sequential files, and **INOUT__FILE** for direct files. It probably wouldn't make sense to create a file with an **IN__FILE** mode, as you would not be able to do anything with it. Any existing external file of the same name is deleted when the new file is **Created**.

Open—is used the same way **Create** is, but the external file must already exist before you can **Open** it.

Close—disconnects the linkage between the external file and the file object **File**.

The system automatically does such things as writing an end-of-file and updating directories when a file is Closed, so be sure to close output files before terminating a program.

Delete—removes the external file associated with the file object File. The external file ceases to exist and the file object File is left closed. Note that the file must be opened before it can be deleted.

Reset—rewinds the file so that reading or writing may resume at the start of the file. (For a Direct__IO file this means that the index is set to one.) Note that this is an overloaded procedure: If a Mode is supplied, the file mode may be changed at this time (from OUT__FILE to IN__FILE, for example, to reread a temporary file).

The functions Mode, Name, and Form return the associated parameters of the file object File. For example, Name(File__One) returns the external name that the file File__One is associated with.

The function Is__Open returns TRUE if File is linked to an external file (is open); otherwise it returns FALSE.

Examples of the file management procedures:

```
with Text_IO; use Text_IO;
- -
Input_File, Output_File : FILE_TYPE;
- -
Open( Input_File, IN_FILE, "B:TEXT.DOC" );
Create( Output_File, OUT_FILE, "B:TEXT.BAK" );
Close( Output_File );
Reset( Input_File, OUT_FILE );
if Mode( Input_File ) = IN_FILE then....
Put( Name( Input_File ) );
if Is_Open( Input_File ) then...
Delete( Input_File );
```

Refer to the examples in this book for the nuts and bolts of using the file management functions.

Package Text__IO

Text__IO contains facilities to open a link to the system's standard input and output devices, normally the keyboard and the display. The links are established automatically to the internal default input and default output files when you with Text__IO. There are also ways to redirect the default I/O streams, and subprograms to output formatted and unformatted text.

The subprograms in Text__IO are:

Create	Set_Output	New_Page	Get
Open	Standard_Input	Set_Col	Get_Line
Close	Standard_Output	Set_Line	Put
Delete	Current_Input	Col	Put_Line
Reset	Current_Output	Line	
Mode	Set_Line_Length	Skip_line	
Name	Set_Page_Length	Skip_page	
Form	Line_Length	End_Of_Line	
Is_Open	Page_Length	End_Of_Page	
Set_Input	New_Line	End_Of_File	

There are four generic elements to **Text__IO**, which must be instantiated before we can use them. They are:

Integer__IO, Float__IO, Fixed__IO, Enumeration__IO

We use **Integer__IO** to I/O integers, subtypes of integer, and derived types of integers. We use **Float__IO** similarly for float, **Fixed__IO** for fixed, and **Enumeration__IO** for enumeration types.

We don't need to make an instantiation for subtypes if the parent type is already instantiated, but we do need to instantiate for each *derived type* (see further discussion in Chapter 8).

Most of the subprograms in **Text__IO** are overloaded to use the default input or output if a **FILE__TYPE** object is not supplied in the call. We will present the nongeneric portions of **Text__IO** grouped according to function, and then the generic portions.

A whole slew of formatting subprograms in **Text__IO** have been moved to the end of this chapter past the subprograms in direct and sequential I/O. These subprograms are not usually implemented in microcomputer Ada subsets, and in fact are not particularly useful for micros.

All of **Text__IO** uses the basic definitions of types and constants shown in Figure 6-1, which has been extracted from the specification of **Text__IO** printed in Appendix D.

Text__IO has six subprograms that deal with the standard input and standard output files:

```
procedure Set_Input ( File : in FILE_TYPE );

procedure Set_Output( File : in FILE_TYPE );

function Standard_Input  return FILE_TYPE;

function Standard_Output return FILE_TYPE;

function Current_Input   return FILE_TYPE;

function Current_Output  return FILE_TYPE;
```

Subprogram	Status	Mode	Name	Exception Error Type Use	Device	End	Data	Layout
Create	*		*	*				
Open	*		*	*				
Close	*							
Delete	*							
Reset	*			*				
Mode	*							
Name	*							
Form	*							
Is_Open								
Set_Input	*	*						
Set_Output	*	*						
Standard_Input								
Standard_Output								
Current_Input								
Current_Output								
Set_Line_Length	*			*				
Set_Page_Length	*			*				
Line_Length	*							
Page_Length	*							
New_Line	*	*						
Skip_Line	*	*				*		
End_of_Line	*	*						
New_Page	*	*						
Skip_Page	*	*				*		
End_of_Page	*	*						
End_of_File	*	*						
Set_Col (IN_FILE)	*					*		
Set_Col (OUT_FILE)	*							*
Set_Line (IN_FILE)	*					*		
Set_Line (OUT_FILE)	*							*
Col	*							*
Line	*							*
Page	*							*
Get	*	*			*	*	*	
Put	*	*			*			*
Get_Line	*	*			*	*		
Put_Line	*	*			*			

Table 6-1. **Text__IO** *Exceptions*

```
type FILE_TYPE is limited private;
type FILE_MODE is (IN_FILE, OUT_FILE);
subtype FIELD is INTEGER range 0..Implementation_Defined;
subtype NUMBER_BASE is INTEGER range 2..16;
type COUNT is range 0..Implementation_Defined;
subtype POSITIVE_COUNT is COUNT range 1..COUNT'last;
type TYPE_SET is (LOWER_CASE, UPPER_CASE);
Unbounded : constant COUNT := 0;
```

Figure 6-1. **Text__IO** *Header*

Set__Input—assigns the name file as the new standard input or default input file. All default file **Get** operations will take place from the file named, rather than the standard input device (usually the keyboard).[9] *Example:*

```
with Text_IO; use Text_IO;
procedure Redirect_Input( Name_Of_File : STRING ) is
     Input_File : FILE_TYPE;
begin
     Open( Input_File, Name_Of_File, IN_FILE );
     Set_Input( Input_File );
exception
     when others =>
          Put_Line( "Input Redirection Failed" );
end Redirect_Input;
```

Set__Output—assigns the file named as the new default output file. All default **Put** operations will take place to the named file, rather than the standard output device (usually the screen). *Example:*

```
with Text_IO; use Text_IO;
procedure Redirect_Output( Name_Of_File : STRING ) is
     Output_File : FILE_TYPE;
begin
     Create( Output_File, Name_Of_File, OUT_FILE );
     Set_Output( Output_File );
exception
     when others =>
          Put_Line( "Output Redirection Failed" );
end Redirect_Output;
```

Both procedures given as examples above are very handy for redirection. If using output redirection, remember to close the file to insure that all system housekeeping gets done. This may involve declaring the file object Output_File in a parent unit, because of accessibility problems with limited private types, or using the Default_Output function as a parameter to Close.

Standard_Input and Standard_Output are functions that return values of type FILE_TYPE which correspond to the system's standard input and standard output devices. You could use these functions if the input or output had been redirected and you wanted them switched back to the default setting. Or you could use them as parameters to Put and Get (seen later) to make sure that error messages are printed to the standard output device if default output has been redirected. No exceptions are raised by these two functions:

```
Put( Standard_Output, "FATAL ERROR - press any key" );
Get( Standard_Input, Dummy_Char );
```

Current_Input and Current_Output—return file objects corresponding to the current default input and default output streams. These functions may have very limited utility (see limited private types in Chapter 10 for why this is so), being limited almost exclusively to use as parameters to Text_IO subprograms not overloaded to have a version which writes to the default streams. No exceptions are raised by these two functions.

Text Input/Output

In Ada text files can be treated as lines of characters and pages of lines. This is explored in greater detail at the end of the chapter. For simple I/O, just the line concept will do.

Lines are a sequence of characters, ended with a *line terminator*.[10] In CP/M and MS-DOS systems a line terminator is a carriage return/linefeed pair. Ada ignores them for both input and output unless they are explicitly accounted for.

When text is being output a new line is not generated unless asked for. Unlike BASIC's PRINT statement, which generates a return/linefeed at the end of each line unless suppressed, Ada's Put subprogram outputs exactly what is specified, with no leading or trailing spaces and no automatic linefeed or return.

When inputting, Ada's Get scans only for a data item to match what was requested, whether the scan takes place in an external file or from the user input stream. A Get acts in a peculiar way when scanning for input strings! The return/linefeed will be ignored, and characters from the next line are input as part of the current string. When Getting numeric types, Get skips return/linefeed pairs, spaces, and tabs until it either finds the specified numeric type in the input or it encounters data that do not match the expected type.

To overcome these peculiarities `Text_IO` provides a method of positioning both the input and output (`New_Line` and `Skip_Line`) and a method of controlling input (`Get_Line`), which we'll cover later.

For positioning the output we have:

default file—

```
procedure New_Line( Spacing : in POSITIVE_COUNT := 1);
```

named file—

```
procedure New_Line( File    : in FILE_TYPE;
                    Spacing : in POSITIVE_COUNT := 1 );
```

`New_Line` causes a line terminator (return/linefeed on micros) to be output. If we supply the `Spacing` parameter we can get multiple line terminator output. Calling this procedure with no parameters outputs one line terminator to the default file.

```
New_Line;           -- outputs one return/linefeed
New_Line( 5 );      -- outputs 5 return/linefeeds
New_Line( Myfile, 3); -- outputs 3 return/linefeeds
                    -- to file "Myfile"
```

For positioning input (usually used to skip over any garbage left on the input line by the user) we have:

default file—

```
procedure Skip_Line( Spacing : in POSITIVE_COUNT := 1 );
```

named file—

```
procedure Skip_Line( File    : in FILE_TYPE;
                     Spacing : in POSITIVE_COUNT := 1 );
```

`Skip_Line` scans over the input stream until a line or page terminator is detected. A repeat count may be specified (`Spacing`). *Example:*

```
Skip_Line;          -- skips to start of next line
Skip_Line( Myfile ) -- skips to start of next line
                    -- in file "Myfile"
```

You usually will want to detect an end-of-file condition before an exception is raised. In these cases, **Text__IO** provides a function that returns a Boolean result:

default file—
```
function End_Of_File                            return BOOLEAN;
```
named file—
```
function End_Of_File( File : in FILE_TYPE ) return BOOLEAN;
```

This function returns **TRUE** if an end-of-file is next; otherwise it returns **FALSE**.

Getting Stuff Out There

So far we have looked at most everything in **Text__IO** except for how to actually do input and output. All I/O to text files is through the procedures **Get**, **Put**, **Get__Line**, and **Put__Line**. Two forms of each procedure exist for each defined type: One has no file parameter and operates on the default file, and the other has a file parameter and operates on an open file.

The **Get** procedures all operate on files of mode **IN__FILE**. The **Put** procedures all operate on files of mode **OUT__FILE**.

Several forms of **Get** and **Put** for numeric I/O have formatting parameters, used to adjust the output field size.

All forms of **Get** and **Put** raise the following exceptions:

- **STATUS__ERROR**—if the file is not open.
- **MODE__ERROR**—if the file is of the incorrect mode.

Get procedures raise the exception **END__ERROR** if an attempt to read past the end-of-file mark is made, and the **DATA__ERROR** exception if an attempt to read data of the wrong type is made.

A special version of **Put** that outputs to strings (rather than files) raises the **LAYOUT__ERROR** exception if the output as specified will not fit in the constraints of the string.

Let's look at the character I/O functions:

default file, character—
```
procedure Get(                          Item : out CHARACTER );
```
named file, character—
```
procedure Get( File : in FILE_TYPE; Item : out CHARACTER );
```

```
default file, character—
        procedure put(                                    Item : in  CHARACTER );
named file, character—
        procedure put( File : in FILE_TYPE; Item : in  CHARACTER );
```

Get skips any line or page terminators and places the next character in the stream into the variable **Item**. This is a feature of Ada that will bite you sooner or later.

Put outputs the character in **Item**. If a column count is defined, Put may call **New_Line** before Putting the character (see formatting at end of chapter).

The string I/O functions:

```
named file, string—
        procedure Get       ( File : in FILE_TYPE; Item : out STRING );
default file, string—
        procedure Get       (                      Item : out STRING );


named file, string—
        procedure Get_Line( File : in FILE_TYPE;
                            Item : out STRING
                            Last : out NATURAL );
default file, string—
        procedure Get_Line( Item : out STRING
                            Last : out NATURAL );


named file, string—
        procedure Put       ( File : in FILE_TYPE; Item : in  STRING );

default file, string—
        procedure Put       (                      Item : in  STRING );


named file, string—
        procedure Put_Line( File : in FILE_TYPE; Item : in  STRING );

default file, string—
        procedure Put_Line(                      Item : in  STRING );
```

The string version of Get first determines the length of the parameter **Item** (a string variable) and then, if **Item** has a length greater than 0, calls the character version of Get, which adds characters from the input stream until **Item** is full or an end-of-file is reached. You will recall that line and page terminators are skipped by the character Get.

Get_Line also figures the length of **Item** and tries to fill it by calls to the character version of **Get**. It reacts to an encounter with a line terminator by:

1. Assigning the index of the last character inserted in **Item** to the parameter **Last** so that

```
Item( Last ) = the last character read
```

2. Calling **Skip_Line**.

If **Item** has a length of zero, then:

```
Last = Item'FIRST - 1
```

If the line terminator is reached and **Skip_Line** is called before **Item** is filled (the usual case), the remaining components of **Item** are left undefined. Normally this means they retain whatever value they had before the call to **Get_Line**.

Procedure **Put** outputs string **Item**. **Put_Line** calls string **Put** to output **Item**, and then calls **New_Line**.

Generally, in an interactive environment, you will use the **Get_Line** procedure for user input. A common practice is to use a string that is longer than any conceivable input, and then use the information returned in **Last** to parse the string. For example, when asking a user to enter a file name we can use **Last** to determine the end of a *slice* of the input (see Chapter 8):[11]

```
with Text_IO;
procedure Whatever is

    Filename_Input : STRING( 1..80 );
    Response_Length : NATURAL;
    File_Obj : Text_IO.FILE_TYPE;
    --
    Text_IO.Put( "Please enter a filename: " );
    Text_IO.Get_Line( Filename_Input, Response_Length );
    Text_IO.Open( File_Obj, Filename_Input( 1..Response_Length ),
      OUT_FILE, "" );
    --
```

When writing programs that you want to user proof, you will have to use **Get_Line** and parse the input string (interpret it character by character to determine exactly what the user typed). Ada doesn't do any of the hand holding that BASIC does for you; however, you'll never get a error message messing up your nicely formatted display, either. A word of warning: Some implementations of Ada do not interpret line editing characters, so backspaces and other editing controls will be returned explicitly.

Numeric I/O is a bit more complicated. In addition to the need to instantiate the generic portions of **Text__IO** for each numeric or enumeration type, the numeric **Get** and **Put** procedures have additional parameters that can affect input or output field width. Numeric types also have a number base parameter, and enumeration types have a parameter that specifies the use of upper- or lowercase for the output.

The declarations of all the types used for these parameters are listed in Figure 6-1, the **Text__IO** header.

Text__IO for Integers

Another set of **Get** and **Put** procedures are available for instantiation for integer types. Note the functions included for converting integers to strings, and vice-versa.

Default values for **Default__Width** below is the minimum number of characters required to represent the largest value of the type **NUM**, and the default value for **Base** below is base 10, although we can reach into the instantiated package and change these default values using named notation. The type **NUM** represents the integer data *type__mark* that the package has been instantiated for:

default file, integer__type—
```
      procedure Get( Item  : out NUM;
                     Width : in  FIELD := 0 );
```

named file, integer__type—
```
      procedure Get( File  : in  FILE_TYPE;
                     Item  : out NUM;
                     Width : in  FIELD := 0 );
```

The default file and named file versions of **Get** have identical characteristics. If **Width** is unspecified or zero, leading blanks and line/page terminators are skipped until the number is encountered. The number may be any valid integer literal, including based literals. If **Width** is specified nonzero, then exactly **Width** characters are scanned for the number, up to a line terminator.

This is the garden variety **Get** procedure for integers. Usually it is called without a width parameter:

string-to-integer__type—
```
    procedure Get( From  : in  STRING;
                   Item  : out NUM;
                   Last  : out POSITIVE; );
```

The string version of **Get** is similar to the file versions. The string, rather than the input stream, is scanned for the number. The end of the string is treated as a file terminator. The parameter passed as **Last** is filled with the index of the last character of the string read.

The string version might be used with slices (see Chapter 7) of an input string when parsing user input.

All three of these procedures raise the exception **DATA__ERROR** if a number can't be formed from the input, or if the value obtained is outside the range of the subtype **NUM**:

default file, integer__type—
```
    procedure Put( Item  : in  NUM;
                   Width : in  FIELD := Default_Width;
                   Base  : in  NUMBER_BASE := 10 );
```

named file, integer__type—
```
    procedure Put( File  : in  FILE_TYPE;
                   Item  : in  NUM;
                   Width : in  FIELD := Default_Width;
                   Base  : in  NUMBER_BASE := 10 );
```

The default and named file versions of **Put** have identical characteristics. **Width** defaults to the number of characters required to represent the largest possible value pass as **Item**. Leading blanks are added to pad the output field.

These are the usual versions of **Put** used for integers:

integer__type-to-string—
```
    procedure Put( To    : out STRING;
                   Item  : in  NUM;
                   Base  : in  NUMBER_BASE := 10 );
```

The string version of **Put** outputs to the supplied string. The value for **Width** is taken from the length of the string.

This **Put** is generally used for internal manipulations. For example, you could generate unique external filenames by concatenating the string produced by this **Put** to a fragment of a standard file name.

I/O for floats and fixed is similar to that for integer.[12] We have the six functions, with the **Width** parameter replaced in the **Put** by three specifications: **Fore**, **Aft**, and **Exp**. **Fore** specifies how many places appear before the decimal point; **Aft**, after the decimal point; and **Exp**, the size of the exponent field. **Fore** has leading blanks; **Aft** has trailing zeros; **Exp** has leading blanks, or does not appear if **Exp** is zero. Keep in mind that a decimal point and an **E** appear in the output field:

$$(Fore = 3) + (Aft = 3) + (Exp = 3) /= (Width = 9)$$

```
Fore      Aft      Exp
```

The default formats of the six real I/O procedures are:

for float_types—
```
      Default_Fore : FIELD := 2;
      Default_Aft  : FIELD := NUM'Digits-1;
      Default_Exp  : FIELD := 3;
```

for fixed_types—
```
      Default_Fore : FIELD := NUM'Fore;
      Default_Aft  : FIELD := NUM'Aft;
      Default_Exp  : FIELD := 0;
```

The six procedures are:

named file, real_type—
```
      procedure Get( File  : in  FILE_TYPE;
                     Item  : out NUM;
                     Width : in  FIELD := 0 );
```

default file, real_type—
```
      procedure Get( Item  : out NUM;
                     Width : in  FIELD := 0 );
```

string-to-real_type—
```
      procedure Get( From  : in  STRING;
                     Item  : out NUM;
                     Last  : out POSITIVE );
```

named file, real_type—
```
    procedure Put( File : in   FILE_TYPE;
                   Item : in   NUM;
                   Fore : in   FIELD := Default_Fore;
                   Aft  : in   FIELD := Default_Aft;
                   Exp  : in   FIELD := Default_Exp;
```

default file, real_type—
```
    procedure Put( Item : in   NUM;
                   Fore : in   FIELD := Default_Fore;
                   Aft  : in   FIELD := Default_Aft;
                   Exp  : in   FIELD := Default_Exp;
```

real_type-to-string—
```
    procedure Put( To   : in   STRING;
                   Item : in   NUM;
                   Aft  : in   FIELD := Default_Aft;
                   Exp  : in   FIELD := Default_Exp;
```

As previously mentioned, these six procedures for real types correspond to the six for integer types. In the real-to-string version of **Put**, **Fore** is determined by subtracting the rest of the fields from the string length. The same exceptions apply as for integer types.

Sample outputs using the **Fore**, **Aft**, and **Exp** parameters:

```
X : real_type := -123.4567;   --8 digits
--
put( x );                              -1.2345670E+02
put( x, Fore => 5, Aft => 3, Exp => 2 );  ƀƀƀ-1.235E+2
put( x, 5, 3, 0 );                     ƀ123.457

-- the symbol ƀ means "blank" or "space".
```

Enumeration I/O

Three **Get** and three **Put** procedures are defined for enumeration types.[13] Again, they correspond to the integer **Put**s and **Get**s, and only the differences will be noted.

Something that may not be obvious to you if you are unfamiliar with enumeration types is that when an enumeration value is input or output, what appears is the identifier. For example:

```
type SUIT is ( HEART, DIAMOND, SPADE, CLUB );
Card_Suit : SUIT;
--
-- Instantiate I/O for SUIT somewhere
--
Put( HEART );                                    HEART
Card_Suit := DIAMOND;
Put( Card_Suit );                                DIAMOND
```

Values are output in either upper- or lowercase, controlled by a parameter called **Set**. Values for this parameter are of type **TYPE__SET**, declared in **Enumeration__IO**:

```
type TYPE_SET is ( LOWER_CASE, UPPER_CASE );
```

Two default parameters are also defined:

```
Default_Width    : FIELD := 0;
Default_Setting : TYPE_SET := UPPER_CASE;
```

A **Width** of zero causes the output of only the number of characters actually required to **Put** the identifier; if **Width** is specified, trailing spaces are output after the identifier as required to fill the field.

ENUM in the following represents the enumeration type that the package was instantiated for:

default file, enumeration__type—
```
     procedure Get( Item : out ENUM );
```

named file, enumeration__type—
```
     procedure Get( File : in  FILE_TYPE;
                    Item : out ENUM );
```

string-to-enumeration__type—
```
     procedure Get( From : in  STRING;
                    Item : out ENUM;
                    Last : out POSITIVE );
```

default file, enumeration__type—
```
     procedure Put( Item  : in  ENUM;
                    Width : in  FIELD    := Default_Width;
                    Set   : in  TYPE_SET := Default_Setting );
```

named file, enumeration__type—
```
     procedure Put( File  : in   FILE_TYPE;
                    Item  : in   ENUM;
                    Width : in   FIELD    := Default_Width;
                    Set   : in   TYPE_SET := Default_Setting );
```

enumeration__type-to-string—
```
     procedure Put( To   : out  STRING;
                    Item : in   ENUM;
                    Set  : in   TYPE_SET := Default_Setting );
```

Direct and Sequential I/O

Mercifully, **Direct_IO** and **Sequential_IO** have only a few basic subprograms not already covered in **Text_IO**.[14] The file management routines (**Create, Open**, etc.) all operate as they do in **Text_IO**. The additional subprograms are essentially the same for **Sequential_IO** and **Direct_IO**: **Direct_IO** contains analogs to all procedures in **Sequential_IO**, and has only a few extra subprograms to learn.

Sequential files may have modes of **IN_FILE** or **OUT_FILE**. A file may not be open for both input and output. Direct files may have either of those modes, or a third mode, **INOUT_FILE**.

Sequential files operate about the same as text files. When they are opened, we are positioned at the start of the file. As we input or output to sequential files, we progress toward the end of the file. We can't "back up" in a sequential file, except to go back to the very beginning by using the **Reset** file management procedure.

A direct file has an additional property: the *index*. In a direct file, we can *seek* or *position* ourselves anywhere in the file at any time. A direct file may be thought of as an open-ended array. The index to the file is similar in concept to the index of an array, with one difference: After reading or writing in the direct file, the index is automatically pointed to the next-higher item in the file. Ada keeps track of the index for us, and we don't always have to explicitly specify it.

The subprogram descriptions follow.

```
Subprograms in Sequential_IO
(file management not listed)

Read      Write      End_Of_File
```

```
Subprograms in Direct_IO
(file management not listed)
```

```
Read        Write       End_Of_File
Size        Index       Set_Index
```

We'll list the common subprograms first, and then the subprograms unique to Direct__IO. The common subprograms are:

either direct or sequential—
```
procedure Read( File : in  FILE_TYPE;
                Item : out ELEMENT_TYPE );
```

direct only—

```
procedure Read( File : in  FILE_TYPE;
                Item : out ELEMENT_TYPE;
                From : POSITIVE_COUNT );
```

Read places the value of the next element of **File** in **Item** and then advances to the next item. In the case of a direct file, the second form of **Read** is allowed, in which case the file index is moved to position **From** before the **Read** operation takes place.

either direct or sequential—

```
procedure Write( File : in  FILE_TYPE;
                 Item : out ELEMENT_TYPE );
```

direct only—

```
procedure Write( File : in  FILE_TYPE;
                 Item : out ELEMENT_TYPE;
                 To   : in  POSITIVE_COUNT );
```

Write places the value in **Item** in the next element of **File** and then advances to the next position. In the case of direct files the second form is allowed, in which case the file index is moved to index **To** before the **Write** operation takes place. **USE__ERROR** is raised if file capacity is exceeded (e.g., the disk is full):

either sequential or direct—

```
function End_Of_File( FILE : in FILE_TYPE ) return BOOLEAN;
```

Subprogram	Status	Mode	Name	Use	Device	End	Data
Create	*		*	*			
Open	*		*	*			
Close	*						
Delete	*						
Reset	*			*			
Mode	*						
Name	*						
Form	*						
Is_Open							
Read	*	*			*	*	*
Write	*	*			*	*	*
Set_Index	*						
Index	*						
Size	*						
End-of-File	*	*					

Table 6-2. Exceptions Raised by Direct__IO *and* Sequential__IO

   End__Of__File returns TRUE if the current index is greater than the current file size (i.e., if you're at the end of the file or beyond).

direct only—

```
function Index( File : in FILE_TYPE ) return POSITIVE_COUNT;
```

   Index returns the current index of File.

direct only—

```
procedure Set_Index( File : in FILE_TYPE;
                     To   : in POSITIVE_COUNT );
```

   Set__Index sets the index of File to To. To may exceed the present size of the file.

direct only—

```
function Size( File : in FILE_TYPE ) return count;
```

Size returns the size of File, in units of ELEMENT__TYPE..

Page Formatting: More Text__IO

From Ada's viewpoint, text files are pages with lines and columns. Each page has a page terminator, and each line has a line terminator. In the CP/M and MS-DOS worlds, line terminators are carriage return/linefeeds, and page terminators are form feeds.

When the Put procedure is used a check is made of the current column, and if the next item to be output will not fit on the current line, a new line is begun (except in the special case of output to strings). If a new line will not fit on the current page, a new page is begun.

We can set limits on page length and line length using procedures. These limits are in terms of the subtype POSITIVE__COUNT in the Text__IO header. The constant UNBOUNDED, defined in the header, is used when we don't wish to have limits on line length or lines per page (unformatted output).

When a file is opened or created, line and page lengths are set to UNBOUNDED, and therefore the file defaults to a single line of unlimited length, unless we explicitly output terminators.

The following are the subprograms used in page formatting. All of these have two versions, one where a file is named and one where the default input and output are assumed.

As stated earlier, Ada subsets probably will not implement these subprograms.[15]

default file—

```
procedure Set_Line_Length( To   : in COUNT );
```

named file—

```
procedure Set_Line_Length( File : in FILE_TYPE;
                           To   : in COUNT );
```

default file—

```
procedure Set_Page_Length( To   : in COUNT );
```

named file—

```
procedure Set_Page_Length( File : in FILE_TYPE;
                           To   : in COUNT );
```

default file—

```
function Line_Length( File : in FILE_TYPE ) return COUNT;
```

named file—

```
function Line_Length                         return COUNT;
```

default file—

```
function Page_Length( File : in FILE_TYPE ) return COUNT;
```

named file—

```
function Page_Length                         return COUNT;
```

The procedures above set the format of the output page. Leave all of these alone (set to zero) if no formatting is desired. The exception **USE_ERROR** is raised if the settings are not appropriate to the actual device used.

The functions above return the current settings of the line and page boundaries.

Positioning

For positioning the output, we have:

default file—

```
procedure New_Page;
```

named file—

```
procedure New_Page( File   : in FILE_TYPE );
```

default file—

```
procedure Set_Col ( To     : in POSITIVE_COUNT );
```

named file—

```
procedure Set_Col ( File   : in FILE_TYPE;
                    To     : in POSITIVE_COUNT );
```

default file—

```
procedure Set_Line( To        : in POSITIVE_COUNT );
```

named file—

```
procedure Set_Line( File      : in FILE_TYPE;
                    To        : in POSITIVE_COUNT );
```

default file—

```
function Col                           return POSITIVE_COUNT;
```

named file—

```
function Col ( File : in FILE_TYPE ) return POSITIVE_COUNT;
```

default file—

```
function Line                          return POSITIVE_COUNT;
```

named file—

```
function Line( File : in FILE_TYPE ) return POSITIVE_COUNT;
```

default file—

```
function Page                          return POSITIVE_COUNT;
```

named file—

```
function Page( File : in FILE_TYPE ) return POSITIVE_COUNT;
```

New__Page causes a page terminator to be output. If output is positioned at the start of a page, or if the current column is not zero, a line terminator is output first.

Set__Col causes the output to be positioned to the specified column, by outputting spaces. Since we can't "back up" an output stream, if the requested column number is less than the current column position, a **New__Line** is issued and the output is spaced to the requested column.

Set__Line is similar to **Set__Col**; **New__Line** is called until the current line number is equal to the one requested. If the current line is greater than the requested line, **New__Page** is called first.

Set_Line and Set_Col raise the exception **LAYOUT_ERROR** if the value requested exceeds the set limits for these values.

The functions Col, Line, and Page return the current values regarding the position of the output. If these values exceed COUNT'Last, the exception **LAYOUT_ERROR** is raised.

We may use additional subprograms to position our input streams, in a fashion very similar to the way we position the output streams. The input positioning procedures are:

default file—

```
procedure Skip_Page( Spacing : in POSITIVE_COUNT := 1 );
```

named file—

```
procedure Skip_Page( File    : in FILE_TYPE;
                     Spacing : in POSITIVE_COUNT := 1 );
```

default file—

```
procedure Set_Col ( To      : in POSITIVE_COUNT := 1 );
```

named file—

```
procedure Set_Col ( File    : in FILE_TYPE;
                    To      : in POSITIVE_COUNT := 1 );
```

default file—

```
procedure Set_Line ( To     : in POSITIVE_COUNT := 1 );
```

named file—

```
procedure Set_Line ( File   : in FILE_TYPE;
                     To     : in POSITIVE_COUNT := 1 );
```

Skip_Page scans over the input stream until a page terminator is detected. A repeat COUNT may be specified. for either procedure.

Note that if a page terminator is placed immediately after a line terminator, it always will be skipped when the line terminator is skipped. It is impossible for the "file pointer" to be positioned between a line terminator and page terminator.

Set_Col and Set_Line are used to skip in the input until the requested line or column is reached. Short lines or pages are skipped until a line or page with the desired position is available. The exception **LAYOUT_ERROR** is raised if the requested value exceeds the current bounds.

A Sample I/O Procedure

This example is from the Ada *Language Reference Manual* and shows the use of text I/O facilities in a dialog with a user at a terminal. The user is prompted to type a color, and the program responds by giving the number of items of that color available in stock, according to an array inventory which is initialized for demonstration purposes with dummy values. The default I/O streams are used. The instantiations are all given as part of the procedure; the manual recommends in practice placing them in a separate package for reuse by other similar or associated routines.[16]

```
with Text_IO; use Text_IO;
procedure Dialogue is
    type COLOR is (WHITE, RED, ORANGE, YELLOW, GREEN,
     BLUE, BROWN);
    package Color_IO is new Enumeration_IO( ENUM => COLOR );
    package Number_IO is new Integer_IO( INTEGER );
    use Color_IO, Integer_IO;

    Inventory : array( COLOR ) of INTEGER := ( --initial values
             20, 17, 43, 10, 28, 173, 87 );
    Choice    : Color;

    procedure Enter_Color( Selection : out COLOR ) is
    begin
       loop
          begin                          -- start of a block
             Put( "Enter color: " );     -- user prompt
             Get( color );               -- accepts color, or
             return;                     -- raises exception
          exception
             when DATA_ERROR =>
             Put( "Bad selection, try again." );
             New_Line( 2 );
          end;                           -- end of the block
       end loop;                         -- loop repeats block
    end Enter_Color;                     --  until input valid
```

```
begin                                   -- body of dialog
   Number_IO.Default_Width := 5;        -- named assignment
   loop
      Enter_Color( Choice );            -- get color request
      Set_Col( 5 );  Put( choice ); Put( " items available:");
      Set_Col( 40 ); Put( Inventory( Choice) );
      New_Line;
   end loop;
end Dialogue;
```

Example interaction (underlined characters are user input):

```
Enter color: Black
Bad selection, try again.

Enter color: Blue
     BLUE items available:            173
Enter color: Yellow
     YELLOW items available:          10
```

A Sample I/O Package

Given the stream file concept and the fact that all devices are considered files, it is a relatively simple matter to engineer a package that will do UNIX-style command line redirection.

Command line redirection is a technique whereby the default input and/or default output of a program can be directed from or to a disk file, without the program's intervention. The later versions of MS-DOS have this facility built in. No version of CP/M does.

Consider the following program, written for Janus/Ada version 1.5.0:

```
with Util, IO;
package body Copy is
   use Util, IO;

   Char : CHARACTER;

begin
   while not End_Of_File( Current_Input() ) loop
```

```
      Get( Char );
      Put( Char );
   end loop;
end Copy;
```

Aside from the irregularities of the syntax (note especially the empty parentheses required for the function call Current_Input) and the odd context specification, the meaning of this program is fairly obvious. As the user types on the console, the input should be echoed to the screen. If compiled and run, this program will produce two copies of everything typed (once for the key echo, once for the Put).

If we were to run this program on an operating system that did redirection from the command line, we could use this same program to copy files (by redirecting the input from one file and the output to another), to type files (by redirecting the input and leaving the output as the display), to work as a poor man's text editor (by leaving the input as the keyboard and redirecting the output to a file), as a cheap typewriter program (by leaving the input as the keyboard and redirecting the output to the printer), etc.

The standard convention for command line redirection is to put a file name on the command line and prefix it with a less-than (<) for input redirection, and a greater-than (>) for output redirection:

```
A>COPY <file1 >file2      -- copies file1 to file2
A>COPY <file1             -- TYPEs file1
A>COPY >file1             -- poor man's text editor
A>COPY >LST:              -- cheap typewriter
```

Redirection from the command line is very useful for systems work, especially when writing filters. A filter is a program that modifies the data that passes through it. For example, a directory program (which is not a filter) could output to the screen a list of files on a disk. If this program were redirected to output to a disk file, we would have a snapshot of the disk directory. We then could pass this through an alphabetizing filter and either display the result, or place the output into another file for subsequent use or further filtering.

As well as the redirection arguments, the command line may be used to convey other information to the program, such as options or filenames. In these cases we want any redirection parameters to disappear from the command line, so as not to confuse the program. Remember: For redirection to be most useful it should take place without the program having to take any action regarding it.

With this in mind we have written a package for Janus/Ada version 1.5.0 that will process the command line and perform redirection. Parameters from the command line other than the redirection parameters are placed in an array of strings argv, in the C style, and a variable argc holds a count of the number of command line parameters found.[17]

The package specification and body are presented as Figures 6-4 and 6-5. Many of the concepts have as yet not been covered in this book, and the package relies heavily on the

Janus nonstandard string type, which is modeled after the Pascal MT+ string. After you read the next three chapters you will be able to rewrite this package using regular Ada constructions. Note also that Janus uses a different order of the parameters for **open** and **create** than are used by the standard **Text__IO** procedures.

Using the package is very easy. Once the specification and body have been compiled, simply **with**ing the package will cause the redirection to take place because the initialization statements at the end of the package are executed before the main program. If the package is also **use**d, the array **argv** will be directly visible, and will hold the command line arguments when the main procedure starts executing. Even if not **use**d, the array **argv** and the variable **argc** still will be visible, and can be accessed using dot notation:

```
put( cmd.argv( 1 ) );
```

```
-- CMD - redirection for Janus/Ada version 1.5.0
-- This package creates an array of strings (argv) that
-- correspond to command line arguments. This package
-- also does I/O redirection similar to the UNIX construction,
-- where a "<name" tells the program to accept the standard
-- input from file "name", and ">name2" tells the program to
-- direct the standard output to file "name2".
--      The count of command line arguments is in the variable
-- 'argc'. The redirection parameters are not included in the
-- list or the count.


-- Package specification: These items are exported by this
-- package, and these items only.

with IO, Util, Strlib;
package Cmd is
use IO, Util, Strlib;

   Argv     : array( INTEGER range 1..10 ) of STRING;
   Argc     : INTEGER;

end Cmd;
```

Figure 6-2. *Command Line Redirection: Specifications*

```
-- CMD - body
-- Command line analyzer
--      This package was written for Janus/ADA version 1.5.0 and
-- contains non-standard constructions, noted where they occur:
-- *1 means bad syntax
-- *2 means construction violates array constraint principle
-- *3 means procedure format is not standard Ada, either text_io
--      open/create or substitute for attribute function item'length.
-- Note: we also rely on Janus closing the output file when finished.

with IO, Util, Strlib;
package body Cmd is
  use IO, Util, Strlib;

    Cmd_Line : STRING;            -- Copy of Command Line
    Output   : FILE;              -- Std. Output File Object
    Input    : FILE;              -- Std. Input File Object


-- Next_Word skips leading spaces in string 'Line_In', and then
-- places the following non-space chars in string 'Word_Out'.
-- processed chars are removed from the beginning of string
-- 'Line_In' using the Janus string function 'Remove'.

    procedure Next_Word( Line_In, Word_Out : in out STRING ) is
      In_Ptr : INTEGER := 1;
      Limit  : INTEGER;
    begin
      Word_Out := "";                                        -- *2
      Limit := Length( Line_In );                            -- *3
      while Limit > 0 and then Line_In( In_Ptr ) = ' ' loop
        In_Ptr := In_Ptr + 1;
        Limit := Limit - 1;
      end loop;
      while Limit > 0 and then Line_In( In_Ptr ) /= ' ' loop
        Word_Out := Word_Out & Char_To_Str( Line_In( In_Ptr ) );--*2,*3
        In_Ptr := In_Ptr + 1;
        Limit := Limit - 1;
      end loop;
      Line_In := Remove( Line_In, 1, In_Ptr - 1 );           -- *2, *3
    end Next_Word;
```

Figure 6-3. Command Line Redirection: Body

```
-- Do_Output removes the redirection mark from the string in 'Name',
-- and then creates an output file and directs standard output to
-- that file. No error checking is done.

   procedure Do_Output( Name : in out STRING ) is
   begin
     Name := Remove( Name, 1, 1 );              -- *2, *3
     create( Output, Name, Write_Only );        -- *3
     Set_Output( Output );
   end Do_Output;




-- Do_Input Removes the redirection mark from the string in 'Name',
-- and then opens an input file and redirects the standard input. No
-- error checking is done for 'open', so the program crashes if the
-- file does not exist.

   procedure Do_Input( Name : in out STRING ) is
   begin
     Name := Remove( Name, 1, 1 );              -- *2, *3
     Open( Input, Name, Read_Only );            -- *3
     Set_Input( Input );
     In_Done := TRUE;
   end Do_Input;




-- This is the body initialization part of CMD. We read the command
-- line into our own string, and have the procedure Next_Word hack
-- off chunks of it. A test is made for the redirection chars '>'
-- and '<', if not present the "word" is left in our argv array. If
-- redirection requested, the suitable action is taken. Note that
-- these actions are carried out automatically BEFORE execution of
-- the main program when this package is 'withed'.

begin
  Argc := 0;
  Cmd_line := Command_Line();                   -- *1, *2
  loop
    Next_Word( Cmd_line, Argv( Argc + 1 ) );
```

Figure 6-3 continued

```
          exit when Length( Argv( Argc + 1 ) ) = 0;          -- *3
          if Argv( Argc + 1 )( 1 ) = '>' then
            Do_Output( Argv( Argc + 1 ) );
          elsif Argv( Argc + 1 )( 1 ) = '<' then
            Do_Input( Argv( Argc + 1 ) );
          else
            Argc := Argc + 1;
          end if;
        end loop;
      end Cmd;
```

Figure 6-3   continued.

Another I/O Package

When writing Ada programs, sooner or later you'll have to interface to files created by another processing system. An example is a statistical processor written in Ada. Chances are you'll need to be able to read files created by database managers or BASIC programs.

The formats of these files vary widely, but the most common is the *common delimited record*, where values for a given record are separated by commas, and the record is terminated with a carriage return/linefeed pair.

Reading this sort of file with the I/O procedures of **Text__IO** can be inconvenient, as an exception will be raised when trying to read a numeric value and a comma is encountered instead.

It would be nice to have a package that would scan a text file and pull out numeric values from surrounding commas and other garbage. A specification for reading these System Delimited Format (SDF) files might read like Figure 6-4.

Given procedures as specified in Figure 6-4, when reading the following:

```
-1, 2, 5          -or-
dogface -1 ducksuits + 2 //? garbage cans 5          -or-
-1 [return/linefeed] 2,5
```

we should in all three cases obtain the numbers −1, 2, and 5 from successive calls to **Get__Int**.

The body of this specification could be implemented as shown in Figure 6-5. The body includes the two procedures noted in the specification and it also includes some supporting routines hidden from any other package that **withs** this package.

```
-- SDF - System Delimited Files for CP/M and MSDOS
-- Reads integers and floats from a comma delimited
-- Text file under CP/M or MSDOS, such as is output by
-- dBASE II in the SDF mode
-- Janus/Ada version

-- with Text_IO; -- Standard Ada
package Sdf is


-- Get_Int retrieves the next integer from the text file
-- 'Input', skipping any non-numeric data. It then skips
-- any trailing non-numeric data, and returns the value
-- in 'Item'.

-- Standard Ada version:
--    procedure Get_Int( Input : in Text_IO.File_Type;
--                       Item  : out INTEGER );
-- Janus/Ada version:
      procedure Get_Int( Input : in FILE;
                         Item  : out INTEGER );


-- get_float does for standard-format (not exponential
-- notation) floats what Get_Int does for integers.

-- Standard Ada version:
--    procedure Get_Float( Input : in Text_IO.File_Type;
--                         Item  : out FLOAT );
-- Janus/Ada version:
      procedure Get_Float( Input : in FILE;
                           Item  : out FLOAT );

end Sdf;

--------JANUS/ADA--------------
-- Filename:    SDF.LIB
-- Compile:     A>JANUS SDF.LIB
-- Link:        not applicable
-- Run:         not applicable
```

Figure 6-4. SDF Specification

```
-- SDF - System Delimited Files for CP/M and MSDOS
-- Reads integers and floats from a comma delimited
-- Text file under CP/M or MSDOS, such as is output by
-- dBASE II in the SDF mode. Actually, anything not valid
-- as numeric data will delimit the numbers. No error
-- checking is performed.
-- Janus/Ada version

with IO, Sfloatop;
package body Sdf is
   use IO, Sfloatop;

   Ungot_Char : CHARACTER;            -- used for backing up the
   Ungot_Flag : BOOLEAN := FALSE; -- input stream


-- Unget() backs a character into the input stream, for
-- re-use later by getchar().

   procedure Unget( Char : CHARACTER ) is
   begin
      Ungot_Char := Char;
      Ungot_Flag := TRUE;
   end Unget;


--Getchar() gets the next character out of the input
--stream.

   procedure Getchar( Input : in FILE;
                      Item  : out CHARACTER ) is
   begin
      if Ungot_Flag then
         Item := Ungot_Char;
         Ungot_Flag := FALSE;
      else
         Get( Input, Item );
      end if;
   end Getchar;

-- Skip passes over non-numeric characters in the input
-- file.
```

Figure 6-5. SDF Body

```
      procedure Skip( Input : in FILE ) is
         Char : CHARACTER;
      begin
         while not End_Of_File( Input ) loop
            Getchar( Input, Char );
            exit when Char in '0'..'9' or Char = '-';
         end loop;
         if not End_Of_File( Input ) then

            Unget( Char );
         end if;
      end Skip;
```

-- Get_int returns the next integer it can form from the
-- input stream. The Skip() at the end is so that trailing
-- blanks won't interfere with the host's end-of-file test.

```
      procedure Get_int( Input : in FILE;
                         Item  : out INTEGER ) is
         Sign : INTEGER := 1;
         Char : CHARACTER;
      begin
         Skip( Input );
         Item := 0;
         loop
            Getchar( Input, Char );
            exit when Char not in '0'..'9' and Char /= '-';
            if Char = '-' then
               sign := -1;
            else
               Item :=  Item * 10 + (CHARACTER'pos( Char ) -
               CHARACTER'pos( '0' ) );
            end if;
         end loop;
         Item := Item * Sign;
         Skip( Input );
      end Get_int;
```

-- Get_Float returns the next float it can form from the
-- input stream. The Skip() at the end is so that trailing
-- blanks won't interfere with the host's end-of-file test.

Figure 6-5   continued

```
       procedure Get_Float( Input : in FILE;
                             Item  : out FLOAT ) is
      Sign          : FLOAT := 1.0;
      Dp_Found      : BOOLEAN := FALSE;
      Value         : FLOAT;
      Scale_Factor  : FLOAT := 10.0;
      Char          : CHARACTER;
   begin
      Skip( Input );
      Item := 0.0;
      loop
         Getchar( Input, Char );
         exit when Char not in '0'..'9' and Char /= '-'
          and Char /= '.';
         if Char = '-' then
            Sign := -1.0;
         elsif Char = '.' then
            Dp_Found := TRUE;

         else
            Value := FLOAT( CHARACTER'pos( Char ) -
            CHARACTER'pos( '0' ) );
            if Dp_Found then
               Item := Item + Value / Scale_Factor;
               Scale_Factor := Scale_Factor * 10.0;
            else
               Item := Item * 10.0 + Value;
            end if;
         end if;
      end loop;
      Skip( Input );
      Item := Item * Sign;
   end Get_Float;
end Sdf;

-----------JANUS-----------
--Filename:     SDF.PKG
--Compile:      A>JANUS SDF
--Link:         not applicable
--Run:          not applicable
```

Figure 6-5 continued.

The two procedures that may seem odd are **Unget** and **Getchar**, which are modeled after the C standard functions of similar names. These two procedures allow for us to scan through the input file, passing over garbage, and then to replace the first nongarbage character we run across. Think of **Unget** as a kind of "oops, too far" error fixer.

The **Skip** procedure actually does the scanning mentioned in the last paragraph. **Skip** runs through the input until it finds a character that could be the first character in a number.

Get_Int accumulates an integer by skipping any garbage characters and then picking up any unary minus sign and contiguous digits. After the number is formed, trailing garbage is skipped, to force an end-of-file condition in case the number is the last in a file and has trailing blanks or carriage returns.

Get_Float is more complicated than **Get_Int** because we have to account for decimal points. Most of the additional code is involved with this operation.

These simple routines will work in many cases, but a lot of odd cases aren't accounted for. For example, a floating-point number encountered by **Get_Int** will have the integer portion returned, leaving the fractional portion next-up in the input stream.

Conclusion

This was a long and dreary chapter, something you have to put up with for I/O in any language. At first glance the I/O for Ada seems clumsy, especially when text and numeric data are used.

When you take a closer look at and actually use the routines described herein, you will see that they aren't really much harder to use than the **PRINT USING** of BASIC or the *printf()* of C with their escape codes and trailing parameters. You also will find that Ada's routines are a lot more obvious when rereading the code. The portability resulting from the I/O procedures being written in Ada is a great advantage over having the I/O statements as part of the language itself, as they are in BASIC, FORTRAN, and other languages.

7
Composite Types: Arrays and Records

So far in our discussion of Ada we have used only scalar data types—with the exception of the string type, which we haven't treated in much detail. Scalar representation, where there is a one-to-one mapping of a single value to a single symbol, is useful for many purposes.

Where we need more than one value to describe a single concept (the x–y coordinates defining a point on a plane, for example), Ada provides us with *composite data types*. Composite types collect a number of elements into a single logical unit, or *object*.

Ada has two flavors of composite types: the *array*, a collection of components of the same type, and the *record*, a collection of components of different types.

Arrays

An array is a composite of components all of the same type:

- a list of the all the finishing times of the 1980 Boston Marathon
- the term grades for all the members of a freshman class
- last week's daily high temperatures

You might think of an array of the last kind (let's call it highs) like this:

day →	1	2	3	4	5	6	7
highs →	78	82	85	90	89	88	92

or:

```
highs(1) = 78
highs(2) = 82
highs(3) = 85
highs(4) = 90
highs(5) = 89
highs(6) = 88
highs(7) = 92
```

The temperatures range from 78° on Monday to 92° on Friday; each temperature is a value in our seven-component, one-dimensional array. The components are referenced with a two-part notation: **<array name> (<index>)**

The index of an array is the position of a particular component. We can refer to the second component of our array of temperatures with the index *2* (assuming that the index range starts at 1: it doesn't always in Ada). In BASIC we would call an "index" a "subscript".

There are at least three types involved in any array:

- The type of the array object itself;
- the type of the index(es) (always a discrete type);
- the type of the components (any data type).

Declaring Array Types

In line with Ada's use of similar constructs for similar tasks, the declarations of array and scalar types are very similar.

Ada puts no limit on the size of an array. Of course, your microcomputer has a limit to its memory, and an array can take up lots of room!

The declaration of the array states the type(s) and range constraint(s) of the index(es), and the type of the component in each cell of the array. The range constraint of the index determines the size of the array. The type of the index must be a discrete type: the predefined types and subtypes of integer, character, or Boolean, or user-defined enumeration types.

We can declare an array directly if we wish:

```
Highs : array( INTEGER range 1..7 ) of INTEGER;
```

This declares an anonymous array called **Highs**, with seven components of type integer. The array is anonymous because there is no associated *type_mark*. An anonymous array is one-of-a-kind.

More often we will need more than one array of a particular type, or we will need to use attribute functions to determine array characteristics. In these cases we declare a new data type, and use the type to create array objects.

As an example, let's take a look at our system which takes the high temperature reading every day, and dumps them once a week.

```
subtype TEMPERATURE is INTEGER range -30..100;
type DAYS is ( SUN, MON, TUE, WED, THU, FRI, SAT );

type WEEK_OF_TEMPERATURES is array( DAYS ) of TEMPERATURE;

This_Weeks_Temp_Readings : WEEK_OF_TEMPERATURES;
```

Later, if we wish to see the temperature on Wednesday, we can access the value like this:

```
Put( This_Weeks_Temp_Readings( WED ) );
```

We can use two different methods to specify the range constraint of an array index. First, we can use the **type_mark** of a discrete type, as we used the enumerated type **DAYS** to define the single index of **WEEK_OF_TEMPERATURES** above. The compiler will recognize that we mean the entire range possible in the type **DAYS**, from **SUN** to **SAT**.

Second, we can use a subtype indication to state that only some of the possible values will be used to index the array:

```
type WEEK_OF_TEMPERATURES is array( DAYS range MON..FRI)
    of TEMPERATURE;
```

We could instead have declared an integer subtype to use for indexing, like this:

```
subtype DAYS is INTEGER range 1..7;
```

It is usually better technique to use realistic indices as we did in the example, if it makes the program clearer.

A fairly common practice, and one that is recommended, is to use a unique numeric type (see *derived types* in Chapter 8) or an enumeration type as an index, to take advantage of the compiler's type checking to spot errors.

This practice is especially useful when a multidimensional array is used.[1] A multi-dimensioned array has two or more indices and is comparable to a matrix in mathematics. To continue the temperature example, we can make a table of temperatures, with a high, low, and average reading for each day:

```
subtype TEMPERATURE is INTEGER range -30..100;
type DAYS is ( SUN, MON, TUE, WED, THU, FRI, SAT );
type READING is ( LOW, AVERAGE, HIGH );

type WEEK_OF_TEMPERATURES is array( DAYS, READING ) of TEMPERATURE;

Temp_Readings : WEEK_OF_TEMPERATURES;
```

To display the Wednesday high:

```
Put( Temp_Readings( WED, HIGH ) );
```

Since we are using a unique type for each index, our compiler will alert us if we inadvertantly reverse the indices.

Arrays of two or more dimensions are less common in Ada than in other languages, especially arrays like the last example. A two-dimensional array like the one above would probably be better expressed as a record. (This concept is covered later in this chapter). In Ada, multidimensional arrays are used mainly for matrix arithmetic and other mathematical complexities.

Unconstrained Arrays

The array types and objects we have declared so far have been *constrained*. The bounds of a *constrained array* are static; its size is fixed.[2]

The exclusive use of *constrained* arrays in Pascal is one of Pascal's major shortcomings. Conversely the total absence of constraints of any sort in C is why C programmers find it so easy to trash the operating system. Ada has a middle ground, in the form of *unconstrained arrays*. Their declarations use a special symbol—the box <>— which in effect says "range supplied later". Recall how the string type is defined in **Standard**:

```
type STRING is array( range <> ) of CHARACTER;
```

```
array <Type_Name> is array ( <Range_Specification> ) of <TYPE>;

--<Type_Name>becomes the name of the array type, and is
    used as a type_mark.
--<Range_Specification>sets the bounds of the array. See
    Figure 5-2.
--<TYPE>is a previously defined discrete type_mark
```

Figure 7-1. *Array Type Declaration Template*

```
<DISCRETE_SCALAR_TYPE> range <Low_Value>..<High_Value> {, repeat }
```

```
--<DISCRETE_SCALAR_TYPE>is any discrete scalar type,
   including enumeration types. The type is the same as
   will be used to index the array. If omitted, omit also
   range, and integer will be assumed. Can also
   use a subtype.
--<Low_Value>is the lower boundary of the array index.
--<High_Value>is the upper boundary of the array index.
-- range may be unconstrained using <> notation.
```

Figure 7-2. Array Range Specification Template

When we want to declare a string object, we simply supply the range at run time. Ada *elaborates* objects, which includes reserving storage space for them, when a program unit is invoked (at runtime). When we create an object from an unconstrained array type, it can be elaborated with different range constraints each time a subprogram is called:

```
Name : STRING( 1..Name_Size );
```

In this case, **Name__Size** is a variable which has already been elaborated at this point in the program (it could be a global variable, for example) and determines the upper bound of the array **Name**. We can use a simple expression for the lower boundary, the upper boundary, or both. Once the array is declared it is constrained to the range given in the declaration.

Constraints are passed along with arrays when arrays are used as parameters. When an unconstrained array type is given for a subprogram formal parameter, the actual parameter provided when the subprogram is called determines the constraints in effect during that call. If we pass an array of 20 elements to a subprogram expecting an unconstrained array, the subprogram is constrained to 20 elements for the duration of the call. For example:

```
-- A formal parameter with an unconstrained type:
--
function String_Size( Input_String : STRING ) return INTEGER is
--
--
-- Two subsequent calls to string_size
--
Put( String_Size( "Hello" ) );                          5
Put( String_Size( "Goodbye" ) );                        7
```

In the first call to **String__Size** above, the array **Input__String** would be constrained to range 1..5. During the second call, **Input__String** would be constrained to range 1..7.

Arrays of Arrays

Arrays can consist of objects of any kind, as long as they are of the same type. Since an array is itself an object, we can have an array of arrays. A frequently encountered array of arrays is an array of the predefined (array) type **STRING**—a list of names, for example:

```
type NAME_LIST is array ( range 1..100 ) of STRING( 1..20 );
```

When accessing the string as a whole, we use only a single index:

```
Class_roster : Name_List;
--
--
Class_Roster( 1 ) := "Smith              ";
```

When accessing an element of the inner array, say the second letter of the name "Smith" above, we use two sets of parentheses, with the index of the outer array appearing first:

```
Class_Roster( 1 )( 2 ) := 'm';
```

Our array of arrays was declared as a type (**NAME__LIST**), and we can extend the principle and declare a type that is an array of arrays of arrays:

```
type ROSTER is array ( range 1..100 ) of STRING( 1..20 );
type SCHOOL_MASTER is array( range 1..10 ) of ROSTER;
Master : SCHOOL_MASTER;
```

To access the third letter of the individual name "Fisk", which appears as the second name in the first roster, we use the notation:

```
Master(1)(2)(3) := 's';
```

Again, the index to the outer array is listed first. Arrays of arrays are not limited to single dimensioned arrays. Each array may have any number of indices. We won't show any examples, as they are needlessly complicated and probably should be avoided anyhow.

Ada defines operators for use with arrays. Some work only with arrays of a single dimension. All require that the arrays be of the same type, and most require that the arrays have identical constraints.[3]

Concatenation

The symbol **&** is used to concatenate single-dimensioned arrays, for example:

```
Word_One : STRING := "Hello";
Word_Two : STRING := " World";
Phrase_One : STRING := Word_One & Word_Two;
```

results in **Phrase__One = "Hello World."**

The concatenation operator is overloaded in the case of type *STRING* to allow concatenation of a character to either end of a string, for example:

```
Word_One : STRING := "Hello";
Char_One : CHARACTER := ',';
--
--
Put( Word_One & Char_One );                    Hello,
Put( Char_One & Word_One );                    ,Hello
```

Assignment

The standard assignment operator := can be used to make an aggregate assignment of one array to another array. The arrays *must* be of equal constraint. Again using type **STRING** as an example,

```
String_Variable : STRING( 1..10 );
--
--
String_Variable := "0123456789";    -- is legal
String_Variable := "01234";         -- is not legal
String_Variable := "01234      ";   --is legal
```

The first example is legal: We are assigning a string literal array of length 10 to a string array object of length 10. The second is illegal because we are attempting to assign a string literal array of length 5 to a string array object of length 10. The third example is the way the second should have been—legal now because we padded the string with blanks to give it a length of 10 characters.

Logical

Ada provides the four logical operators **and**, **or**, **xor**, and **not** for use with arrays of Boolean components only. The result is an array of equal constraint, which may be assigned or passed as a parameter.

Membership

The membership "operators" **in** and **not in** may be used for arrays:

```
"Hello" in STRING( 1..5 )
```

Relational

The six relational operators $=$, $/=$, $>$, $>=$, $<$, and $<=$ are defined for arrays of discrete components.[4] The equality and inequality operators operate on arrays of the same type and size. The other four operators operate on arrays of the same type but not necessarily of the same size.

```
"Hello  " > "Goodbye"
"Hello" /= "hELLO"
```

When unequally constrained arrays are compared, the individual elements are compared, starting at the first element and continuing until a discrepancy is found.

Array Attributes

Ada provides attribute functions for arrays.[5] They are formally described in Appendix G. We'll describe them informally here, and use examples based on the following object declarations:

```
String_Var : STRING( 1..10 );
Roster     : array( INTEGER range 5..7,
   INTEGER range 3..8 ) of STRING( 4..6 );
```

Address—Returns the address of the first storage unit (memory location) used by the array, this attribute function is implementation dependent. Return type is **ADDRESS**, defined in the package **system**.

```
Put( INTEGER( String_Var'address ) );  -- if conformable
```

base—Returns the component type of the array type given, and is allowed only as a prefix to another attribute. *Example:*

```
STRING'base = the type CHARACTER
```

We need to use this as a prefix to another attribute:

```
STRING'base'first = ASCII.NUL
```

This attribute function is especially useful in generics.

first—When used with arrays, **first** returns the lower bound of the first index:

```
String_Var'first = 1
```

For other indices, write **Object_Name'first(x)**, where **x** is an integer universal expression. **x** names the **x**th index of **object_name**:

```
Roster'first( 2 ) = 3
```

last—**last** is similar to **first**, returning the upper bound of an index:

```
Roster'last = 7
Roster'last( 2 ) = 8
```

length—Returns the number of elements in the first or specified index range of an array:

```
String_Var'length = 10
Roster'length( 2 ) = 6
```

range—Returns the range value of the first or specified index of the array:

```
String_Var'range = 1..10
Roster'range( 2 ) = 3..8
```

This attribute is especially useful for setting the limits of a **for** loop.

```
-- This procedure fills a string with blanks.

procedure Blank( Input_String : in out STRING ) is
begin
     Input_String := ( others => ' ' );
end Blank;
```

Figure 7-3. String Blanking Procedure

size—Returns the number of bits (*NOT* bytes) needed to hold the array. In a typical microcomputer:

```
STRING( 1..10 )'size might be 80
(10 bytes = 10 times 8 bits = 80)
```

Aggregate Assignment to Arrays

When declaring arrays, or when reusing them, it is sometimes useful to assign values to the whole array at once. We can do this in Ada using the aggregate assignment notation, either when the array is declared or in the executable portion of the subprogram.[6]

We can loosely compare Ada's aggregate assignment to a BASIC READ/DATA operation:

```
1000 DIM A( 10 )
1010 FOR B = 1 to 10 : READ A(B) : NEXT B
1020 DATA 5,3,7,23,1,3,5,6,3,0
```

A variety of notations are allowed, and they may be intermixed with each other to some extent. Here are some examples of one dimensional aggregate assignments:

```
type SIMPLE_ARRAY is range 1..4 of FLOAT;
Array_Object : SIMPLE_ARRAY;
--
--
```
```
(1)      Array_Object := ( 0.0, 0.0, 0.0, 0.0, );    -- positional
(2)      Array_Object := ( 1 => 0.0, others => 2.0 ); -- named
(3)      Array_Object := ( 1..2 => 1.5, 3..4 => 3.0 ); -- range
(4)      Array_Object := ( others => 0.0 ); -- named
(5)      Array_Object := ( 1 ¦ 3 => 2.5, others => 0.0 ); -- choice
```

The results of the above aggregate assignments would be

index →	1	2	3	4
(1)	0.0	0.0	0.0	0.0
(2)	0.0	2.0	2.0	2.0
(3)	1.5	1.5	3.0	3.0
(4)	0.0	0.0	0.0	0.0
(5)	2.5	0.0	2.5	0.0

A few notes about aggregate assignments:

- All components must be exhausted in an aggregate assignment. You must have a value assignment specified for each and every component; you can't just assign to one or two components.
- If an **others** clause is used with additional named or positional notation clauses, it must be the last in the list.
- An **others** clause may appear by itself, in which case all elements of the array *usually* will be assigned the same value (see next point).
- The assigned values may be expressions as well as literals, as our examples show. When assigning the same value to more than one component, as with an **others** clause or when using a range, the expression is evaluated for each component. Therefore an expression that evaluates to a different value each time (such as an allocator, seen in Chapter 8, or a random number function) will assign different values to each array component.
- The vertical bar notation in the last example of the above list reads "or": "If component is 1 or 3, assign the value 2.5."

Aggregates for Multidimensional Arrays

An aggregate for a multidimensional array has a slightly different form. A multidimensional aggregate is an aggregate of aggregates. Consider this two-dimensional array:

```
type MATRIX is array( range 1..4, range 1..5 ) of FLOAT;
Matrix_Object : MATRIX;
--
--
```

```
Matrix_Object := (
    ( 0.0, 0.0, 0.0, 0.0, 0.0 )
    ( 1..3 => 2.2, others => 5.5 )
    3 ¦ 4 => ( 2.2, 3.3, 4.4, 5.5 )
    );
```

The resulting array is:

```
0.0  0.0  0.0  0.0  0.0
2.2  2.2  2.2  5.5  5.5
2.2  3.3  4.4  5.5  6.6
2.2  3.3  4.4  5.5  6.6
```

If you examine this example carefully, you can infer some rules:

- The assignment of a two-dimensional array is like assigning aggregate components to a one-dimensional array. If we look at the inner parentheses aggregates as a unitized object, the declaration can be rewritten like this:

```
type MATRIX is array( range 1..4 ) of UNITIZED_OBJECT;
Matrix_Object : MATRIX;
--
--
Matrix_Object := (
    Unitized_Object1,
    Unitized_Object2,
    3 ¦ 4 => Unitized_Object3
    );
```

An aggregate component is an *Object* in Ada, very similar in analogy to a string literal. It is a collection of components, separated by commas, enclosed in parentheses.

- When building a multidimensional array we start with the leftmost index as the outer set of parentheses and move to the rightmost indices as we go deeper into the parentheses nesting, assigning progressively less complicated aggregates as we go.
- The *type* of an aggregate may be ambiguous. Consider the following:

```
type TABLE_ONE is array( range 1..10 ) of INTEGER;
type TABLE_TWO is array( range 1..20 ) of INTEGER;
.          .
.          .
...( 1..3 => 0, others => 50 ) ...
    -- literal aggregate
```

A compiler is unable to determine the type of the above aggregate literal except by context because the aggregate could be assigned to an object of either type **TABLE_ONE** or type **TABLE_TWO** (because the size is uncertain due to the **others** clause). Usually context will be a clue, but in some cases that may not be enough. We can *qualify* an aggregate in the same way we qualify an ambiguous overloaded enumeration element: by placing a **type_mark** and apostrophe before the aggregate and making a *qualified expression*:

```
... TABLE_ONE'( 1..3 => 0, others => 50 ) ...
```

The qualification removes any ambiguity (caused by uncertain size) regarding the type of the aggregate.

Array Slices

At times it is useful to refer to a portion of an array as a unit, especially when doing string work. In Ada, we can mark off a section of one dimension of an array as a unit called a **slice**.[7]

To refer to a slice, we use the dot-dot range notation:

```
Str_Var1 := "one  two  threefour five  ";
Str_Var2 := Str_Var1( 1..5 );  -- assigns "one  "
Str_Var3 := Str_Var2( 11..15 );-- assigns "three"
Str_Var1( 1..5 ) := Str_Var1( 4..8 );
```

Note the last example, where we assign a slice of **Str_Var1** to another slice of itself. Ada has been designed so that the programmer doesn't need to worry about overlapped slices in arrays. The result is always the same as if there were no overlap.

You can use a qualified expression with slices to change the type of a slice to another type, as long as the base elements are the same in the original array type and the target array type, and range constraints are satisfied.

Unfortunately, array slices are not implemented in many Ada subsets. The use of slices is essential to efficient string operations.

Slices are limited to arrays of a single dimension. Sometime, just for fun, tell an Ada compiler designer that multiple-dimension slices have been added to the Ada specification, and watch him or her faint dead away!

Records

The second kind of composite type in Ada is the **record**. A record is a collection of logically related components that are usually (but not necessarily) of dissimilar type.

Records are usually collected in a set of records, frequently as an array of records.

As a result we almost always declare a record type that becomes the base component for the set of records we want. Consider a classic example, an employee information record:

```
type EMPLOYEE_RECORD is
    record
        Name : STRING( 1..30 );
        Pay_Rate : FLOAT;
        Employee_Number : INTEGER range 1..9_999;
    end record;
```

The reserved words **record** and **end record** delimit the list of three components of types **STRING**, **FLOAT**, and **INTEGER**, three different kinds of data needed to give basic pay information for a single person. The enclosed pieces of information form a single object of type **EMPLOYEE__RECORD**. In languages without record structures (e.g., FORTRAN IV) we would have to declare three different arrays to represent the same information. Figure 7-4 illustrates the record type declaration template.

The closest construct in most dialects of BASIC, the random access file with its fields, is limited by convention to use with disk files; all information is of type **string**, with tortuous functions to convert to and from numeric types.

Ada's records are both easier to use and more effective. Any data type may be a record component, with all operations for that type allowed for the component.

This means we can create nested records; one record may have other, previously defined records as components:

```
type <TYPE_NAME> ( <Discriminate_List> ) is
    record
        <Object_Declaration_List>;
    end record;

--<TYPE_NAME>is any legal identifier.
--<Discriminant_List>is optional, and if omitted, also omit enclosing
  parentheses. If present, has the same
  form as function formal parameter lists.
--<Object_Declaration_List>is a list of object
  declarations, just as in a subprogram declaration
  section, which determine the components of the record.
  In a variant record, a case construction may also be
  used.
```

Figure 7-4.   Record Type Declaration Template

```
type PERSON is
    record
         Work : EMPLOYEE_RECORD;
         Home : PERSONAL_RECORD;
    end record;
```

Given a record of type **EMPLOYEE__RECORD**, as defined in the first example, we can access each component of the record using notation similar to that used to access a **with**ed package element:

```
Employee : EMPLOYEE_RECORD;
    .        .

    .        .
Employee.Name      := "Smith                ";
Employee.Pay_Rate  := 5.25;
Employee.Number    := 126;
```

If a record contains a component that is also a record, we can reference it in a way similar to the one we use with arrays of arrays—by nesting the dot notation:

```
type PLANT_RECORD is
    record
        Employee  : EMPLOYEE_RECORD;
        Equipment : EQUIPMENT_RECORD;
end record;
    .        .

    .        .
Plant : PLANT_RECORD;
    .        .

    .        .
Plant.Employee.Name := "Smith                ";
```

When records are components of an array of records, accessing an individual record is also easy. We need to place an index into the array. The indexed array reference replaces the name of the record object, and in effect refers to the record as a whole. Dot notation can be used after the array reference to point to a particular component of that record:

```
type EMPLOYEE_LIST is array( 1..10 ) of EMPLOYEE_RECORD;
Personnel : EMPLOYEE_LIST;
    .        .

    .        .
Personnel(1).Name := "Smith                ";
```

As records are mainly binders to hold logically related information together, the actual operations that can be performed on records as a whole are few. Normally you will be performing operations on components of records, where the operations defined for the component's types are still valid. Operations that can be performed on a record as a whole are:

Assignment—The assignment operator : = assigns one record as a whole to another record. Of course, the records must be of the same type.

Membership—The membership "operators" in and not in may be used on records, mainly with variant records or records with discriminants, which we see later in this chapter. These operators don't get a lot of use with records.

Relational—The relational operators = and / = may be used on records. The other four relational operators are not defined for records, but could be overloaded if a full Ada compiler is available. Normally there is not a relationship of "greater than" or "less than" between records as a whole, even if individual components of those records may have greater/less than relationships. For example, our **EMPLOYEE__RECORD** type probably would be sorted on the name component alone, or the employee number component alone. Sorting on the whole record wouldn't produce useful results.

Record Attributes

Records have attribute functions available; these are formally described in Appendix G.[8] We present an informal description of attributes of record types here.

address and *base*—These are the same as for arrays.

first bit—Returns the offset of a record component from the start of the first storage unit (memory location) used by the record as a whole, to the first bit used by the component. For example, **Employee.Pay__Rate'first__bit** might return 240; typically 30 characters times eight bits are occupied by the first component **Name**.

last bit—This works like **first__bit** but measures to the end of the component. **Employee.Pay__Rate'last__bit** typically might return 264 (240 plus 24 bits for **Pay__Rate**). Note that both **first__bit** and **last__bit** operate on record *objects* rather than *types*.

position—Returns the offset from the first storage unit (memory location) used by the record as a whole to the first storage unit used by the component: `Employee.Pay_Rate'position` might return 30. Again, the prefix is a component of a record *object*.

Advanced Record Features

The basic record described up to this point is more than enough for garden variety microcomputer use. If you need more powerful stuff, read on. Many of the following features are not available in Ada subsets. They are, however, interesting enough that you probably will want to get acquainted with them anyhow.

Record Discriminants

Just as it is convenient to be able to assign array bounds at execution time, so it is convenient to specify what types of data a record can hold at run time. Ada provides a mechanism for this: the *record discriminant*.[9]

Records may take parameters (discriminants) when they are declared as objects in a fashion similar to subprograms. We can pass information into the record structure when we use the record type to declare an object:

```
-- an unconstrained array type.
type ARRAY_MASK is array ( range <>, range <> ) of FLOAT;

type SQUARE_ARRAY( Side_Value : INTEGER := 10 ) is
      record
            Table : ARRAY_MASK( 1..Side_Value, 1..Side_Value );
      end record;
```

The record type `Square_Array` above is guaranteed to have a square matrix as its only component. The discriminant `Side_Value` is written very much like a function parameter, including an optional default value for the discriminant. (*Note:* If more than one discriminant is used, either *all* or *none* of them can have default values.) Records can have more than one discriminant, and we can use either positional parameter passing or named parameter passing when we declare objects of this type:

```
Two_By_Two   : SQUARE_ARRAY( 2 );
Four_By_Four : SQUARE_ARRAY( Side_Value => 4 );
```

A discriminant may only be used directly within the record definition, as we did above. It may not be used as part of an expression. Therefore, the following is illegal:

```
-- illegal use of discriminant
type X( Y : INTEGER ) is
    record
            A : STRING( 1.. 2*Y );
    end record;
```

There are uses for discriminants other than as array bounds, such as the variant type records we'll see later in this chapter.

A discriminant may be passed through and used as a discriminant in enclosed records, if we wish:

```
type CUBES( Edge_Value : INTEGER := 10 ) is
  record
    Cube : array( 1..Edge_Value ) of SQUARE_ARRAY( Edge_Value );
  end record;
```

A record object declared from a type with a default value for its discriminant is said to be *constrained* if we supply a parameter for the discriminant when we declare the object. Using the above type definition:

```
Constrained_Square_Record : SQUARE_ARRAY( 5 );
Unconstrained_Square_Record : SQUARE_ARRAY;
```

In the first case, we supply a discriminant, and so fix the component array size at 5×5 size. This is a *constrained record*. The second case is an example of an *unconstrained record*.

In the second case we don't supply a discriminant, and the initial size is the default discriminant 10. We can alter the discriminant of this record, and therefore the size of the array, during execution of the program. To do this we need to make an assignment to the entire record, including the discriminant, using an *aggregate assignment*, which we will see an example of just after the next section.

Variant Records

While discriminants are useful in unconstrained records, they are essential for *variant records*.

A variant record is a record that may have different components depending on the value of a discriminant. Let's drag the ol' employee record out again, and use it for more examples.

The employee record as we defined it earlier was fine for hourly employees. But we may want to use the same record to hold information on middle- and upper-management personnel as well, or even Programmers.

We can use a discriminant to conditionally add components to a record using the **case** construct we saw in Chapter 4:

```
type PERSONNEL_TYPE is (
    HOURLY, MIDDLE, UPPER, PROGRAMMER);
    -- an enumerated type for the discriminant

type EMPLOYEE_RECORD (Level : PERSONNEL_TYPE := HOURLY) is
    record
        Name : STRING( 1..10 );
        Employee_Number : NATURAL;

        case Level is
            when HOURLY =>
                Pay_Rate : FLOAT;
                Overtime_Rate : FLOAT;
            when MIDDLE | UPPER | PROGRAMMER =>
                Salary : FLOAT;
            when UPPER | PROGRAMMER =>
                Bonus : FLOAT;
            when PROGRAMMER =>
                Company_Car_Number : INTEGER;
            others =>
                null;
        end case;
    end record;
```

Here we have an enumeration type **PERSONNEL_TYPE** that lists possible employee types. We declare a discriminant of this type to use in conditional assembly of a record, and give the discriminant a default value of **HOURLY**.

The vertical bar symbol | means "or" and can be used when more than one but not all possibilities select a component. We also could use a discrete range to select contiguous choices:

```
when HOURLY..UPPER =>
```

The **others** choice is optional and in this case not needed as we have exausted all possibilities (a requirement as in the **case** statement). If the **others** choice is included, it must be last. We use a discriminant of this type to assemble custom records for each type of employee:

```
Hourly_Worker : EMPLOYEE_RECORD( HOURLY );
```

has **Name, Employee_Number, Pay_Rate,** and **Overtime_Rate** components.

```
Upper_Worker : EMPLOYEE_RECORD( UPPER );
```

has **Name, Employee_Number, Salary,** and **Bonus components.**

In the two examples above we have created constrained records that thereafter are not variant because we specified the discriminant when we declared the object. If we wish the record to be unconstrained, and therefore still variant, we declare the object without the discriminant:

```
Employee : EMPLOYEE_RECORD;
```

This declares a variant record using the default discriminant. It follows that for a record *object* to be variant, the type declaration must have a default value for the discriminant.

We can alter the discriminant, and therefore the record components, by making an aggregate assignment to the record. In fact, we can *only* alter the discriminant by assigning a new one as part of an aggregate assignment.

Aggregate Record Assignment

Using the same aggregate, or multiple, assignment notation we used for arrays, we can assign values to a record. If we have an unconstrained record we can alter the components by reassigning the discriminant. If we assign to the discriminant, it must be the first assignment made. Here's an example of an aggregate assignment to an unconstrained variant record of type **PERSONNEL_TYPE** using named association:

```
Employee := (
        Level              => PROGRAMMER,
        Name               => "Krantz      ",
        Employee_Number    => 100,
        Salary             => 4000.0,
        Bonus              => 8000.0,
        Company_Car_Number => 6 );
```

We can initialize records when they are declared using the same notation. We may use any of the other aggregate assignment forms as well, as outlined for arrays. When making a

```
-- HISTOGRAM - A simple Histogram processor, which reads a
-- CP/M or MSDOS delimited file and plots the frequency
-- on a histogram. Package 'sdf', with'ed below, is our
-- system delimited file reader from chapter 6.

with Text_IO, Sdf;
procedure Histogram is

      Lo, hi : INTEGER;                -- range limits
      Input  : Text_IO.FILE_TYPE;      -- input file object



-- Say_Hello does the sign-on message.

      procedure Say_Hello is
      begin
         Text_IO.Put( "Histogram Version 1.0" );
         Text_IO.New_Line( 2 );
      end Say_Hello;



-- Get_Limits finds the lower and upper bounds of the
-- values for the histogram, by asking the user. Of course,
-- we could read the file and determine the high/low from
-- the actual values, too.

      procedure Get_Limits( Lo, Hi : out INTEGER ) is
      begin
         Text_IO.Put( "Enter low limit for histogram: " );
         Text_IO.Get( Lo );
         Text_IO.Put( "Enter high limit for histogram: " );
         Text_IO.Get( Hi );
         Text_IO.New_Line;
      end Get_Limits;



-- Open_File asks for the filename for the input sequence,
-- and then opens the file.
```

Figure 7-5. Simple Histogram Processor

```
procedure Open_File is
   File_Name : STRING( 1..80 );
   Last_In   : INTEGER;
begin
   Text_IO.Put( "Enter input filename: " );
   Text_IO.Get_Line( Item => Filename, Last => Last_In );
   Text_IO.Open( Input, In_File, File_Name( 1..Last_In ) );
end Open_File;



-- Do_Histogram reads the values from the input file and
-- increments the corresponding element in the array
-- 'values'. Items outside the hi/lo range are counted
-- by variable 'Reject'. The histogram is output and the
-- number of rejected values is displayed.

   procedure Do_Histogram( Lo, Hi : in INTEGER ) is
      Values : array( INTEGER range Lo..Hi ) of
       INTEGER := ( others => 0 );
      Reject : INTEGER := 0;
      Item   : INTEGER;
   begin
      while not Text_IO.End_Of_File( Input ) loop
         Sdf.Get_Int( Input, Item );
         if Item in Lo..Hi then
            Values( Item ) := Values( Item ) + 1;
         else
            Reject := Reject + 1;
         end if;
      end loop;
      Text_IO.New_Line( 3 );
      for Index in Lo..Hi loop
         Text_IO.Put( Index, 5 );
         Text_IO.Put( "   " );
         for Inner in 1..Values( Index ) loop
            Text_IO.Put( '*' );
         end loop;
         Text_IO.New_Line;
      end loop;
      Text_IO.New_Line;
```

Figure 7-5 continued

```
            Text_IO.Put( "Number of Values Rejected: " );
            Text_IO.Put( Reject );
            Text_IO.New_Line;
        end Do_Histogram;

begin
    Say_Hello;
    Open_File;                      -- open input file
    Get_Limits( Lo, Hi );           -- ask user for ranges
    Do_Histogram( Lo, Hi );         -- read into array, print
end Histogram;
```

Figure 7-5   continued

positional assignment, the discriminant(s) is listed first. The above assignment could be written like this:

```
employee := (
        PROGRAMMER, "Krantz    ", 100, 4000.0,8000.0, 6 );
```

Care must be taken when using the **others** clause that the types of all unfilled components matches that of the value to be assigned.

Variant records are completely managed by the language. The discriminant can be thought of as another component of the record, with the one restriction that we may only assign to it as part of an aggregate assignment. The discriminant may be referenced using the selected component (dot) notation:

```
<record_name>.<discriminant_name>
```

just as any other component is.

When using variant records in I/O, say to a disk file, it is one of the predefined I/O packages that provides the record management scheme. Therefore, given the variant employee record example, you could randomly write records of different variance to a disk file, and at a later date read them back. The I/O subprogram will arrange that the correct record is generated for each block of information.

A Sample Program Using Arrays

A good example of array usage is a simple program that generates histograms (Figure 7-5). It uses the package **SDF** from the last chapter to read integers from an ASCII file and plot the frequency of each integer's occurrence.

```
Histogram Version 1.0

Enter low limit for histogram: 1
Enter high limit for histogram: 10

Enter input filename:B:HISTO.TST


    1   *
    2   **
    3   ****
    4   ******
    5   *********
    6   **********
    7   *********
    8   ******
    9   ****
   10   **


Number of Values Rejected: 3
```

Figure 7-6.   Sample Output from Historian Program

The program is fairly simple. Four supporting procedures in the declaration part of **Histogram** do all of the work.

Say__Hello just outputs a message when the program is invoked.

Get__Limits prompts the user for high and low limits for the range of values to be displayed.

Open__File asks the user for a filename and then opens an input file. Note the use of an array slice to pass just the part of the string entered by the user to **Open**.

The largest procedure, **Do__Histogram**, declares an array (**Values**) just large enough to hold value counts in the acceptable range. An aggregate assignment initializes this array to zero. This procedure also keeps track of values not in the acceptable range (**Reject**). Finally, the array is output in histogram form at the end of the procedure.

A sample output from this program is given as Figure 7-6. This program could be dressed up, of course.

Conclusion

Ada provides versatile composite types and powerful tools for manipulating them. The use of unconstrained arrays and array slices make Ada's **STRING** type much more usable than ISO Pascal's. Ada's strings have their faults, but it's not hard to beef them up (see Chapter 9).

Ada's records are very nice—especially the variant records. The system's management of discriminants, particularly when output and reinput from disk files, make Ada's I/O seem suddenly much more usable. The strong type checking reduces the chance of error when handling complex data representations.

8

Fine Points

We already have presented most of Ada's simple data types and data structures. In this chapter we will look at some of the more complex scalar data types and related topics, including the real numeric types, derived types, pointers, and dynamic storage allocation and deallocation.

Real Numeric Types

For practical scientific or business uses of a computer, we need to be able to express real numbers—numeric values distinguished from integers by having a fractional part. They can be used to represent quantities in the real world that even mathematicians and computer scientists cannot put into neatly discrete packages. 3.1416 and $1.98 are examples of real numbers that have proven useful in practical applications such as science and marketing.

All implementations of Ada offer at least two predefined real number types: a floating point type (**FLOAT**), and a fixed-point type of the anonymous type universal_fixed. Two characteristics distinguish between floating point and fixed point types:

- the range of values that can be represented by their objects;
- the type of errors occurring in their representation.

Floating point objects can represent a wide range of values with an error that is constant in relation to the value represented.

Fixed-point objects represent a narrower range of values with an effectively constant absolute error.

With floating-point representation, errors accumulate within predictable bounds when values are multiplied or divided, but are inexact when they are added or subtracted. This accounts for the popularity of floating point for scientific or mathematical computation.

In contrast, the properties of fixed-point representation allow for exact handling of values in addition and subtraction, making it suitable for accounting and other business functions.

These are general principles; in practice, fixed point is suited for many scientific uses, while floating point has its place in business.[1]

Floating-point Types

A floating-point number can represent a very large value, such as the number of centimeters that light travels in a century, or a very small one, such as the weight of a quark as a fraction of a ton. The relative error in representing either value in floating point would work out to be the same.

Recall how Ada's floating-point literals are expressed with an "E" separating the mantissa from the exponent, which is treated as a power of 10:

```
1.0E6          -- floating point representation of 1_000_000
1.234567E6     -- floating point representation of 1_234_567
1.23E-6        -- floating point representation of 0.00000123
```

When we create a floating-point type we can specify the number of decimal digits of precision the compiler needs to keep track of. The maximum error in a floating point number is about plus or minus 1/2 the value of the least significant digit.

All implementations of Ada must have a predefined floating point type **FLOAT**.[2] In addition, an implementation may predefine the types **SHORT_FLOAT** and **LONG_FLOAT**, but only if the precision of these optional types is significatntly different from **FLOAT**. Other floating-point types and subtypes may be created as needed.

Floating point types are declared by giving:

```
type T is <floating point constraints>;
```

where **T** is the *type_mark*, and <floating point constraint> is made up of the reserved word **digits**, a static integer expression specifying the number of decimal digits of accuracy you want, and an optional *range constraint*, made up of the reserved word **range** and a range expression:[3]

```
type METERS is digits 10;
type CENTIMETERS is digits 10 range 0.0 .. 100.0;
```

The range expression's high and low bounds are static floating-point expressions. If they aren't literals, and therefore of type *universal real*, their values must be "safe numbers" (as described below) in the declared type.

A floating-point subtype is declared like this:

```
subtype S is T <floating point constraint>;
```

where S is the subtype's type-mark, and T is the parent type's type-mark. The <floating point constraint> is either a digits clause, or a range clause, or both:

```
type METRIC is digits 10;
subtype METERS is METRIC digits 5;
subtype CENTIMETERS is METRIC range 0.01 .. 1.0;
subtype MILLIMETERS is METRIC digits 3 range 0.001 .. 1.0;
```

Note that we can create subtypes with less precision, or less range, or both. If a subtype range is specified, the range limits must fall within the range of the parent type.

Fixed-point Types

A fixed-point Ada object can be used to represent a value that must maintain an absolute constant accuracy, such as your checking account balance *to the penny* or the number of hours worked *to the tenth of an hour*.

An Ada compiler is required at least to appear as if it manages fixed point numbers as a *delta*, the smallest number which can be represented in the type and a *mantissa*, an integer to multiply the delta by to produce our result. For example, if we specify a *delta* of 0.01, the machine might represent 100.0 as:

mantissa	delta	mantissa * delta
10000	0.01	100.00

The delta is the smallest step between the values of a fixed-point type. If the delta can't be exactly represented directly within the computer, then the compiler chooses another format that allows the exact representation and scales the resulting product accordingly.

No rounding errors are allowed in addition or subtraction of fixed-point numbers. In multiplication and division, the rounding errors become relatively larger as the mantissa becomes relatively smaller. Consider this example for a delta of 1.0:

```
5.0/4.0 = 1.0, error of about 25% in result
501.0/4.0 = 125.0, error of less than 1%
```

Fixed-point types are created by declaring the type in the following manner:

```
type T is <fixed point constraint>;
```

where <fixed point constraint> is the reserved word **delta** followed by a simple expression for the smallest nonzero number to be represented. The delta specification can be optionally followed by a range constraint:

```
type DECIMAL_CURRENCY is delta .01
type SAVINGS_BALANCE is delta .01 range 0.0 .. 1000.0
```

Subtypes of a fixed-point type are declared in a similar fashion:

```
subtype US_CURRENCY is DECIMAL_CURRENCY range 0.0 .. 1000.0;
subtype BRITISH_CURRENCY is DECIMAL_CURRENCY delta 0.10;
```

The fixed-point type declaration must always have the delta clause because that's how we distinguish a fixed-point type from all others. A subtype declaration may have a delta clause, a range clause, or both.

The subtype range must be completely enclosed in a parent type's range, and the range values must be compatible with the parent type. The delta of a subtype must be as large or larger than that of the parent type.

Model Numbers and Safe Numbers

Inside a computer, both fixed- and floating-point types may be represented using specialized formats for efficiency. A certain amount of error may occur in conversions between external formats and internal format or in other ways the programmer may not be aware of. Many languages (FORTRAN in particular) require that the programmer be aware of the internal formats and their characteristics. This often results in subtle problems when a program is moved from one computer to another.

To help control errors, and to provide consistency when moving a program from one implementation to another, Ada defines two sets of numbers associated with each real type: *model numbers* and *safe numbers*.

Model numbers—Model numbers can be represented exactly in the specified precision of the type. If we restrict ourselves to operations that produce results (including intermediate results) that are model numbers, we can safely move a program from one implementation to another without worrying about errors. Operations on model numbers are guaranteed to give correct results.

Safe numbers—Safe numbers can be represented exactly in the *implementation* for the given type. They include all the model numbers, for the given type, but they may also include extra numbers.

Because it would be wasteful to have distinct math operations for every different number of digits of precision, compilers usually have two or three sets of real number math routines built in, say, one set for up to six digits of precision, and one set for up to 14 digits of precision. The six-digit routines will be faster than the 14-digit routines.

A floating-point type with three digits of specified precision is only guaranteed to have the same model numbers as any other implementation's model numbers for three-digit precision, but would actually be represented and manipulated as if it had six digits of precision. The safe numbers for this three-digit type would be the model numbers for the same implementation's six-digit precision floating-point type.

Model numbers can be represented exactly in the precision *specified* (by you) for that type. Safe numbers can be represented exactly in the actual *implementation* of the type (by the particular compiler).

For a microcomputer user, these fine distinctions are probably unimportant; for a numerical analyst, these distinctions are very important indeed. If you are working in a situation where precision is critical, consult a numerical analyst or the language reference manual for the formulas required to compute model numbers. Safe numbers will be implementation dependent.

Operations on Real Types

Real types (fixed and float) have similar operations, and they are passed on to subtypes and derived types. The basic operations are assignment, membership, qualification, and explicit conversion between the real types and other numeric types. Implicit conversion is available to convert real literals (which are instances of the type *universal_real*) to real types.

Attribute functions also exist for both fixed-point types and floating-point types. These attribute functions are mostly related to determining precision and the largest and smallest values in a type, and have been relegated to Appendix G.

Besides the basic operations, all the operators available to type **INTEGER**, with the exception of **mod** and **rem**, are defined for real types. Precedence for these operators is the same as for the equivalent integer operators.

Derived Types

Sometimes it is desirable to segregate data types that have similar or identical characteristics to make them incompatible with each other. For example, suppose we have a complex system of X-Y coordinates, and we need to pass values of type X and type Y thru some hairy equations that we don't even begin to understand, and suppose, we have a tendency when writing our code to mix variables of type X with type Y. It takes us weeks to track down all the bugs.

If we could make variables of type Y incompatible with variables of type X in our equations, the compiler would spot a lot of the mixups for us.

Or, as a better example, suppose we are writing financial software where we are dealing with both U.S. and British currency, which have identical numeric representations, but different values. It would be nice to be able to keep values of these two types distinct.

Or, to use a real-world example, suppose we are doing software development on one compiler, which only supports type **INTEGER**, and the software later will be compiled in a system that supports both **INTEGER** and **LONG__INTEGER**. It would be very helpful to do limited simulation with an **INTEGER** type simulating **LONG__INTEGER**, but yet keep the type checking of two distinct types.

In Ada we can do this using *derived types*. A derived type is essentially a copy of another type (called the *parent type*). The derived type inherits all the operators, attributes, and members of the parent type, but the derived type is distinct from the parent type. In effect a derived type is a subtype of the parent that is incompatible with the parent. Our hypothetical examples aren't enough reason to build this sort of feature into a language, of course.

We have other, more valid reasons for the segregation of data types, such as representation clauses (covered in Chapter 11) that allow us to do such things as specify a new storage format for a particular type.

We create a derived type by using the reserved word **new** in a type declaration:

```
type T is new <subtype indication>;
```

where **T** is the derived type's **type__mark**, and **<subtype indication>** is any allowable subtype expression for the parent type. For example:

```
type US_MONEY is new DECIMAL_CURRENCY;
type UK_MONEY is new DECIMAL_CURRENCY;
type INT is new INTEGER;              -- a copy of INTEGER
type MY_FLOAT is new FLOAT digits 5;  -- A less precise FLOAT
type INDEXER is new POSITIVE;         -- same range as POSITIVE
```

Any constraints, bounds, deltas, limitations, etc. of the parent type are passed to the derived type, and any new limits specified in the declaration also are imposed.

The only tricky part of derived types is conversion to another type. As you may remember, free conversion exists between a subtype and other subtypes of the same parent— not so, however, for derived types. A derived type must be explicitly converted to its parent type, and it can only be converted upward to its parent type (free conversion exists between a parent derived type and its subtypes).

As an example, let's look at converting between three different types, using the following objects:

```
Var_Float     -- an object of type FLOAT
Var_Integer   -- an object of type INTEGER
Var_Derived   -- an object of type MY_INT, derived from INTEGER
```

Given the above three objects, the following conversions must be applied:

```
Var_Float   := FLOAT(Var_Integer);            -- INTEGER to FLOAT
Var_Float   := FLOAT(INTEGER(Var_Derived));   -- MY_INT to FLOAT
Var_Integer := INTEGER(Var_Float);            -- FLOAT to INTEGER
Var_Integer := INTEGER(Var_Derived);          -- MY_INT to INTEGER
Var_Derived := MY_INT(INTEGER(Var_Float));    -- FLOAT to MY_INT
Var_Derived := MY_INT(Var_Integer);           -- INTEGER to MY_INT
```

Even if we have two types derived from the same parent, to convert between the two derived types we first have to convert up to the parent type, and then down to the other derived type. This rule requires us to write each potential conversion explicitly, thus forcing us to think about the correctness of the type conversion:

```
--
Bucks   : US_MONEY;
Pounds  : UK_MONEY;
--
Bucks := US_MONEY( Pounds ) * Conversion_Factor;
```

Access Types

Ada goes out of its way to avoid the use of the word *pointer* when describing data types. In Ada, pointers are referred to as *access types*.[4] We'll call the types "access types", although we may refer to objects of access types as "pointers", as it's more convenient and maybe a little more understandable.

An access type object (constant or variable) is an object which holds the address of (a *pointer to*) an object of another type, called the *designated type*. The object being pointed to is called the *designated object* and must have been created by an *allocator*. Each access type may have only one designated type associated with it—an access object could not, for example, designate either an **INTEGER** or a **CHARACTER**; it must designate one or the other (or another type altogether).

More than one access object may point at the same designated object. Interestingly enough, if no access object points at a designated object, the designated object disappears!

Ada's pointers can't be used in the same fashion one uses pointers in a language like C. We can't just hack off a conveniently sized hunk of memory and start aiming pointers into it. (Actually, you can, but you really have to work at it.)

While we don't want to get into a debate on the relative merits of languages, let's just say that while some pointer operations are easier to do in a language such as C, where pointers and pointer arithmetic are strong features, other pointer operations are easier in

Ada, and you are a lot less likely to stab the operating system in the heart with a loose pointer in Ada.

When an access type is created, it is assigned the value null as a default value. null is a literal of the language, and is defined for all access types. If a pointer has been assigned the value null it is guaranteed not to point at anything, and Ada will tell you if you try to use it as if it were pointing at something.

We can make a pointer quit pointing at something by reassigning null to it:

```
<access object> := null;
```

Declaring Access Types

When we declare an access type we use the reserved word *access* and we designate what we are pointing to:

```
type INT_POINTER is access INTEGER;
```

We aren't limited to designating scalar types. We can designate any other type, including other access types, as long as they have been declared. Much of the power of access types lies in the fact that we can point to complex data structures such as records and arrays. An access type is said to be *bound* to the type it designates.

When we have our access type all ready, and we declare pointers, we're all ready to start pointing at things. How do we go about it?

Allocators are used to create objects to point to, and to show where to point. An allocator is the reserved word **new** and a type mark. The following creates an access type of **INT__POINTER**, and then uses an allocator to create an integer and point **Ptr** toward the integer.

```
type INT_POINTER is access INTEGER;
Ptr : INT_POINTER;
--
Ptr := new INTEGER;
```

We can initialize the pointer when it's declared, or the integer when it's allocated, or both:

```
Ptr : INT_POINTER := new INTEGER;
--
Ptr : INT_POINTER := new INTEGER'( 0 );
--
Ptr := new INTEGER'( 21 );
```

As you can see, initializing the pointer is along the same lines as any other initialization.[5] The initialization of the designated object takes the form of a qualified expression. The qualified expression is any expression legal for the type; in the case of a record or array we can use an aggregate if we wish, as long as it is qualified.

Now that have our pointers working, and pointing at something, it's nice to be able to refer to the value contained in what we're pointing at, which, after all, is the idea in the first place.

The reserved word *all* is used to designate the object being pointed to by a pointer. If a pointer **Ptr** is pointing at an integer, then **Ptr.all** refers to the integer itself, in a manner very similar to record component selection. If we want to assign a value to the integer, and then print it out we can do it this way:

```
Ptr.all := 27;
Put( Ptr.all );
```

Objects created by allocators may in theory be deallocated as soon as nothing is pointing at them anymore, but no sooner. The language rules state that if the following sequence is followed, **Ptr2** still will be pointing at a valid allocated object:

```
Ptr, Ptr2  :  INT_POINTER;
--
Ptr    := new INTEGER;
Ptr2   := Ptr;
Ptr    := null;
```

In practice it is too much trouble for the run-time system to make sure that there are no pointers pointing to an object, so deallocation usually takes place when the scope of the access type declaration expires. If we use a global access type, then in all probability no deallocation will take place while the program is executing. If an access *type* (NOT an access type object) is declared in a subprogram, when the subprogram is finished, objects allocated during the subprogram may be deallocated when the subprogram is done.

We can also explicitly deallocate objects using the **Unchecked_Deallocation** procedure presented in Chapter 11. It is roughly analogous to the C function **free** or the Pascal procedure **Dispose**.

Operations available for the access types are assignment, qualification, allocators, membership tests, and explicit conversion. The literal **null** is implicitly declared for all access types.

So, What Good Are Access Types, Anyhow?

If you have used pointer types before, you probably know how useful they are, and you can just nod and say "Uh-huh" and feel smug as you read along.

If you've never used a pointer before, you are probably mystified as to the need for them. You may be wondering why we don't just create the objects and dispense with the pointers.

There are lots of applications for pointers, and we'll present two examples here. Additional examples of pointer use may be found in the next chapter. The two we'll see here are *linked lists* and *array sorts*.

Linked Lists with Pointers

When writing system utilities it's a good idea to make them as general and as system independent as possible. That way, we can pass out copies to our friends, who will revere us for our unmitigated genius and programming skills.

Suppose we get an idea for a program that will require us to read from a disk file an undetermined number of ASCII text lines of various sizes. We have some slick operation planned (unspecified here, perhaps an alphabetical sort?) that requires that all of the lines be in memory at one time.

Setting up an array of strings would be inefficient. If we decide to limit the number of strings to what our system memory will hold, we waste space on a larger system and run out of memory on a smaller system.

We could read the file through once, and count the number of lines, and then try for an array, but that means we have to rewind the file, and read it again. Two passes will be required for each file.

Using pointers, we can set up a linked list to hold our information. A linked list is a series of information records. Each record contains a unit of information, and also holds a reference as to where to find the next piece of information. Our program can define these records using a recursive type definition, where a record contains a pointer to a record of the same type. Because a designated type has to be declared before its access types, we need to use an *incomplete type declaration*, an animal used only for recursive or mutually dependant declarations:[6]

```
type NODE;                  -- incomplete type declaration
type LIST_POINTER is access NODE;

type NODE is
    record
        Info : STRING( 1..80);
        Size : NATURAL;
        Next : LIST_POINTER;
    end record;

Root : LIST_POINTER;      -- the start of the list;
```

We can load the linked list like this:

```
procedure Load_List is
      Temp   : LIST_POINTER;
begin
      while not End_Of_File loop
            Temp := new NODE;
            Get_Line( Temp.all.Info, last => Temp.all.Size );
            Temp.all.Next := Root;
            Root := Temp;
      end loop;
end Load_List;
```

In procedure **Load__List** we set up a simple **while** loop to allow us to read the default file a line at a time, until we hit the end of the file. If we have an empty file we don't execute the loop even once.

The first thing we do in the loop is allocate a record of type **NODE**, and assign **Temp** to point at it. We read a line of information from our file to the string in the record pointed to by **Temp**, along with the size of the string.

So far, it's pretty straightforward. Now comes the tricky part.

We assign the **Next** pointer in **Temp** to point at the same thing **Root** is pointing at, which initially will be **null**. Then we assign **Root** to point at the new object created and assigned to **Temp**.

The next time through, a new object will be assigned to **Temp**; **Temp.all.Next** will be assigned to point to the first object created; and **Root** will point to the object last allocated.

This little linked list loader will load our linked list (try saying that real fast three times) so that **Root** will always point to the last line read from the file. As new lines are added, the first line read will move farther and farther away from **Root** in the linked list. We load this particular list in reverse. If we wanted to print the list (in reverse) we could write a little procedure like this:

```
procedure Print_List is
      Temp : LIST_POINTER;
begin
      Temp := Root;
      while Temp /= null loop
            Put_Line( Temp.all.info( 1..Temp.all.Size) );
            Temp := Temp.all.Next;
      end loop;
end Print_List;
```

We could combine these two procedures with file redirection like package **CMD** from

Chapter 6, and have a nice little program to reverse the order of lines in a text file. (Imagine the fun at the office when you reverse all of the word processor files!)

Lists don't have to be linked backwards, of course. There are more complicated algorithms, two-way linked lists, binary tree linked lists, etc. A characteristic of pointers and linked lists is that you end up with nice powerful little procedures that are very hard to understand if you are unaccustomed to pointers.

Array Sorts

Another reason to use pointers is in sorting situations. When sorting we are trying to arrange things which are in one kind of order into some other order, hopefully the correct one. Sorting techniques almost always involve moving the data to be sorted.

Let's write a bubble sort to sort an ASCII file using an array of access types. What's the advantage of using access types as opposed to an array of strings?

When bubble sorting, as with Quick or Shell sorts, we need to swap values that are out of order. If we use an array of strings, when we swap we have to move one string to a temporary holder, move the other string into the spot where the first string was, and then move the first string from the temporary holder into the spot where the second string was. Any swap normally takes at least three moves.

Swapping an 80+ byte string from one place to another is going to take time. If we use access types to point at the strings, we still have to swap, but we can swap the *pointers* and leave the strings in place. In a microcomputer, an access value is probably only two or three bytes long. We can move a two byte pointer a lot faster than we can an 80-character string.

We also need only allocate an array of pointers when we start. We can allocate string space as needed, making the memory requirements for our sort routine much more flexible.

Let's start by declaring the types and globals we'll need first:

```
N : constant := 100    -- limit on list size
type LINE is
    record
        Info : STRING( 1..80 );
        Size : NATURAL;
    end record;
type LINE_POINTER is access LINE;
type LIST_ARRAY is array( POSITIVE range 1..n ) of LINE_POINTER;
List : LIST_ARRAY
```

We declare an access type for our line record, an array type for objects of this access type, and an array object called **List** which will hold our pointers. Now we need a procedure to get our lines into the array:

```
procedure Load_Lines( Lines_Read : out NATURAL ) is
     Index : NATURAL := 0;
begin
     while not End_Of_File loop
          Index := Index + 1;
          List( Index ) := new STRING;
          Get_Line( List( Index ).all.Info,
                    Last => List(Index).all.Size );
     end loop;
     Lines_Read := Index;
end Load_Lines;
```

Note that we return the number of lines read as an out parameter to **Load_Lines**. Now we need to bubble sort the array:

```
procedure Bubble_Sort( Lines_Read : in NATURAL ) is
   No_Swap_Made : BOOLEAN;
   Temp         : LINE_POINTER;
begin
OUTER:
   loop
      No_Swap_Made := TRUE;
INNER:
      for Index in 1..Lines_Read - 1 loop
         if
            List(Index).all.Info(1..List(Index).all.Size)
            > List(Index+1).all.Info(1..List(Index+1).all.Size)
         then
            Temp := List( Index );
            List( Index ) := List( Index + 1 );
            List( Index + 1 ) := Temp;
            No_Swap_Made := FALSE;
         end if;
      end loop INNER;
      exit OUTER when No_Swap_Made;
   end loop OUTER;
end Bubble_Sort;
```

We just need to print our results out now. Here's a procedure to write the list back, in order:

```
procedure Write_Lines( Lines_Read : in NATURAL ) is
begin
   for Index in 1..Lines_Read loop
```

```
        Put( List(Index).all.Info(1..List(Index).all.Size);
      end loop
  end Write_Lines;
```

Our main procedure could look like this:

```
begin
    Load_Lines( Lines_Read );
    Bubble_Sort( Lines_Read );
    Write_Lines( Lines_Read );
end;
```

Again, adding the redirection package **CMD** from Chapter 6 will give this simple program some real versatility.

Conclusion

In this chapter we saw Ada's numeric real types. Floating-point types are useful for scientific and other work where very large or very small numbers are important. Fixed-point types are needed for financial work where precision is crucial. It is interesting to note that fixed-point types are the only real types used in many embedded applications—one reason that Ada's fixed-point facilities are so complete.

We also looked at Ada's access types (a.k.a. pointers) and two simple applications of pointers. Pointers have as much potential for abuse as for worthwhile use, although Ada safeguards reduce the chance of pointers coming loose and spraying the insides of your computer with extra bits.

9

A Package of the Third Kind

As the title indicates, in this chapter we will develop a package of the third kind—a data type and its associated operators, all collected in a single package.[1]

In Chapter 7 we saw some of the restrictions on the one dimensional array type **STRING**. Strings are fairly difficult to deal with using the operators and facilities provided in Ada.

Consider the simple entry of a file name by the user. We have been using **Get_Line** and extracting a slice of the input to pass to **Open**. This is a sorry state, as we need to keep track of two values for a single logical concept: a value for the string and a size for the same string.

What the language designers probably said was, "Well, any decent implementation will have a variant string handling package. . . ."

Since you probably will have a subset of Ada, you may not have a string handling package. Or you may have a situation similar to the earlier versions of Janus/Ada, where type **STRING** is an intrinsic base type, with nonstandard (and therefore nonportable) string operations.

Subsets of Ada are an embarrassing problem, especially when writing a book about Ada. Reading Chapter 1 of this book probably gave you the impression that all your portability problems were done with. Well, they are if you have full Ada, but they're just starting if you have a subset with nonstandard features.

What we will do in this chapter is to develop a set of varying string subprograms that can be placed in a package and then **with**ed, just like **Text_IO**. These programs will be as portable as possible, and yet will operate in nonstandard environments.

The string handling package may need some minor tweaking when it is moved from one compiler to another, but programs depending on the package will not (although if the string package is modified, dependent programs will have to be relinked).

The idea is to move toward the Ada goal of program portability; and, though the string package itself may vary between compilers, if we use the subprograms in the package (and don't get tricky), programs depending on the string package will be completely portable.

The normal way to create a varying string type is to embed the string in a record with a default discriminant:

```
type VARYING_STRING( Size : POSITIVE := 80 ) is
    record
            Value : STRING( 1..Size );
    end record;
```

When we need to change the size of the string, we make an aggregate assignment to the record:

```
    Vary_String : VARYING_STRING;
    New_Value   : STRING := "Any string";
    --
    --
    Vary_String := ( Size => New_Value'length, Value =>
New_Value );
    --
```

We can directly access the string portion of the record using named component notation:

```
Put( Vary_String.Value );
```

And we can determine the current size by using attribute functions:

```
Put( Vary_String.Value'length );
```

This is one of the ways a varying string operation could be carried out in full Ada. A problem arises when using a subset that lacks records with discriminants, or length attribute functions, or aggregate assignments, or named component notation, or any of the other advanced features of Ada that seem to get left out of subset compilers.

The first step is to declare a type which can be handled even on a simple subset. An analysis of the requirements for varying strings tells us we need to know three things about a varying string object:

- the current value of the string;
- the current length of the string; and
- the maximum possible length of the string.

We can create a record with this information and use it as our basic varying string type.

To avoid a conflict with the Janus/Ada string type, let's not use the predefined string type available in Ada at all.

```
MAX_STRING_SIZE : constant := 80;

type VARYING_STRING is
   record
     Size  : NATURAL := 0;
     Valu  : array( 1..MAX_STRING_SIZE ) of CHARACTER;
   end record;
```

We are using the named number **MAX__STRING__SIZE** as our maximum string size component. You may, of course, change the value from 80 to whatever size you want. Just remember—the full amount of storage always will be allocated.

The actual format of the varying string type is unimportant if we don't use any of the details of the record in our programs depending on this package. But if, for example, we start modifying individual components of our record in our main programs, we won't be able to change the record format later without modifying all of our dependent main programs.

Objects of type **VARYING__STRING** are declared just like any other object:

```
Name_Of_File : VARYING_STRING;
```

Now let's start writing subprograms to manipulate our new string type.

Copy

Starting with the basics, we need to write a subprogram which will assign a value to our varying string type variable. We will overload it to accept either regular **STRING** arguments or **VARYING__STRING** arguments.

The toughest subprograms we are going to write will be the ones that translate from our varying string type to a fixed-string type.

There are four possibilities when copying string values between the varying type we have defined and the predefined (we'll call it the "intrinsic") Ada **STRING** type. They are:

1. intrinsic	:=	intrinsic
2. intrinsic	:=	varying
3. varying	:=	intrinsic
4. varying	:=	varying

Of these four possibilities, #1 and #4 should be available from the compiler. We will write a copy routine for version #4 just in case we move to a subset that can't assign a record

```
-- Copy: For copying one Varying string to another Varying
-- string.

   procedure Copy( Destination : in out VARYING_STRING;
                   Source : in VARYING_STRING ) is
   begin
      Destination.Valu := Source.Valu;
      Destination.Size := Source.Size;
   end Copy;



-- Copy: Above function overloaded to copy an intrinsic string
-- type to a Varying string.

   procedure Copy( Destination : in out Varying_String;
                   Source : in STRING ) is
   begin
      Destination.Size := Length( Source );
      for Index in 1..Length( Source ) loop
         Destination.Valu( Index ) := Source( Index );
      end loop;
   end Copy;



-- Copy: Above function overloaded to copy a Varying string to
-- an intrinsic STRING type. Value truncated if the destination
-- string is too short; blank padded if destination string is
-- too long.

   procedure Copy( Destination : out STRING; Source :
                   VARYING_STRING ) is
   begin
      for Index in 1..Length( Destination ) loop
         if Index > Source.Size then
            Destination( Index ) := ' ';
         else
            Destination( Index ) := Source.Valu( Index );
         end if;
      end loop;
   end Copy;
```

Figure 9-1. **Copy** *Procedures*

to another record, so we will end up with our **Copy** procedure overloaded three times (see Figure 9-1).

Note in our copy routines the use of a function **Length**. Since some subsets do not define the length attribute, in particular the version of Janus/Ada the authors used to compile this package, we are using a substitute function built-in to the compiler. In full Ada, we would use the length attribute:

```
Length = String_Object'length
```

If you have this attribute available, you can write a length function that returns the same value as the length attribute:

```
function Length( Item : STRING ) return NATURAL is
begin
    return Item'length;
end Length;
```

Add this function to the package, rather than trying to change every instance where the Janus **Length** function appears. This approach will simplify conversion of the package from subset to subset and will give us a form similar to that required for determining the length of a varying string, where an attribute function is not defined. We will need a length function for varying strings which will look something like that shown in Figure 9-2.

Value

The **Copy** procedures will allow us to get intrinsic string types in and out of our varying strings fairly nicely. Many times, though, we will want just the value of a varying string without having to assign it to an intrinsic string variable. We can write a function that will just return the value of a varying string, as opposed to the **Copy** procedure, which fills an existing string variable. We can **Put** the value or use it in other ways.

```
--Length: to return the length of a Varying string

function Length( Source : VARYING_STRING ) return INTEGER is
begin
    return Source.Size;
end Length;
```

Figure 9-2. **Length** *Function*

```
-- Has non-standard Ada parts
-- Value: Returns an intrinsic string type corresponding to the
-- value of a Varying string.

   function Value( Source : VARYING_STRING ) return STRING is

      Value_Part : STRING; -- Not standard Ada
-- Value_Part : STRING( Source.Size ); -- standard Ada

   begin

-- start nonstandard Ada - Nothing required in Ada
      Value_Part := "";
      for Index in 1..Source.Size loop
         Value_Part := Value_Part & " ";
      end loop;
-- end nonstandard Ada

      for Index in 1..Source.Size loop
         Value_Part( Index ) := Source.Valu( Index );
      end loop;
      return Value_Part;
   end Value;
```

Figure 9-3. **Value** *Function*

This will be the only subprogram in our string package that has nonstandard Ada constructions as we write it in Janus/Ada. The problems arise from Janus's base type of string, which is already varying, but not within the limits of the language. The nonstandard portions are marked in Figure 9-3.[2]

Compare

A frequent operation performed on strings is a comparison of position alphabetically with another string.

Most subsets will not allow the overloading of operators, so we will not be able to use the familiar operators =, >, and < on our varying strings. The = operator should be defined to work on the records, but will yield unreliable results because we are leaving the ends of our varying strings uninitialized.

Since we won't be writing our comparison function as overloaded operators, we will follow the C example of string comparison (**strcmp** and **strncmp**) and write a single

```
-- Compare: to compare Varying strings of unequal length, with a
-- limit on how many characters are examined for equality.
-- return values:
-- Relation => equal if strings are equal.
-- Relation => greater_than if left string > right string
-- Relation => less_than if left string < right string

   Function Compare( Left, Right : VARYING_STRING;
                     Limit : POSITIVE ) return Relation is

       Index_Limit : INTEGER;

   begin
      if Left.Size > Right.Size then
         Index_Limit := Left.Size;
      else
         Index_Limit := Right.Size;
      end if;

      if Index_Limit > Limit then
         Index_Limit := Limit;
      end if;

      for Index in 1..Index_Limit loop
         if Left.Valu( Index ) > Right.Valu( Index ) then
            return Greater_Than;
         elsif Left.Valu( Index ) < Right.Valu( Index ) then
            return Less_Than;
         end if;
      end loop;

      return Equal;
   end Compare;


-- Compare: Generalized version of above. Same return values, but
-- strings are examined over the entire length.

   function Compare( Left, Right : VARYING_STRING ) return Relation is

       Max_Length : INTEGER;
```

Figure 9-4. **Compare** Function

```
begin
   if Left.Size > Right.Size then
      Max_Length := Left.Size;
   else
      Max_Length := Right.Size;
   end if;
   return Compare( Left, Right, Max_Length );
end Compare;
```

Figure 9-4   continued

function that will return a value indicating equality, greater than, and less than. We will enumerate the possible return values as **EQUAL**, **GREATER_THAN**, and **LESS_THAN**, as these will be easy to remember.

```
type RELATION is (LESS_THAN, EQUAL, GREATER_THAN);
```

It also is useful to be able to compare only a part of two strings. We will overload the compare function we write so that we can specify a limit on how far the comparison will be carried out. Then we can say in effect, "Compare the first X characters of string number one to the first X characters in string two."

For code efficiency, and to save us some typing, we can write one compare function in terms of the other. It is easiest to write the general case compare in terms of the limited case compare (see Figure 9-4).

Concatenate

Concatenation is an essential operation for string types. We should include concatenation procedures to join two varying strings or to join an intrinsic string or string literal to a varying string. For convenience we will write these procedures to modify one of the input varying strings, rather than returning a new string, as the Ada concatenation operator does. Of course, given Ada's nonvarying string type, a constraint error would be raised if we tried to extend the length of a string. Our procedures are shown in Figure 9-5.

Slices of Varying Strings

In a full Ada compiler it is relatively easy to extract a portion of a string, by using slices:

```
--Concatenate: to concatenate a Varying string to a Varying string

   procedure Concatenate( Destination : in out VARYING_STRING;
           Source : in VARYING_STRING ) is
   begin
      if Source.Size = 0 then
         return;
      end if;
      for Index in 1..Source.Size loop
         Destination.Valu( Index + Destination.Size ) :=
            Source.Valu( Index );
      end loop;
      Destination.Size := Destination.Size +
         Source.Size;
   end concatenate;


-- Concatenate: to concatenate an intrinsic string type to a
-- Varying string

   procedure Concatenate( Destination : in out VARYING_STRING;
                          Source : in STRING ) is

      Source_Length : INTEGER;

   begin
      Source_Length := Length( Source );
      if Source_Length = 0 then
         return;
      end if;
      for Index in 1..Source_Length loop
         Destination.Valu( Index + Destination.Size ) :=
            Source( Index );
      end loop;
      Destination.Size := Destination.Size + Source_Length;
   end Concatenate;
```

Figure 9-5. **Concatenate** *Procedure*

```
String_Var : STRING( 1..12) := "Hello there!";
--
    Put( String_Var( 4..8 ) );          "lo th"
```

We will need this feature occasionally for our varying strings. Let's borrow from MicroSoft BASIC, and add functions equivalent to **MID$**, **LEFT$**, and **RIGHT$**, to extract from the middle, left side, and right side of a varying string, respectively. We could express **LEFT$** and **RIGHT$**, in terms of **MID$**, or **MID$** in terms of **LEFT$** and **RIGHT$**, in our programs, but it is more obvious to use the one of the three which is most appropriate.

That doesn't mean that we have to write our basic functions without referring to each other, though. We can write the **Middle__Portion** function, and then express **Left__Side** and **Right__Side** in terms of **Middle__Portion** as we do in Figure 9-6.

Position

Another handy function is one that will locate an occurrence of a smaller string within a larger string, or tell us it is not there at all. We can write a function **Position** to tell us where our **target** string begins within our **Source** string. An equivalent function in BASIC is **INSTR$**, and in C is **index**. Our **Position** function will return a zero if the target string is not contained in the source string, or the starting position of the target within the source (see Figure 9-7).

Case Sensitivity

When comparing or otherwise processing strings, we often have no control over the case used. Comparing an uppercase 'A' to a lowercase 'a' will result in an unequality. Sometimes this is okay, but when alphabetizing or looking for names, titles, etc. the case should not matter to a comparison. In other instances we may want to make sure that a string appears in uppercase or in lowercase, for the sake of either readability or consistency.

We will present four subprograms, two to convert varying strings to either upper- or lowercase, and two to return intrinsic string upper- or lowercase equivalents of varying strings.

To help us write these subprograms we will write two character functions and bundle them into the rest of our string package. The two character functions are **To__Upper** and **To__Lower**. **To__Upper** will convert a lowercase letter to an uppercase letter. For the sake of convenience, we will have **To__Upper** pass uppercase and nonalphabetic characters

```
--Middle_Portion: To return a section of a Varying string as a
-- Varying string. Give a starting position, and a count of
-- how many characters to return.

    function Middle_Portion( Source : VARYING_STRING;
       Start, Count : POSITIVE ) return Varying_string is

       Ret_String : VARYING_STRING;

    begin
       for Index in 1..Count loop
          Ret_String.Valu( Index ) :=
            Source.Valu( Index + Start - 1 );
       end loop;
       Ret_String.Size := Count;
       return Ret_String;
    end Middle_Portion;


--Left_Side: Returns the left 'Count' characters of a Varying
-- string as a Varying string.

    function Left_Side( Source : VARYING_STRING; Count : POSITIVE )
          return VARYING_STRING is
    begin
       return Middle_Portion( Source, 1, Count );
    end Left_Side;

------------------------------------------------------------------
--Right_Side: Returns the right 'Count' characters of a Varying
-- string as a Varying string.

    function Right_Side( Source : VARYING_STRING; Count : POSITIVE )
          return VARYING_STRING is
    begin
       return Middle_Portion( Source, Source.Size - Count + 1, Count );
    end Right_Side;
```

Figure 9-6. Substring Functions

```
--Position: To determine if a Varying string appears as a substring
-- of another Varying string.
-- Returns index of target string within source string, or
-- zero for no match found.

   function Position( Source, Target : VARYING_STRING )
    return NATURAL is
   begin
      for Index in 1..(Source.Size - Target.Size + 1) loop
         if Compare( Middle_Portion( Source, Index,
          Target.Size ), Target ) = equal then
             return Index;
         end if;
      end loop;
      return 0;
   end Position;
```

Figure 9-7. **Position** *Function*

through unchanged. This will eliminate any need to test a character to be sure that it is lowercase before we run it through **To_Upper**. **To_Lower** will be very similar to **To_Upper**, except that it will convert uppercase letters to lowercase (see Figure 9-8 on page 200).

Our four subprograms to make strings upper- and lowercase are given as Figure 9-9 on page 201.

Pulling It All Together

Now that we have all of our subprograms written we need to bundle them into a package that we can **with** and **use**. Let's make it a complete system, with a separate specification and body.

In a later chapter we'll show you how to protect the varying string type from misuse. Since the point of this package is portability as well as convenience, we want to hide the details of how varying strings are implemented. For now, don't write shortcuts into programs that **with** the string library. For example:

```
Dyn_Str : VARYING_STRING;
Len : INTEGER;
--
--
Len := Dyn_Str.Size;        -- WRONG! Don't do this!
Len := Length( Dyn_Str );  -- Right.
```

In this example the wrong way depends on a characteristic of the varying string record, which could change. The right way shows us using a string library function.

If you should need extra subprograms when handling strings, write them in as general a way as possible and add them to your string library, rather than using tricks and patching them into your main program. This method has two advantages. First, you'll only have to write the subprogram once, and it will be easy to use it in another program later. Second, when you buy your shiny new compiler, after your subset-burning party, you'll only have to resolve compiler dependencies in one place.

All of our subprograms in this chapter are written for Janus/Ada version 1.5.0 because it is one of the more common subsets. 1.5.0 is as far as Janus will evolve in CP/M, and it will be good for you to see subset dependencies.

Bundling these subprograms into a package is fairly simple. The body of the package will be made up of all of the subprograms presented here, plus any you wrote as exercises. In Janus we need a context that includes Strlib, the Janus string library. In SuperSoft "A", or a real Ada compiler, we don't need any context.

The package specification has the same context requirements. In addition we will place the type definitions for export: VARYING__STRING and Relation. Then we need a declaration for each of the subprograms which we will be exporting. We should leave out To__Upper and To__Lower, because they aren't really string functions; but they are useful functions and we'll want them available.

The specification is also a good place to put the comments regarding usage of each of the subprograms. You don't ever want to have to refer to the body for usage information.

The specification need never change, unless new subprograms are added to the package. If and when you change the body, only the body will need to be recompiled. Also, no programs withing the string package will have to be recompiled, though they will need to be relinked.

We have collected the subprograms into a specification and body for you. The specification is Figure 9-10, on pages 202–205, and the body is Figure 9-11, on pages 206–212.

Conclusion

This package is useful in enough places that you'll probably end up attaching it to most of your programs. Later on we will provide examples of several programs using it.

```
--To_Upper utility function used by make_upper. Returns the
-- uppercase equivalent of the argument character. A useful
-- character function.

   function To_Upper( Char : CHARACTER ) return CHARACTER is

      Offset : constant := CHARACTER'POS( 'a' ) -
              CHARACTER'POS( 'A' );

   begin
      if Char in 'a'..'z' then
         return CHARACTER'VAL( CHARACTER'POS( Char ) - Offset );
      else
         return( Char );
      end if;
   end To_Upper;


--To_Lower: utility function used by make_lower. Returns the
-- lowercase equilavlent of the character argument. A useful
-- character function.

   function To_Lower( Char : CHARACTER ) return CHARACTER is

      Offset : constant := CHARACTER'POS( 'a' ) -
              CHARACTER'POS( 'A' );

   begin
      if Char in 'A'..'Z' then
         return CHARACTER'VAL( CHARACTER'POS( Char ) + Offset );
      else
         return Char;
      end if;
   end To_Lower;
```

Figure 9-8. **To_Upper** *and* **To_Lower** *Functions*

```
-- Make_Uppercase: Makes a Varying string into its uppercase
--   equivalent.

    procedure Make_Uppercase( Right : in out VARYING_STRING ) is
    begin
       for Index in 1..Right.Size loop
          Right.Valu( Index ) := To_Upper( Right.Valu( Index ) );
       end loop;
    end Make_Uppercase;


-- Make_Lowercase: makes a Varying string into its lowercase
--   equivalent

    procedure Make_Lowercase( Right : in out VARYING_STRING ) is
    begin
       for Index in 1..Right.Size loop
          Right.Valu( Index ) := To_Lower( Right.Valu( Index ) );
       end loop;
    end Make_Lowercase;


--Uppercase: Returns an intrinsic string equivalent to the
-- uppercase value of a Varying string.

    function Uppercase( Right : VARYING_STRING ) return STRING is

       Temp : VARYING_STRING;

    begin
       Copy( Temp, Right );
       Make_Uppercase( Temp );
       return Value( Temp );
    end Uppercase;


--Lowercase: returns an intrinsic string equivalent to the
-- lowercase value of a Varying string.

    function Lowercase( Right : VARYING_STRING ) return STRING is

       Temp : VARYING_STRING;
```

Figure 9-9. Upper/Lowercase String Functions

```
begin
   Copy( Temp, Right );
   Make_Lowercase( Temp );
   return Value( Temp );
end Lowercase;
```

Figure 9-9   continued

```
with strlib;
package Varystr is
   use Strlib;

   MAX_STRING_SIZE : constant := 80;

   type VARYING_STRING is
      record
         Size  :  NATURAL;
         Value :  array( 1..MAX_STRING_SIZE ) of CHARACTER;
      end record;

    type RELATION is ( LESS_THAN, EQUAL, GREATER_THAN );

-- For compilers which have the length attribute defined for
--   arrays: Not required for Janus.

   function Length( Right : STRING ) return INTEGER;

-- To_Upper: utility function used by make_upper. Returns the
--   uppercase equivalent of the argument character. A useful
--   character function.

   function To_Upper( Char : CHARACTER ) return CHARACTER;

-- To_Lower: utility function used by make_lower. Returns the
--   lowercase equivalent of the character argument. A useful
--   character function.

   function To_Lower( Char : CHARACTER ) return CHARACTER;
```

Figure 9-10.   Varystr Package Specification

```
-- Copy: For copying one varying string to another varying
--   string.

    procedure Copy( Destination : in out VARYING_STRING;
                    Source : in VARYING_STRING );


-- Copy: Above function overloaded to copy an intrinsic string
--   type to a varying string.

    procedure Copy( Destination : in out VARYING_STRING;
                    Source : in STRING );


-- Copy: Above function overloaded to copy a varying string to
--   an intrinsic string type. Value truncated if the destination
--   string is too short; blank padded if destination string is
--   too long.

    procedure Copy( Destination : out STRING;
                    Source : VARYING_STRING );


-- Value: to return the value of the varying string as an
--   intrinsic string type.

    function Value( Source : VARYING_STRING ) return STRING;

-- Length: to return the length of a varying string

    function Length( Source : VARYING_STRING ) return INTEGER;


-- Concatenate: to concatenate a varying string to a varying string

    procedure Concatenate( Destination : in out VARYING_STRING;
                Source : in VARYING_STRING );


-- Concatenate: to concatenate an intrinsic string type to a
--   varying string
```

Figure 9-10   *continued*

```
        procedure Concatenate( Destination : in out VARYING_STRING;
                                Source : in STRING );


    -- Compare: to compare varying strings of unequal length, with a
    --  limit on how many characters are examined for equality.
    --  return values:
    --    RELATION => EQUAL if strings are equal.
    --    RELATION => GREATER_THAN if left string > right string
    --    RELATION => LESS_THAN if left string < right string

        Function Compare( Left, Right : VARYING_STRING;
                          Limit : POSITIVE ) return RELATION;


    -- Compare: Generalized version of above. Same return values, but
    --  strings are examined over the entire length.

        function Compare( Left, Right : VARYING_STRING ) return RELATION;


    -- Middle_Portion: To return a section of a varying string as a
    --  varying string. Give a starting position, and a count of
    --  how many characters to return.

        function Middle_Portion( Source : VARYING_STRING;
           Start, Count : POSITIVE ) return VARYING_STRING;


    -- Left_Side: Returns the left 'count' characters of a varying
    --  string as a varying string.

        function Left_Side( Source : VARYING_STRING; Count : POSITIVE )
           return VARYING_STRING;


    -- Right_Side: Returns the right 'count' characters of a varying
    --  string as a varying string.

        function Right_Side( Source : VARYING_STRING; Count : POSITIVE )
           return VARYING_STRING;
```

Figure 9-10   continued

```
-- Position: To determine if a varying string appears as a substring
--   of another varying string.
--   Returns index of target string within source string, or
--   zero for no match found.

    function Position( Source, Target : VARYING_STRING )
        return natural;


-- Make_Uppercase: Makes a varying string into its uppercase
--   equivalent.

    procedure Make_Uppercase( Right : in out VARYING_STRING );


-- Make_Lowercase: makes a varying string into its lowercase
--   equivalent

    procedure Make_Lowercase( Right : in out VARYING_STRING );


-- Uppercase: Returns an intrinsic string equivalent to the
--   uppercase value of a varying string.

    function Uppercase( Right : VARYING_STRING ) return STRING;


-- Lowercase: returns an intrinsic string equivalent to the
--   lowercase value of a varying string.

    function Lowercase( Right : VARYING_STRING ) return STRING;

end Varystr;
```

Figure 9-10 *continued*

```
with Strlib;
package body Varystr is
  use Strlib;


--For compilers that have the length attribute defined for
--arrays: Not required for Janus.

    function Length( Right : STRING ) return INTEGER is
    begin
       return Length'Right;
    end Length;


--All standard Ada

   function To_Upper( Char : CHARACTER ) return CHARACTER is

      Offset:constant := CHARACTER'Pos( 'a' ) - CHARACTER'Pos( 'A' );

   begin
      if Char in 'a'..'z' then
         return CHARACTER'Val( CHARACTER'Pos( Char ) - Offset );
      else
         return( Char );
      end if;
   end To_Upper;

--All standard Ada

   function To_Lower( Char : CHARACTER ) return CHARACTER is

      Offset:constant := CHARACTER'Pos( 'a' ) - CHARACTER'Pos( 'A' );

   begin
      if Char in 'A'..'Z' then
         return CHARACTER'Val( CHARACTER'Pos( Char ) + Offset );
      else
         return Char;
      end if;
   end To_Lower;
```

Figure 9-11. Varystr Package Body

```
--All standard Ada

   procedure Copy( Destination : in out VARYING_STRING;
                   Source : in VARYING_STRING ) is
   begin
      Destination.Valu := Source.Valu;
      Destination.Size := Source.Size;
   end Copy;


--All standard Ada

   procedure Copy( Destination : in out VARYING_STRING;
                   Source : in STRING ) is
   begin
      Destination.Size := Length( Source );
      for Index in 1..Length( Source ) loop
         Destination.Valu( Index ) := Source( Index );
      end loop;
   end Copy;

--All standard Ada

   procedure Copy( Destination:out STRING; Source : VARYING_STRING )is
   begin
      for Index in 1..Length( Destination ) loop
         if Index > Source.Size then
            Destination( Index ) := ' ';
         else
            Destination( Index ) := Source.Valu( Index );
         end if;
      end loop;
   end copy;

--Has non-standard Ada parts

   function Value( Source : VARYING_STRING ) return STRING is

      Value_Part : STRING; -- Not standard Ada
     --Value_Part : STRING( Source.Size ); -- standard Ada
```

Figure 9-11   continued

```
  begin

--start non-standard Ada - Nothing required in Ada
    Value_Part := "";
    for Index in 1..Source.Size loop
       Value_Part := Value_Part & " ";
    end loop;
--end non-standard Ada

    for Index in 1..Source.Size loop
       Value_Part( Index ) := Source.Valu( Index );
    end loop;
    return Value_Part;
  end Value;


--All standard Ada

  function Length( Source : VARYING_STRING ) return INTEGER is
  begin
     return Source.Size;
  end Length;


--All standard Ada

  procedure Concatenate( Destination : in out VARYING_STRING;
          Source : in VARYING_STRING ) is
  begin
     if Source.Size = 0 then
        return;
     end if;
    for Index in 1..Source.Size loop
       Destination.Valu( Index + Destination.Size ) :=
       Source.Valu( Index );
     end loop;
     Destination.Size := Destination.Size +
       Source.Size;
  end Concatenate;
```

Figure 9-11 continued

```
--All standard Ada

   procedure Concatenate( Destination : in out VARYING_STRING;
                          Source : in STRING ) is

      Source_Length : INTEGER;

   begin
      Source_Length := Length( Source );
      if Source_Length = 0 then
         return;
      end if;
      for Index in 1..Source_Length loop
         Destination.Valu( Index + Destination.Size ) :=
            Source( Index );
      end loop;
      Destination.Size := Destination.Size + Source_Length;
   end Concatenate;


--All standard Ada

   Function Compare( Left, Right : VARYING_STRING;
                     Limit : POSITIVE ) return RELATION is

      Index_Limit : INTEGER;

   begin
      if Left.Size > Right.Size then
         Index_Limit := Left.Size;
      else
         Index_Limit := Right.Size;
      end if;

      if Index_Limit > Limit then
         Index_Limit := Limit;
      end if;

      for Index in 1..Index_Limit loop
         if Left.Valu( Index ) > Right.Valu( Index ) then
            return GREATER_THAN;
         elsif Left.Valu( Index ) < Right.Valu( Index ) then
            return LESS_THAN;
```

Figure 9-11   continued

```
            end if;
        end loop;

        return EQUAL;
    end Compare;


--All standard Ada

    function Compare( Left, Right : VARYING_STRING ) return RELATION is

        Max_Length : INTEGER;

    begin
        if Left.Size > Right.Size then
            Max_Length := Left.Size;
        else
            Max_Length := Right.Size;
        end if;
        return Compare( Left, Right, Max_Length );
    end Compare;


--All standard Ada

    function Middle_Portion( Source : VARYING_STRING;
        Start, Count : POSITIVE ) return VARYING_STRING is

        Ret_String : VARYING_STRING;

    begin
        for Index in 1..Count loop
            Ret_String.Valu( Index ) :=
              Source.Valu( Index + Start - 1 );
        end loop;
        Ret_String.Size := Count;
        return Ret_String;
    end Middle_Portion;
```

Figure 9-11   *continued*

```ada
-- All standard Ada

   function Left_Side( Source : VARYING_STRING; Count : POSITIVE )
        return VARYING_STRING is
   begin
      return Middle_Portion( Source, 1, Count );
   end Left_Side;


--All standard Ada

   function Right_Side( Source : VARYING_STRING; Count : POSITIVE )
        return VARYING_STRING is
   begin
      return Middle_Portion( Source, Source.Size - Count + 1, Count );
   end Right_Side;


--All standard Ada

   function Position( Source, Target : VARYING_STRING )
    return NATURAL is
   begin
      for Index in 1..(Source.Size - Target.Size + 1) loop
          if Compare( Middle_Portion( Source, Index,
          Target.Size ), Target ) = EQUAL then
             return Index;
          end if;
      end loop;
      return 0;
   end Position;


--All standard Ada

   procedure Make_Uppercase( Right : in out VARYING_STRING ) is
   begin
      for Index in 1..Right.Size loop
         Right.Valu( Index ) := To_Upper( Right.Valu( Index ) );
      end loop;
   end Make_Uppercase;
```

Figure 9-11   continued

```
--All standard Ada

   procedure Make_Lowercase( Right : in out VARYING_STRING ) is
   begin
      for Index in 1..Right.Size loop
         Right.Valu( Index ) := To_Lower( Right.Valu( Index ) );
      end loop;
   end Make_Lowercase;


--All standard Ada

   function Uppercase( Right : VARYING_STRING ) return STRING is

      Temp : VARYING_STRING;

   begin
      Copy( Temp, Right );
      Make_Uppercase( Temp );
      return Value( Temp );
   end Uppercase;


--All standard Ada

   function Lowercase( Right : VARYING_STRING ) return STRING is

      Temp : VARYING_STRING;

   begin
      Copy( Temp, Right );
      Make_Lowercase( Temp );
      return Value( Temp );
   end Lowercase;

end Varystr;
```

Figure 9-11   continued

10

Software

Components

As we defined it in Chapter 5, a package of the third kind includes an encapsulated data type and its operators; the string package in the last chapter is a good example. There we have a distinct data type (**VARYING_STRING**) and operators for that type (**Copy**, **Compare**, etc.), all collected into a package ("encapsulated"). In this chapter we look at how to refine this sort of package further, and at some other ways of encapsulating software to create interchangeable software parts: software components.

The first step in encapsulating a data type is to move the type declarations, operator functions, associated procedures, and any local types, variable, constants, and subprograms from a main program environment to a separate package. We have already done this with our string package **Varystr**.

The next step is to decide what parts of the package to *export*, or make available to other packages and programs, and what part we wish to hide—that is, have available for local use only. We do this by separating the specification part of the package from the body. Exportable items go into the specification; things we want to hide away for local use only, we tuck away in the body, where they can be considered hidden as far as the outside world is concerned. This was done in our string package.

Ada provides an additional kind of hiding, or rather *partial* hiding: private types. These types are both visible and available to an external user, but the details of their implementation are kept hidden. We do this by separating the specifications of a package into a *visible* part, and a *private* part.

```
package A is
    --
    type PARTIALLY_HIDDEN is private;
    function Check return PARTIALLY_HIDDEN;
    --
```

```
private
    --
    <type declaration of PARTIALLY_HIDDEN>
    --
end A;
```

The visible part of a specification is the first part. If we take no action to make part of a specification private, all of the specification is visible.

The private part of a specification is everything that occurs after the reserved word **private**. Here in the source code the implementation of the type is spelled out in the usual way; but these details are not made visible or available to the user.

What aspects of a specification do we want to make private, and what do we want to make visible in a package? In general, we want everything to be private except what absolutely has to be known to the user.

In our package **Varystr** we would need to have all the subprogram declarations visible so they could be used by another program. That's the point of the package. We also would need the details of the type **relation** known to the other packages, so that relational tests can be interpreted.

One thing we don't want known is the details of how our varying strings are implemented. We don't want someone playing around with the record components directly, because we may want to change the implementation of the package when we get a better compiler.

We can't hide this string type completely, though, or the user won't be able to declare objects of type **VARYING_STRING**. If the type definition is completely hidden, as far as other packages are concerned, it doesn't exist. The solution is to declare the type in the visible part of the specification as a *private type*, and then to place the full definition of the type in the private part of the package:

```
package Varystr is
    type VARYING_STRING is private;
    --
    <declarations of subprograms using type
    VARYING_STRING parameters>
    --
private

    type VARYING_STRING is
        record
            Size : NATURAL;
            Valu : array( 1..MAX_STRING_SIZE ) of CHARACTER;
        end record;
end Varystr;
```

This allows the type name to be exported but hides the details of the implementation from the user. Even if the user can see the private part by dumping the source file, the compiler will reject references to the components of an object of type VARYING_STRING.

If you prepare a package for sale, you can distribute the visible part of the declaration along with the compiled specification and body, and protect your valuable ideas, as well as keep hacks and sloppy programmers away from where they don't belong.

In kinder words, if a programmer knows too much about the implementation of a data type, he or she can make his or her program dependent on the implementation in such a way that the package body can't be changed without affecting his program.

As they say around SIGAda, the visible part of the specification is the contract between the package and another program using the package. What you see is what you get.

To further encapsulate our varying string type, we can make our constant MAX_STRING_SIZE into a *deferred constant*. (It's actually a named number now, because of the absence of a type name.)[1] A deferred constant is a constant whose name is visible, but whose value is not. We declare a deferred constant like this:

```
<name of constant> : constant <type_mark> ;
```

For example:

```
package Varystr is
--
--
MAX_STRING_SIZE : constant POSITIVE;
--
--
private
--
MAX_STRING_SIZE : constant POSITIVE := 80;
--
end Varystr;
```

What's the use of a deferred constant? In our package Varystr we might change the value of the constant MAX_STRING_SIZE at some time. If we leave the present value visible, as sure as the sun rises some joker is going to hard-code the value 80 into his or her program because he or she doesn't like to type long names. When you change your package, this programmer's program won't work right anymore, and you'll get the blame. There's no justice in the computer world. Making MAX_STRING_SIZE a deferred constant allows the user to use the constant in expressions, but discourages the user from abusing it.

Between the time a private type is declared and the time its full declaration is listed in the private part, it can only be used (1) as a *type__mark* in the declaration of subprogram parameters or of task entries, or (2) as the *type__mark* of deferred constants. It can't be used to create objects, or in representation clauses, or with allocators, or nearly anything else you can do with types in a package specification.

A private type is designed to work with the subprograms defined in its own package. It may be used freely by the package that declares it, but to another package importing the private type the only operations allowed are:

- creating objects of that type;
- comparison of equality and inequality;
- assignment;
- membership tests;
- explicit conversions;
- selecting discriminants if a record type; and
- a very limited number of attribute functions.

Any other operations must be in the form of explicitly declared functions contained in the package that declares the type, such as the **compare** and **concatenate** operations in our package **Varystr**.

Limited Private Types

If we wish to further restrict the allowable operations on a private type, we can use a *limited* declaration when declaring the type:

```
type FILE is limited private;
```

If a type is declared as **limited private**, outside the package where the type is declared we can use some of the same operations as for a private type. We can:

- create objects of that type;
- make membership tests;
- select discriminants of a record type; and
- perform a very limited number of attribute functions.

Note that we can't make comparisons for equality and inequality, and we can't make assignments to an object of **limited private** type.

The creator of the package has complete control over his or her limited private types, so a limited private type is useful where we don't want any user meddling at all. For example, the type **FILE_TYPE** used for I/O is limited private. Within the I/O package type **FILE_TYPE** may be a record with the file name, a system File Control Block, an I/O buffer and associated pointers, a "needs flushing" flag, etc. A user could really mess up file operations if, for example, he or she was allowed to assign to a file object.

Limited private types are used for complete encapsulation of the type. You can be assured that the only practical operations on a limited type are those provided by you in your package.

As another example, suppose we have defined a type to represent *rational numbers*, where fractions are always represented by an integer numerator and an integer denominator:

```
-- Examples of rational numbers
```

$$\frac{1}{3} \qquad \frac{3}{4} \qquad \frac{4}{2} \qquad \frac{7}{8} \qquad \frac{5}{9}$$

Rational numbers are useful in certain operations where exact representations are required. The fraction $\frac{1}{3}$, for example, has no precise decimal representation.

A record for this type could be declared as limited **private**:

```
--
type RATIONAL is limited private;
--
private
      type RATIONAL is
            record
                  Numerator   : INTEGER;
                  Denominator : INTEGER;
            end record;
```

The package declaring this type also would provide operators to act on the type. If we allow the user, say, to perform equality tests using the predefined equality operators, they are going to get inaccurate results if they compare $\frac{-1}{2}$ with $\frac{1}{-2}$, or $\frac{2}{4}$ with $\frac{1}{2}$, which are defined by the rules of rational arithmetic to be equal, but will show as unequal with the predefined equality test.

Don't make the mistake of assuming that **private** and **limited private** types are a boondoggle of the DoD and have to do with National Security. They have legitimate uses in everyday programming.

In a strongly typed language like Ada it is difficult to write subprograms to serve a general purpose, because parameter types need to be known when the subprogram is written. The I/O subprograms are a perfect example. To output enumerated types, and preserve type checking, we would have to have a Put procedure in our library for every possible enumerated type. This is not only impractical, it's impossible.

To deal with the problem, Ada uses *generic units*. A generic unit is a program unit which is all ready except for information specific to the task required of it. When you need it you *instantiate* it with the required information. The instantiation process basically takes the new information provided (usually a type__mark), and clones a new program unit for the particular purpose at hand.

In the case of Put and an enumeration type we supply the generic package Enumeration__IO in Text__IO with the type name of an enumeration type, and out pops a custom package (called and *instance* of the original) suited to the type supplied:

```
package Boolean_IO is new Enumeration_IO( BOOLEAN );
--
--
Boolean_IO.Put( TRUE );
```

Using generic programs is easier than writing them. As most subsets of Ada don't implement generics, you may want to skip the how-to part, or maybe just scan it for tips on instantiation of existing packages. At least one subset plans to include a requirement for fake instantiation of numeric and enumerated I/O, just to make sure your programs will be more portable.

Generic Declarations

A generic declaration consists of the word *generic*, followed by a *generic specification*, followed by a program unit which will be the generic template.[2] The general form is:

```
generic
<generic specification>
<program unit>
```

For example:

```
generic
    type STACK_ITEM is ( <> );
function Pop return STACK_ITEM is
--
```

```
-- template body
--
end Pop;
```

The generic specification contains a listing of the things that may vary when we instantiate the generic unit. The items in this list are called *generic fromal parameters*. In the example above, we are saying that STACK__ITEM is a type which will be defined when the function is instantiated. Until instantiation, we can't determine what type of value the function Pop will return (although we can tell because of the form of the type declaration that it will be a discrete type). The type STACK__ITEM is a generic formal parameter.

Generic formal parameters come in three varieties: They may be *objects*, such as variables or constants; they may be *types*, as the example above is; or they may be *subprograms*. We'll look briefly at all three varieties.

Generic Objects

Objects are declared as generic using exactly the same syntax that a procedure formal parameter uses:

```
generic
        Size : in INTEGER := 40;
package...
```

As with procedures we have modes of in and in out (but not out); we declare a type; we optionally can have a default assignment.

When an object is declared as a generic formal parameter of type in, we can use it throughout the template body as a constant. The actual parameter used when instantiating the generic unit will replace the formal parameter throughout the new instance of the body.

If the actual parameter is a global variable, each time we call the new instance the current value of the actual global variable will be used for whatever computations you have selected.

If the generic formal parameter has a mode of in out, we can actually modify global variables within the new instance.

Generally, generic object parameters are not used very often. It is considered poor practice to have to instantiate a generic package with a global in out variable, as that is contrary to structured programming techniques. Information that might be passed as in objects can often be calculated from the attributes of the other parameters passed to the generic unit.

An example of parameters which might be passed to a generic unit as object parameters would be a terminal size specification passed to a generic display package:

```
generic
     Rows    : POSITIVE := 24;
     Columns : POSITIVE := 80;
package Display is...
```

We might pass information of this type to a generic unit as generic information rather than as subprogram parameters, because an optimizing compiler could then produce faster and more compact code.

The type name used when declaring objects doesn't have to be a predefined type—it also can be a type name you defined that is visible to the generic unit, or a generic parameter, as long as it appears before the object parameter in the generic declaration. We'll see an example in the next section.

Types as Generic Formal Parameters

The most common item passed to a generic unit is a type. As you might expect, since this is the most used feature it is the most complicated. Because code may be generalized to different degrees depending on the job to be accomplished, there are different levels of restrictions on the types of generic unit may be instantiated with. The many forms of generic type parameter passing correspond to how general you can make the code in the body of the generic unit.

For example, a generic procedure to swap the values of two objects can be pretty general. Any type can be used that allows creation of another object of that type, and allows assignments:

```
generic
     type ITEMS is private;
procedure Swap( Item1, Item2 : in out ITEMS ) is
     Temp : ITEMS
begin
     Temp  := Item1;
     Item1 := Item2;
     Item2 := Temp;
end Swap;
```

Conversely, a different procedure, say one that shifts the elements of an array one position left, requires that the type passed be an array of one dimension. We would have to use a generic formal parameter that indicates both to the compiler and the user that only a one-dimensional array is suitable as a parameter:

```
generic
   type ELEMENT is private;
   type SHIFT_ARRAY is array( INTEGER range <> ) of ELEMENT;
procedure Shift_Left( Item : SHIFT_ARRAY ) is ...
```

Notice that we have declared both the component type of the array and the array type itself as generic formal parameters. According to this declaration, the component type can be any type (including another array type), but the array type must be one dimensional. After we declare the formal parameter *type_marks*, we can use these *type_marks* just as we use any other *type_mark* of a similar class.

When we instantiate this procedure, we have to specify both the component type **ELEMENT**, and the array type **SHIFT_ARRAY**. There's no such thing as a "default" type declaration.

Four different forms of the box notation <> are used in limiting allowable types of a formal generic type:

```
(<>)            indicates any discrete type
range <>        indicates any integer type
digits <>       indicates any floating point type
delta  <>       indicates any fixed point type
```

For example:

```
type ANY_DISCRETE is (<>);
type ANY_INTEGER  is range <>;
type ANY_FLOAT    is digits <>;
type ANY_FIXED    is delta <>;
```

"Any discrete type" means integer and enumeration types. Ranges for **FLOAT** and **FIXED** types are inherited from the actual parameter used when instantiating the generic unit.

Some other forms of generic formal type declarations are:

```
type WHATEVER is limited private;
```

We use a **limited private** restriction to match any type at all. The restrictions on using this type, and objects created from this type, within the generic unit, are the same as for any **limited private** type. Essentially all we can do with objects created of type **WHATEVER** is to create them, and pass them as parameters to other procedures that can accept them. We can't assign to them, and we can't test them.

A **private** restriction allows us to create objects, assign to them, and test them for equality and inequality.

```
type ANY_TYPE is private;
```

An access restriction allows us to instantiate the generic unit with any access type that points to objects of type **OTHER_TYPE**. If **OTHER_TYPE** is also a generic formal parameter, we can specify both the access type and the target type in the instantiation:

```
type OTHER_TYPE is private;
type ACCESS_TYPE is access OTHER_TYPE;
```

Array types can be declared using the same form as when declaring them any other place. By using the box notation and mixtures of generic formal parameter types and predefined types, we restrict allowable instantiations to whatever degree is necessary:

```
type BOOL_ARRAY is array(INTEGER range 1..8) of BOOLEAN;
```

This declaration says we can only instantiate an array of Boolean components, with integer indices, and an index range of 1..8.

```
type BOOL2_ARRAY is array(INTEGER range <>) of BOOLEAN;
```

This declaration says we can only instantiate an array of Boolean components, with integer indices, but any range constraint will do.

```
type INDX is (<>);
type BOOL3_ARRAY is array( INDX range <>) of BOOLEAN;
```

With these two declarations, we can first pass a discrete type for **INDX**, which can be any integer or enumeration type. Then we can pass an array of Boolean components, with an index type matching the one instantiated for **INDX**, and any range constraint.

```
type INDX is (<>);
type COMPONENT is private;
type GEN_ARRAY is array( INDX range <>) of COMPONENT;
```

With these three declarations, we first can pass the index type, any discrete type, and then pass the component type, which can be any type. The array passed then can be virtually any one-dimensional array. Once we get inside the generic unit, we can perform operations on the array.

Operations also may be performed on the components, as long as the operations are suitable for a private type (in this case).

There are other variations to restrict arrays, but you've probably gotten the point by now.

Arrays of more than one dimension can also be passed to a generic unit. The formal declaration form involves the same sorts of modifications to a standard array declaration as we made to the single-dimensioned arrays declared above.

Records are not really suited to generics. A record type may be passed as a whole, and assigned as a whole, but operations on components of generic records are very, very inefficient, and you probably shouldn't consider using them.

Subprograms as Generic Formal Parameters

Subprograms may be passed to generic units in a manner analogous to passing types. Take, for example, a generic device controller package, which inputs or outputs a string to a device. If we instantiate the package for a printer we would need a different **Output** function than if we were to instantiate the package for a modem. We can pass different **Tx** and **Rx** procedures to the generic package as formal parameters by using the reserved word **with**:

```
generic
     with procedure Tx( Char : in CHARACTER );
     with procedure Rx( Char : out CHARACTER );
package Device_IO is...
```

The requirements for using subprograms as generic formal parameters are that the actual parameter subprograms used when instantiating the generic unit must match the formal parameters in type, number, position, and also return type if the subprogram is a function. Of course, by using types as previous formal parameters we can generalize the requirements for typing in the formal subprograms.

Predictably, there are various forms to the subprogram formal declaration. We can specify a default subprogram for the formal subprogram, as long as the default subprogram name is visible at the point of instantiation, by using the reserved word **is**:

```
generic
     with procedure Tx( Char : in CHARACTER ) is Put;
     with procedure Rx( Char : out CHARACTER ) is Get;
package Device_IO is...
```

Of course the above declaration would generate a compiler error. Can you see why? What the heck, we'll tell you. You have to remember that the **Get** and **Put** procedures both have default parameters not accounted for in the above declarations.

The last form of a subprogram as a generic formal parameter is the box notated form. If we replace the default name with a *box*, the compiler will use as the default any subprogram visible at the point of instantiation, whose name matches the *formal parameter name* and whose parameter and return types match that of the formal subprogram:

```
generic
     with procedure Tx( char : in CHARACTER ) is <>;
     with procedure Rx( char : out CHARACTER ) is <>;
package Device_IO is...
```

Given the above generic declaration, if this package was to be instantiated with no **Tx** and **Rx** parameters given for the instantiation, the compiler would look at the point of instantiation for visible procedures called **Tx** and **Rx**, that have character parameters.

The box default form of subprogram formal generic parameter is a convenience to the programmer, and is not recommended because of human reader ambiguity problems.

Instantiation and Parameter Passing

Instantiation is a fairly straightforward process, thank goodness. It involves stating a new name for the instance of the generic unit and specifying actual parameters corresponding to the formal parameters of the generic unit. Two methods of parameter passing may be used: positional and named association. The named association is the recommended method. Here is a sample of instantiation of our generic procedure **swap**:

The generic unit, to jog your memory:

```
generic
     type ITEMS is private;
procedure Swap( Item1, Item2 : in out ITEMS ) is
     Temp : ITEMS
begin
     Temp  := Item1;
     Item1 := Item2;
     Item2 := Temp;
end Swap;
```

The instantiations:

```
-- named association
procedure Swap_Int is new Swap( ITEMS => Integer );

-- positional association:
procedure Swap_Vary is new Swap( VARYING_STRING );
```

Now that you have a better grasp of generics you should look at the specifications for the I/O packages of your compiler and see exactly how they can be customized for a particular application.

Conclusion

Packages with self-contained types and operators, generic program units, and separate compilation give software designers in Ada the facilities to set up the production of large-scale programs the way a production engineer handles the manufacturing specifications of a car: a brake rotor can be defined to be stamped out as though by a cookie cutter, whether the cutter is in Detroit or Osaka. That's fine for DoD procurement; but for microcomputer applications developers, the emergence of truly reusable software components, even software parts houses, for Ada programming will be truly revolutionary.

11
Machine Dependencies and Representation Specifications

In this chapter we examine the implementation dependent features of Ada: representation specifications and other features used in systems-level programming.[1]

The designers of a high-level language with systems programming capability face a special problem. They want to keep the language portable by representing data in as abstract a way as possible. Yet they know that if we are going to use the language to control the hardware of a particular machine, we need to get down and root around with that hardware.

While the language can be portable, no reasonable programmer would expect a disk operating system that controls an IBM-PC disk system to run on an Osborne 1 without any sort of modification. A reasonable programmer could, however, expect to use the same high-level source code for the operating system by modifying the way the program represents the disk controllers and other hardware as objects.

Ada handles machine dependencies by separating the physical representation of objects from their logical properties.

The Separation Principle

The separation principle in Ada works like this: First we define an object logically. For example, we declare an object of type **INTEGER**. This declaration defines for both compiler and programmer all the logical properties of the object, the operations that can be performed on it, and the types and subtypes it is compatible with.

Second, the representation of the object in the underlying hardware of the system is defined, either by the compiler or by the programmer. Usually it's the compiler that decides how the object will be represented and where it will be stored. In the case of our integer object, a microcomputer compiler might decide to keep it on the stack, stored in two consecutive bytes, with the low-order byte stored in the lower address and the high-order byte kept in the higher address. This might be a default representation, chosen by the compiler.

Normally the programmer doesn't (and shouldn't) care about how the integer variable is stored. In some cases, however, as in our disk controller example, it is important how our data and objects are represented in the machine, and so Ada provides a mechanism for specifying representation.

Once we are sure that we have correctly represented our disk controller we can concentrate on writing the algorithm to manipulate it. As long as the algorithm is correct, even if the underlying representation has to be changed (as when a new type of controller chip is installed), we have only to change the representation, not the algorithm.

Because Ada is a strongly typed language it is convenient to specify the representation of *types* rather than the objects of those types. The advantage is that the compiler (and you) never have to remember that two objects of the same type have different machine representations. In other words, two objects of the same type need never be converted to be conformable with each other. The disadvantage is that the only convenient way to implement different representations of what seems (logically) the same type is by using derived types and specifying a different representation for each of the derivations. An explicit type conversion function must be used when mixing two or more of these types in a single expression. This reminds the programmer that there may be a representation conversion, with accompanying overhead, between objects of different types. (Type conversion is limited to *conformable* types, that is, types which are logically equivalent. It is not possible to convert, for example, an integer to a record type).

Representation is specified at two levels. The first level is the *pragma*, and the second is the *representation clause*.

Representation Pragmas

A *representation pragma* tells the compiler that we want to change the representation of a type, even though we don't say exactly how.

For example, all compilers are required to recognize the **pack** pragma, although they don't actually have to do anything about it. We can see an example of the **pack** pragma in **Standard**:

```
type STRING is array( POSITIVE range <> ) of CHARACTER;
pragma pack( STRING );
```

pack tells the compiler to use a little space as possible for objects of type string. A microcomputer compiler likely will ignore this pragma, especially as it applies to **STRING**, since at most one bit per character could be saved. A good compiler might not pack strings, but would probably pack arrays of Boolean values, with a saving of seven bits/component. A great compiler would figure you knew what you were doing, and would pack whatever you asked.

You should consider tradeoffs before packing arrays, however. It almost will always be faster to retrieve an unpacked component, as the component does not have to be realigned before processing. The code required for realignment occupies program space, and realignment will take time, at least in a microcomputer system. If a huge array is involved, however, packing might be required to get it into memory. Trial and error are often the best way to decide whether or not to pack arrays and what the time and code space tradeoffs are for your particular machine.

The **optimize** pragma also may affect storage representation. All compilers must accept (again, they need take no action) the pragmas:

```
pragma optimize( TIME );
pragma optimize( SPACE );
```

As might be inferred, the first form above instructs the compiler to consider code speed over code space, while the second instructs it to do the opposite. Speed and space consideration may affect how the compiler handles the representation of data internally.

Representation Clauses

When the exact form of the internal data is important, as when we are constructing bit tables or addressing hardware, we can spell out to the compiler exactly how to store values.

Since the DoD Ada specifications give the compiler writer some latitude in how far to go along with a representation clause (they say, basically, "Do it if it's feasible", and don't define "feasible"), and because representation clauses seem to be among the last things added to a subset compiler, we will not delve too deeply into them.

A full Ada compiler is required to have a manual with an Appendix F (even if there aren't any other appendices) that spells out the implementation dependencies of the compiler. This is where specific information about representation will be found, as opposed to general information of the kind presented here. We will present a brief overview of representation, and leave it at that, as even a validated Ada compiler is not required to implement any of the following features.

A representation clause may be applied to a type or to a *first named subtype*, a type declared with anonymous or universal ranges. An example of a first named subtype:

```
type BYTES is range 0..255;
```

When a type or a first named subtype is defined, any representations clauses desired must follow it in the same declaration section. For the sake of the human reader it should appear immediately after the type declaration in the text. The same applies to an object for which you specify an address clause.

There are certain situations which imply that the representation of a type has already been determined. For example, an object of a certain type may have already appeared in the assignment expression of a constant. This is called a *forcing occurrence*. After a forcing occurrence of a type, you may no longer apply a representation clause to it. A similar restriction applies to address clauses of objects.

Length Clause

A length specification is used to control the amount of storage allocated to an object of a particular type. The general form of the specification is:

```
for <attribute> use <simple_expression>;
```

<attribute> is an attribute function, for which the prefix is a type name or first named subtype. The only allowed postfixes are size, storage_size, and small.

<simple_expression> is of a numeric type and is evaluated during elaboration of the length clause (a simple expression contains no function calls). For example:

```
Type BYTES is range 0..255;
for BYTE'size use 8;
```

The size specification <simple_expression> must be static. The value specifies the maximum number of bits to use when representing an object of that type. This size must be at least large enough to hold any possible value of the type.

The storage_size attribute is used with access types to limit the amount of storage allocated for any and all objects of that access type. <simple_expression> need not be static. storage_size also may be used with a task type to determine the amount of storage space (excluding code) used when a task is activated. This space includes any internal overhead required for memory management, so the actual number of objects that can be stored will vary from compiler to compiler.

The small attribute is used only with a first named subtype of a fixed-point type. The simple static expression must evaluate to a real type and cannot be greater than the delta of the type. The expression value specifies to the compiler how to represent the numbers of this type. The small clause can be used to specify extra *guard* bits when representing fixed-point numbers, to reduce loss of precision due to rounding when dividing or multiplying.

The size specification is allowed for access types, task types, or fixed-point types, even if another length clause has been or will be given.

We can specify the internal codes used to represent enumeration literals by using a form similar to an aggregate assignment. For example:

```
type DISK_COMMANDS is( CLEAR, STEP_IN, STEP_OUT, READ, WRITE );
for DISK_COMMANDS'size use 8;
for DISK_COMMANDS use ( CLEAR    => 2#00000001#,
                        STEP_IN  => 2#00000010#,
                        STEP_OUT => 2#00000100#,
                        READ     => 2#00001000#,
                        WRITE    => 2#00010000# );
```

The internal codes we supply must be integers. In addition we must declare them in the same order as they appear in the type declaration, and they must be in ascending numeric order.

Note that they need not be contiguous. The Ada manual specifies that indexing, the **pred**, **succ**, and **pos** attributes, case statements, and iteration using noncontiguous representation act as they would if the representation were contiguous, even if it isn't. That's for the sake of consistency. In practice, given the extra overhead involved in implementing this consistent action (the overhead is in the features using noncontiguous types where a contiguous type might be better suited, such as array indexing and loops, not in the actual assignment of codes), you are better off not doing it unless absolutely required to by the application.

When we store an entity of type **DISK_COMMANDS**, as defined above, at a memory location, we are actually writing the bit pattern to the memory location. Note that we have used a **size** representation to ensure an 8-bit storage format.

Only one enumeration map may be applied to any one enumeration type.

Record Representation Clauses

Records may have the order and bit alignment of their individual components, including any discriminants, partially or completely specified. In addition the address alignment of the record also may be specified.

The form of a record representation clause is:

```
for <type_name> use
    record <alignment_clause>
        <component_clause>
        --
    end record;
```

The <alignment_clause> is optional; it forces the compiler to store objects of this type on addresses which are multiples of the <alignment_clause> expression. An alignment clause looks like this:

```
at mod <simple_expression>;
at mod 4;
```

The <component_clause> looks like this:

```
<component_name> at <offset> range <bit_range>;
Index_Hole at 0 range 0..0;
```

The <component_name> is the name of one of the record components. <offset> is the offset in storage units from the start of the record. <bit_range> is the bit positions within the storage unit to use for the component, in dot-dot notation.

Storage units are implementation-defined—in a microcomputer they usually will be eight, but sometimes 16, bits. The first storage unit of a record is numbered zero.

Bit numbering is also implementation defined. Either the least or the most significant bit will be bit zero.

You may specify at most one component clause per component and you need not specify all components if you don't want to ("components" include any discriminants).

Components of a particular form of a record can't overlap each other. The only time overlap is allowed is with variant records, and then overlap can't occur for any two components of the same variant.

The implementation will specify whether a single component can overlap two or more storage units.

An example of where record representation might be used is a disk controller:

```
type DISK_CONTROLLER_OUTPUT is
    record
            Index_Hole : BOOLEAN;
            Lost_Data  : BOOLEAN;
            CRC_Error  : BOOLEAN;
            Ready      : BOOLEAN;
            Data       : BYTE;
    end record;

for DISK_CONTROLLER_OUTPUT use
    record at mod 2;
            Index_Hole at 0  range 0..0;
            Lost_Data  at 0  range 2..2;
            CRC_Error  at 0  range 3..3;
            Ready      at 0  range 5..5;
            Data       at 1  range 0..7;
    end record;
```

The record **DISK_CONTROLLER_OUTPUT** describes the readable portions of a disk controller chip. Two 8-bit memory locations are involved, with the first being the status port and the second being the data port. The design of the chip makes it certain that the status port will always be an even address, while the data port is always the next odd address. We can force this alignment on our record with the alignment clause: **record at mod 2**.

We specify that **Index_Hole** is bit 0 (**range 0..0**) of the first storage unit (**at 0**), and so on for the other Boolean flags. The data port is specified as being bits 0 thru 7 (**range 0..7**) of the second storage unit (**at 1**).

Only one record representation map may be used for any one type.

Address Clauses

We use an address clause when we need to align an object with a specific machine address. If we declared an object of type **DISK_CONTROLLER_OUTPUT** and wanted to match that object to the actual address of the disk controller, we would declare the object and then use a clause of the following format:

```
for <name> use at <simple_expression>;
```

where <name> is the name of the object and <simple_expression> is of type **ADDRESS** (implementation defined) specifying the address to use. We could place a variable like this:

```
WX1770 : DISK_CONTROLLER_OUTPUT;
for WX1770 use at 16#2400#;
```

Only one address clause may be applied to any one object.

In-line Assembler Code

Inclusion of assembler code inline according to the Ada standards is so cumbersome that you probably will try to avoid doing it. This inconvenience appears to be deliberate on the part of the Ada design team. They were well aware of the pitfalls of allowing in-line assembler code with compiler-generated code, especially when the aggregate code is intended to be heavily optimized. They were, however, also aware of the need to add occasional assembly instructions for a particular machine or operating system. The decision was to make in-line assembler allowable, but not easy.

The subset compilers usually have a facility for including assembler in a nonstandard fashion. The standard way is implementation dependent as to mnemonics and so forth, so consult your system manual.

Inter-language Interface

A compiler may optionally have an **interface** pragma that can call in object code from other language libraries, such as FORTRAN libraries, at link time. The details are messy enough to implement in a compiler that you probably won't see this feature except on the largest mainframes.

Unchecked Conversion

At times it is necessary to convert between two normally incompatible types. The classic example is when writing your own memory manager. An address maintained as an integer in your memory management scheme can't be assigned to an access type under the rules of Ada.

In the case where a value must be converted between incompatible types, Ada provides a generic function called **Unchecked_Conversion**. This function must be **with**ed and then instantiated for each conversion. The conversion function simply transfers an uninterpreted bit pattern from one type object to another. The requirement for **with**ing and instantiating is to discourage you from indiscriminate use of this function.

Suppose we have two types, called **TYPE1** and **TYPE2**, which are incompatible. If we have to convert from **TYPE1** to **TYPE2** the process goes like this:

```
with Unchecked_Conversion;
--
-- -- we instantiate the function 'convert'
function Type1_to_Type2 is new
          Unchecked_Conversion( Source => TYPE1,
                              ( Target => TYPE2 );
--
--
Object_Of_Type2 := Type1_To_Type2( Object_Of_Type1 );
```

It is the programmer's responsibility that converted values fit physically and logically into the target type.

You may recall when we discussed access types that, in practice, deallocation of objects created by allocators takes place when the scope of the type declaration bound to that allocation expires. We aren't changing the story now, but consider that usually we declare these types either as a global type or **with** a package containing the type declaration. In practice, the scope of access types hardly ever expires. This means that we can't count on the system's garbage collection mechanism to reclaim memory no longer needed by the access types.

Ada provides a method for deallocating access objects when convenient, similar to C's **free** function. The generic procedure **Unchecked_Deallocation** may be **with**ed and instantiated in a manner similar to that for **Unchecked_Conversion**.[2]

The danger to using this procedure is that Ada will not check for other access pointers that point to the object being deallocated, which can leave pointers pointing at garbage or erroneous data. Such is life in the big city.

The procedure for instantiating the unchecked deallocation of an object of type **OBJECT_TYPE**, pointed to by an access type of **POINTER_TYPE** is this:

```
with Unchecked_Deallocation;
--
procedure Free is new
    Unchecked_Deallocation( OBJECT_TYPE, POINTER_TYPE );
--
```

When we wish to deallocate an object we can call **Free** with an access type parameter which points to that object:

```
with Unchecked_Deallocation;
--
type SECTOR_BUFFER is array( INTEGER range 1..128 ) of CHARACTER
type BUFFER_POINTER is access SECTOR_BUFFER;
Ptr : BUFFER_POINTER := new SECTOR_BUFFER;
--
procedure Free is new Unchecked_Deallocation( SECTOR_BUFFER,
                    BUFFER_POINTER );
--
--
Free( Ptr );
```

After executing the above **Free** procedure, Ptr will have a value of null. If Ptr was already null, no action would have been taken. If Ptr was not null when Free was called, the memory used by the object pointed to by Ptr would have been assigned back to the memory manager for reuse, and would no longer be available as an object of type **SECTOR_BUFFER**.

In this chapter we have discussed several machine specific topics, and end-run around Ada's type checking, and the release of storage no longer required. In most cases you as an Ada programmer won't need to use these features, since the compiler normally manages them for you. Look twice at your needs before using these features.

12
Programming Techniques for Micros

In this chapter we will try to reduce our barrage of raw information and present some applications of what you have learned in the earlier chapters.

Learning Ada as a second or third programming language is like learning a second or third spoken language: Eventually, you reach the stage where you realize that a literal translation from one to another doesn't work very well. To write elegantly in any language requires that you be able to think in that language.

When approaching a problem from the standpoint of BASIC, you generally take a "Start coding at line 10, and plug the holes as I go" approach to problem solving. When using C, you take a micro-efficient approach, where you as the programmer essentially specify the optimization path by liberal use of nested assignments and C's rich operator set. If writing in Pascal you spend a lot of time trying to circumvent the language restrictions.

When approaching a problem from the Ada standpoint, other considerations dominate. What we will do in this chapter is describe and demonstrate some of the approaches to problems from the Ada angle.

Optimization

Ada was designed for human readability. It doesn't allow assignments nested in expression; it doesn't have pointer arithmetic, or even bitwise logical operators (e.g., `integer XOR integer` returns `integer`). These features are useful if we don't plan on using an efficient optimizing compiler. The intent of Ada's language structure is to make it easy for a person to read programs. Efficient object code is left up to heavy-duty optimizing compilers.

The effect is to relieve the programmer of the responsibility for code micro-efficiency, allowing him to concentrate on code macro-efficiency.

Of course, this only works out right if we have that heavy-duty optimizer cranking out well-optimized code. In the case of microcomputer compilers the state of the art when this book was written was compilers that didn't even remove unreachable code, let alone do peephole optimization. An optimizer that produces indirectly derived code (code rearranged for the same effect, only more efficiently) wasn't even on the horizon.

What this means for the microcomputer programmer is that for now, no matter what you do, your Ada program isn't going to be ultra-fast. That's not to say it will run as slow as a BASIC equivalent, but it won't be faster than an equivalent C program.

Eventually we will have optimizers that will run on microcomputers, and Ada programs then will probably run as fast as programs produced by good C compilers. They may be even faster, because Ada allows the programmer to provide the compiler with information that languages like C and BASIC do not.

In the interim, grit your teeth, write using good Ada style, and don't try to circumvent the language. Take heart: A better day is coming for Ada programmers.

An Ada Approach to a Problem

As an example of the sort of rethinking needed when programming in Ada, especially when dealing with data representations inherited from other languages, consider the WordStar document file. A WordStar document mode file is a stream of characters comprising the document. WordStar indicates formatting information by setting the high bit of certain characters.

For example, a *soft return* is a return/linefeed combination within a paragraph inserted by WordStar when doing word wraps. Reformatting the paragraph may cause the soft return to move elsewhere, while a hard return, one entered by the typist, is not movable. The high bit on the soft return tells WordStar that it's okay to move it if necessary.

Certain other conditions cause the high bit of a character to be set in WordStar. Spaces inserted for justifying a line are marked by raising the high bit of the last character in each word.

Now suppose we want to write an Ada utility to act on a WordStar text file. Let's say we decide that we want to strip the soft spaces and soft returns from the file. We don't want to just set the high bits off, as that will leave the flagged characters where they are, looking just like other characters entered by the user. We'll have to look at each character with a high bit set and decide whether to discard the character, or strip the high bit and pass the character along to the output file.

In a systems language like C, or a teaching language like BASIC, neither of which has any interest in type checking, we read the characters as eight bit values and can use a bitwise **AND** to test for the high bit, just as in assembler.

In Ada this approach just won't fly. In the first place, the first time you try to stuff a flagged character into a type **CHARACTER** variable you'll get a constraint error because the ordinal value will be outside the range of the ASCII character set.

Then if you decide to use an 8-bit numeric type (the type **BYTE** usually provided in microcomputer environments) to read the characters, you'll discover that Ada doesn't have the bitwise **AND** operator. An involved relational test and subtraction process will be involved to compute the character value.

The answer to these problems is to rethink the approach. What exactly are we looking at in a WordStar file? It's a series of characters, each of which has a 1-bit flag distinguishing whether it has formatting significance, or whether it's a garden variety character. In Ada we can use a representation that reflects the organization of the data:

```
type WORDSTAR_CHAR is
    record
            Format : BOOLEAN;
            Value  : CHARACTER;
    end record;
```

We would use a *representation specification* to force the organization of this record into a 1-byte space ("storage unit"). Now we can write our decision algorithm this way:

```
Input_Char : WORDSTAR_CHAR;

if Input_Char.Format then
    case Input_Char.Value of
            ASCII.CR  =>    Reject;
                            Reject_Following_Linefeed;
            ' '       =>    Reject;
            others    =>    Accept;
    end case;
else
    Accept;
end if;
```

Unfortunately, representation specifications are among the last features to appear in an Ada subset. Even so we should write as much of our code as possible using Ada techniques, so in the future we can limit the damage caused by moving to a new system. We could front-end the decision algorithm like this:

```
Input_Value : BYTE -- implementation's "byte"
package Byte_IO is new Sequential_IO( element => BYTE );
--
    Get( Input Value );
```

```
if Input_Value > 16#7F# then
     Input_Char.Format := TRUE;
     Input_Char.Value := CHARACTER'val(Input_Value-128);
else
     Input_char.Format := FALSE;
     Input_char.Value := CHARACTER'val(Input_Value);
end if;
```

Another Ada Approach

A related exercise in rethinking is hardware control. Take a communications program as an example.

Nearly all communications programs for microcomputers require direct access to the machine hardware, because micro operating systems rarely provide support for modems.

Modem status and control ports can be thought of as arrays of Boolean flags. We could write a record to represent the Intel 8251A UART's readable ports like like this:

```
type INTEL_8251_READ is
    record
         Data_Set_Ready      : BOOLEAN;
         Sync_Detect         : BOOLEAN;
         Framing_Error       : BOOLEAN;
         Overrun_Error       : BOOLEAN;
         Parity_Error        : BOOLEAN;
         Transmitter_Empty   : BOOLEAN;
         Receiver_Ready      : BOOLEAN;
         Transmitter_Ready   : BOOLEAN;

         RX_Port             : BYTE;
    end record;
```

If we were ambitious we would use a variant record with discriminants of **READ** and **WRITE**, to represent not only the status and received data ports as above, but also the control and transmitted data ports.

We still need to use a representation specification to align the Boolean values properly against the actual bit pattern of the ports. When we create the object of type **INTEL_8251_READ** we can use a representation address specification to place the object at a given memory location.

```
for INTEL_8251_READ use
     record at mod 2              -- normal alignment
          Data_Set_Ready         at 0 range 1..1;
```

```
      Sync_Detect              at 0 range 2..2;
      Framing_Error            at 0 range 3..3;
      Overrun_Error            at 0 range 4..4;
      Parity_Error             at 0 range 5..5;
      Transmitter_Empty        at 0 range 6..6;
      Receiver_Ready           at 0 range 7..7;
      Transmitter_Ready        at 0 range 8..8;

      RX_Port                  at 1 range 1..8;
end record;
```

This works fine if we have both representation specifications and memory mapped I/O. Many computers have port mapped I/O and in these cases you will have to use assembly language to interface with the ports. The assembly language portion can either stuff values directly into the proper positions of an object of type **INTEL_8251_READ**, or return an object of that type. Alternatively the complier may have a built-in **In_Port** subprogram for target machines that allow port mapping.

A experienced assembly language programmer is going to wonder why we go to all the fuss in the first place. A type declaration, followed by a record representation specification, giving the address of the object—it's a lot of typing just to look at **TxRDY** and **RxRDY** in a measly 8251. Well, aside from the fact that Ada requires it, there's one good reason for it: documentation.

After you're done writing the code specifications for the 8251, you won't have to look back at the *Intel Component Data Catalog*—the information is all in the code. The bit layout, the names—all are executable program stuff. If you didn't write it out as type declarations, you'd have to write it all as comments, or risk the curses of subsequent programmers who lent their copy of the *Intel CDC* to Bob, and forgot to get it back.

As long as you're thinking Ada, you can go one step further and put all the 8251 information into a package. The package could even automatically initialize the chip, if you wish—remember the initialization code part of packages?

It could be very convenient just to put

```
with Uart8251; use Uart8251;
```

at the head of a program, and in one bang have the pins defined as nice Boolean values, the port automatically initialized, and a couple of procedures to test status and to transmit and receive. It sure beats digging through your old XMODEM.ASM files looking for the place you put those equates—or did you use hex constants in that one? And where did you put those comments? Was it XMODEM301 or XMODEM303? If this strikes a distant chord, it's time to start thinking in Ada.

While many problems suggest Ada-style solutions of the sort outlined above, many others will submit to the standard methods used in any high-level language (BASIC implicitly excluded here). A good example is the obligatory binary tree, always expounded upon in this kind of book.

Binary Tree Structure

A binary tree is a simple method of sorting and maintaining information in a linked list. While not always easy to grasp at first glance, once the principle of binary tree structure is understood you can write simple, elegant code to manage trees.

The basic requirements for a binary tree *node* is a piece of information to use as the *sorting key*, and two pointers, pointing to branches of the tree which lead to keys that have a lower and higher value than the value of the key at the current node.

Binary trees have a *root*, which represents the base of the tree, or the starting position in the linked list.

Consider, if you will, a program which prints word frequency in a text file. In other words, how many times every distinct word appears in a document, as an analog to the Kernighan and Ritchie tree functions presented in *The C Programming Language*.

We can organize a *node* of the required tree like this:

```
type NODE;

type NODE_POINTER is access NODE;
type STR_POINTER  is access STRING;

type NODE is
    record
            Lower      : NODE_POINTER;      -- := null;
            Higher     : NODE_POINTER;      -- := null;
            Key_Word   : STR_POINTER;
            Count      : POSITIVE := 1;
    end record;
```

We use an *incomplete type declaration* (**type NODE;**) because we need a recursive type definition—we have to declare an access type for **NODE** before we declare type **NODE**. Binary trees can be marvels of recursion.

The type **NODE_POINTER** will be used as our link pointers to lower and higher nodes of the tree.

We use a string pointer to refer to the word associated with each node to reduce storage requirements. We will expect to have each word from a document presented as a **VARYING_STRING**, which will not be an efficient storage mechanism (it requires about 85 bytes per string if you are using the package as defined in Chapter 9). We will allocate an instrinsic string for each unique word in our document, and use an access type to **STRING** to keep track of the allocation.

The last component of the record is **Count**, a natural variable to track the count of each word.

Note that we commented out initialization of the **NODE_POINTER**s in our record. A full Ada compiler will assure that access types are initialized to **null**—a subset may not. Check you compiler, and if access types are not initialized be sure that you explicitly set all access types to **null** as they are created. The success of the following functions and procedures depends on it.

The same goes for the initialization of **Count**. If your compiler won't initialize record components, be sure to set **Count** to 1 as each node is allocated.

Now for the algorithm. We'll assume a function **Get_Word** exists which will return the next word in the input stream as a **VARYING_STRING**. We'll need a function to insert the word into the binary tree if the word is not already present there, or to increment **Count** if it is:

```
function Load_Tree( Word      : STRING;
                    This_Node : NODE_POINTER; )
                                        return NODE_POINTER is
begin
    if This_Node = null then
        -- we have to add a new node - 'word' not in tree.
        This_Node := new NODE;
        This_Node.all.Key_Word := new STRING( 1..Word'length )
        This_Node.all.Key_Word := Word;
    elsif Word > This_Node.Key_Word then
        -- we have to look higher for 'word'.
        This_Node.all.Higher :=
         Load_Tree( Word, This_Node.all.Higher );
    elsif Word < This_Node.all.Key_Word then
        -- we have to look lower for 'word'.
        This_Node.all.Lower :=
         Load_Tree( Word, This_Node.all.Lower );
    else -- 'word' must be in this node.
        This_Node.all.Count := This_Node.all.Count + 1;
    end if;
    return This_Node;
end Load_Tree;
```

We load or update the tree by calling **Load__Tree**:

```
with Varystr;
Root     : NODE_POINTER;    -- := null;
Word_In : Varystr.VARYING_STRING;
--
-- probably a loop structure starts here

    Get_Word( Word_In );
    Root := Load_Tree( Varystr.Uppercase( Word_In ), Root );

-- end loop structure
```

The **Load__Tree** function works like this: A word is presented, along with the value of **Root**, to **Load__Tree**. The first time, **Root** will equal **null**, and so a node will be created and **Word** will be assigned to a new **STRING** allocated in the minimum space required for **Word**. The balance of the conditional will be bypassed and the access value (pointer) for the new node will be returned and assigned to **Root**.

The next time we call **Load__Tree** we may have a different word. The initial test for **null** will be false, as **Root** has the pointer to the first node created. We then pass to the second and third tests, where the current word is checked for its relation to the word associated with the current node. If the new word is less than the word at the current node, we look lower in the tree, and if it's greater than, we look higher.

Notice that we assign the **Higher** and **Lower** pointers each time we look down the tree. This is so that in case a new mode is created, we can keep track of it and its relation to the other nodes of the tree.

Should all of our tests fail the value in **Word** must be equal to the word associated with the current node, and so we increment the word count. We used our **Varystr** function **Uppercase** to generate the words, to remove case sensitivity.

If this is unclear, see Figures 12-1, 12-2, and 12-3 for examples of different words and how they would load. Note that the order of loading is important—a random load makes a better tree. Follow the program for each word as it's added, and remember that the load function is recursive.

After loading the tree we can print it with this procedure:

```
procedure Print_Tree( This_Node : NODE_POINTER ) is
begin
    if This_Node.all.Lower /= null then
        Print_Tree( This_Node.all.Lower );
    end if;
```

Words loaded in this order:

Apple Baker Charlie Delta Echo Foxtrot Golf Hotel India

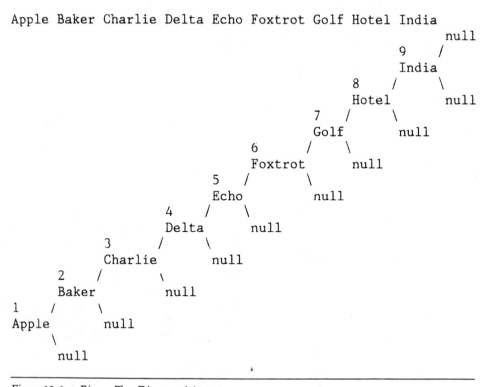

Figure 12-1. Binary Tree Diagram (1)

```
Put( This_Node.all.Key_Word );
Put( "      " );
Put( This_Node.all.Count );
New_Line;

if This_Node.all.Higher /= null then
    Print_Tree( This_Node.all.Higher );
end if;
end Print_Tree;
```

Words loaded in this order:

Echo Charlie Golf India Hotel Foxtrot Baker Apple Delta

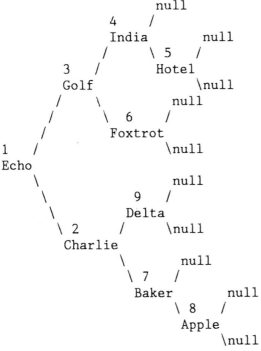

Figure 12-2. Binary Tree Diagram (2)

This procedure prints all of the words in the tree, in alphabetical order, and the frequency of each word. Follow the diagrams of Figures 12-1, 12-2, and 12-3 and see how this works.

Binary tree functions are not the most efficient way to maintain data, but they are easy and reliable. The basic tree load and print functions can be easily modified to do other things, such as count how many different words appear in our tree:

```
function Count_Tree( This_Node : NODE_POINTER;
                     Count     : NATURAL )
                                         return NATURAL is
    Local_Count : NATURAL := Count;
begin
```

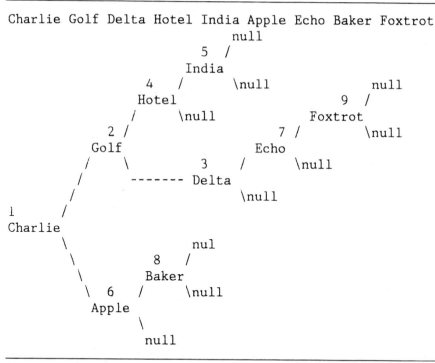

Charlie Golf Delta Hotel India Apple Echo Baker Foxtrot

Figure 12-3. Binary Tree Diagram (3)

```
        if This_Node.all.Lower /= null then
            Local_Count :=
                Count_Tree( This_Node.all.Lower, Local_Count );
        end if;

        Local_Count := Local_Count + 1;

        if This_Node.all.Higher /= null then
            Local_Count :=
                Count_Tree( This_Node.all.Higher, Local_Count );
        end if;
        return Local_Count;
    end Count_Tree;
--
-- call like this:
--
    Put( Count_Tree( Root, 0 ) );
```

Once the techniques are mastered you can use the basic algorithms to carry other information. The node requires that we have a sorting key and two pointers included, but any other information can be taken along, too. For example, a personal directory program might use a record like this:

```
type NODE;

type NODE_POINTER is access NODE;

type NODE is
    record
        Lower           : NODE_POINTER;      -- := null;
        Higher          : NODE_POINTER;      -- := null;
        Name            : Varystr.VARYING_STRING;
        Address         : Varystr.VARYING_STRING;
        City_State_Zip  : Varystr.VARYING_STRING;
        Phone           : Varystr.VARYING_STRING;
    end record;
```

A program using a record like this would likely have a subprogram to look up a given name, and return either a null to indicate that the target name does not appear in the tree, or an access value to the node:

```
function Lookup( Target     : Varystr.VARYING_STRING;
                 This_Node   : NODE_POINTER; )
            return NODE_POINTER is
begin
    -- assumes ">" and "<" overloaded for varying_string!
    if This_Node = null then
        return null;
    elsif Target > This_Node.all.Name then
        return Lookup( Target, This_Node.all.Higher );
    elsif Target < This_Node.all.Name then
        return Lookup( Target, This_Node.all.lower );
    else
        return This_Node;
    end if;
end Lookup;
```

As a last look at binary tree functions we will look at the deallocation of a binary tree.

According to the Ada *Manual*, objects created as access objects must be available as long as they are accessible in some manner. If we lose track of Root, for example, the above trees become inaccessible and the memory manager could reclaim any storage used by the tree.

Ada doesn't guarantee the reclamation ("garbage collection"), though, and in practice if reclamation is performed, it is done when the scope of the type declaration is finished (not when the scope of the procedures that create the objects is finished).

If we want to explicitly deallocate a binary tree we can run through the tree, "pruning" it, starting at the bottom levels, by using **Unchecked_Deallocation**. Here is an example of this deallocation:

```
    procedure Prune is new Unchecked_Deallocation(
     NODE, NODE_POINTER );
    --
    --
    procedure Chop_Tree( This_Node : NODE_POINTER );
    begin
        if This_Node.all.Lower /= null then
            Chop_Tree( This_Node.all.Lower );
        end if;

        if This_Node.all.Higher /= null then
            Chop_Tree( This_Node.all.Higher );
        end if;

        Prune( This_Node );
    end Chop_Tree;
    --
--  call this procedure like this:
--   Chop_Tree( Root );
```

Conclusion

In this chapter we looked at some of the techniques used in programming micros. These style guidelines aren't comprehensive, of course, but they should give you an idea of what the Ada "way" is.

Using Ada to rewrite assembly language or BASIC programs without examining some of the fundamental differences in approaching a problem will leave you frustrated and convinced that Ada is just another flash-in-the-pan, while starting a problem from the Ada point of view will allow you to write powerful, elegant programs.

13
Multitasking

Multitasking, Ada's special contribution to embedded computer systems, is possibly its most powerful feature. Like generics, it is generally among the last features to be added to a compiler on its way to validation, especially in the microprocessor environment.

One reason Ada compilers validated under the CP/M and MS-DOS operating systems have been slow to appear is that the priority of Ada's concurrent tasks must be specifiable by the programmer. CP/M and MS-DOS don't have any facility for the kind of resource management and scheduling required for tasking applications (although MP/M and concurrent versions of CP/M and MS-DOS may have some promise).[1]

Some of the compiler builders are getting around this by writing proprietary operating systems to provide an Ada environment. Telesoft had a compiler for the IBM-PC nearing validation at the time this book was written, which runs under the Telesoft OS for the IBM.

The Task Process

Like several other features of Ada, tasking presents a whole new set of terms and concepts. Let's start by getting a general view of the task process.

A task is a process that may run concurrently with other processes. Any main program is implicitly a type of task, which is called into execution by the operating environment, which itself keeps operating. The main program may have other explicit tasks embedded within it.

A task is not a compilable unit in Ada, with the special-case exception of the main program. A task must be a part of another program unit and it is placed in the other unit's declarative part. We can place a task inside a block, a subprogram body, a package body, or even another task body's declaration part. The parent of a task is the unit within which a task is declared.

Like other program units, tasks can be textually divided into two parts: specification and a body. The specification of a task defines the interface between the task and the rest of the program. The body of a task defines the actions the task will take.

Tasks communicate with other units via *entries*. An entry looks just like a procedure call, with parameters and parameter modes. The entries are used to synchronize tasks with other tasks and the main program. Entry declarations are basically the only things allowed in a task specification, because entries are the only things a task can export. A task specification might look like this:

```
task Keyscan is
     entry Next_Char( Char : out CHARACTER );
end Keyscan;
```

This task might manage a type-ahead buffer. The entry **Next_Char** could be called by the main program to retrieve characters typed by the operator.

This type of task is called a *server* task because it is called by other units, either other tasks or the main program, and it "services" these calls. Server tasks themselves don't call other tasks.

Another type of task is the *customer* task. A customer task has no visible means of communication (no entries). A customer task typically calls other tasks. A main program can be considered a customer task.

An intermediate sort of task, the *messenger* task, calls other tasks and can itself be called.

Tasks have properties somewhat like data strucutures, and are in fact handled very much like records. A task specification can be converted into a *task type* declaration and we can declare task objects using this declaration, just as we can declare records using a record **type_mark**. When we refer to task entries we use dot notation, with the name of the task, a dot, and the entry name, just as in our references to record components:

```
Keyscan.Next_Char( Any_Char_Var );
```

You can envision a task as a "smart record", which can internally compute and recompute values for its components, as well as do jobs for you on the side while you're doing something else.

Tasking really shines in embedded systems, where we may have several processors sharing resources. One or more task could be assigned to each processor by the Ada environment, and all can communicate and keep synchronized by *entry* calls to each other. Many real-time applications use multiple processors. Consider the arcade video game, which may use several processors, all sharing display memory and user controls, and synchronizing between screen updates.

Writing assembly language code for multitasking or distributed processing environments can be a real experience. Using Ada, all the details of scheduling and communication are hidden by the language.

Even applications software can benefit from multitasking. As an example of server tasks and customer tasks in a microcomputer multitasking system, consider the problem of a huge data sorting operation being carried on by the main program (the parent task). If a sort is written in C or any other nontasking high-level language, the system is essentially dedicated to the sorting operation for its duration, and the only control on your computer that would respond during the sort is the reset button.

With Ada you could write a customer task to look at incoming characters from the modem, and a customer task to look at the keyboard. The modem task would call a server to display incoming characters on the screen and the keyboard task would call a server task to send keyboard characters to the modem. We could activate these tasks at the start of our monster sort routine and use our computer as a terminal while the data were being sorted.

Tasks are activated at the end of the declarative part of the unit in which their bodies are elaborated. If we embed our terminal emulator tasks in the declarative part of our sorting routine, they will automatically become active when the sorting routine is elaborated.

Once tasks start running, the parent has to hang around until all the tasks are either terminated or ready to terminate. In our terminal example running on top of the sort routine, the sort routine would have to wait until the terminal tasks all were terminated before it could disappear. Termination can be handled either in the parent or in the task.

A task can have more than one other task attempting to call it at a time. The call to a task is called a *rendezvous*. If a task is not ready, or is engaged in another rendezvous, a call is placed into a task *queue*, on a first-come, first-serve basis. Each entry to each task has its own queue associated with it.

If we have a given task that may be used more than once, we can declare the task specification as a *task type*, and then use this task type to declare task objects where we need them. For example, we might have a dedicated printer keeping a log. Obviously only one task can output to the printer at a time. If several portions of a system are competing for the printer, we don't want the system hung up while waiting for the printer resource to become available. We could declare the task type like this:

```
task type LOG_DRIVER is
    entry Put( Message : in STRING );
    entry Verify;
end LOG_DRIVER;
```

Tasks of this type then would be declared in the declaration part of procedures or packages that need to be logged:

```
Log_This_Job : LOG_DRIVER;
```

The task would activate on elaboration and wait for the Put entry to be made. We could do this at the head of the package:

```
Log_This_Job( "Scanning Core Coolant Sensors" );
```

This task includes a Verify entry, to be sure that the log message is recorded before going on. We could call the Verify entry at the end of the procedure or package to be sure that the message was delivered:

```
Log_This_Job.Verify;
```

By calling the **Put** entry at the top of the package, and the **Verify** entry at the bottom, the parent can continue processing (in this case, checking the core cooling system) while the server task **Log__This__Job** is waiting for the printer. The parent could not continue until the message was logged. (Technically, in this case the **Verify** entry is superfluous because of a rule stating that the parent can't terminate until all child tasks terminate. However, if the task object isn't declared in the caller's declaration section, the **Verify** entry is needed. It's a minor point, but it's just the sort of thing Ada "language lawyers" love to see in print.)

When declaring a task type we still need a body for the task. The body for a task type is exactly the same as for an anonymous type task. The name of the task body is the same as the task *type__mark*.

Since tasks are treated almost as data types in Ada (*limited private* types, to be exact), we can have arrays of tasks (families of tasks); we can have arrays of entries to a particular task (families of entries); and we can have access types to task types, allocate tasks, and even pass tasks as subprogram parameters. Most of these features are beyond the scope of this book, not because of the mechanics of using tasks like this, but because of the applications which use tasks in these fashions.

Task Bodies

Associated with every task specification or task type is a task body. A task body is similar to a procedure body: it has a declaration, a sequence of statements, and an optional exception handler. At the point where the task is elaborated the declaration is elaborated, and then the sequence of statements starts executing. When the execution of the statements reaches the end of the body, the task terminates.

A whole group of new and redefined statements are used for tasks. The most important is the *accept* structure.

An **accept** statement is used to synchronize the task with a caller and pass any information required. When the task encounters an **accept** statement it will wait until the matching entry call is made. We need at least one **accept** statement for each entry. The form of an **accept** statement is:

```
accept <entry name> do
--
--
end <entry name>;
```

The accept structure for our Keyscan task looks like this:

```
task Keyscan is
    entry Next_Char( Char : out CHARACTER );
end Keyscan;

task body Keyscan is
    -- any declarations
begin
    accept Next_Char( Char : out CHARACTER ) do
        -- whatever actions are required
        --
    end Next_Char;
end Keyscan;
```

Note that the **accept** statement reproduces the formal parameters, if any, of the **entry** declaration. When the **Keyscan** task is activated the first statement executed is the **accept** statement. The task waits until another unit calls the **Next_Char** entry. When this happens the task performs the statements in the **accept** block and then waits to terminate.

Quite often we will want our task to do something over and over again. Our **Keyscan**, for example, is not really useful if we only get one character from it. Typically a task body contains a big loop:

```
task body Keyscan is
    -- any declarations
begin
    loop
        accept Next_Char( Char : out CHARACTER ) do
            -- whatever actions are required
            --
        end Next_Char;
    end loop;
end Keyscan;
```

An entry doesn't have to do anything. We can use a task to schedule events by using empty accept blocks (in an empty **accept**, we omit the **do..end** portions of the block). For example, a space war game may have separate tasks drawing the space background, adding ships, computing scores, and displaying results. We could sequence these tasks using a scheduling server task like this:

```
task Sched is
    entry Draw_Done;
    entry Start_Ships;
    entry Ships_Done;
    entry Re_Draw;
```

```
        end Sched;

        task body Sched is
        begin
            loop
                    accept Draw_Done;
                    accept Start_Ships;
                    accept Ships_Done do
                        Score;
                        Display;
                    end Ships_Done;
                    accept Re_Draw;
            end loop;
        end Sched;
```

In the above sequence the task that draws the background calls **Sched.Draw__Done** when the background is complete. The task that placed the ships over the background is waiting for the rendezvous with **Sched.Start__Ships**, which can't take place until the task that draws the background makes its rendezvous with **Sched.Draw__Done**. The ship placement task will call **Sched.Ships__Done** when the ships are in place, and **Sched** then can compute the score and display the results. The background drawer will be waiting to rendezvous with **Sched.Re__Draw**, and can then redraw the background.

The advantage to this scheme is that the background redraw task can be computing a new background while ships are being placed, and scoring and display are taking place, and ship positions can be computed while the background is being updated.

The rules of rendezvous state that if one task is waiting to rendezvous with another which is not ready, the waiting task will continue to wait until the other task is ready. Hopefully the environment will put the waiting task to sleep until the rendezvous can take place. A task that is put to sleep (not using processor resources) is said to be in a *sleeping wait*.

Task Timing

The Ada specification defines a package called **Calendar**, which exports types and functions useful for real-time work. Specifically there is a predefined type **TIME**, which is used for expressing the time of day, a predefined function **Clock** which returns the time of day as type **TIME**, and a predefined type **DURATION**, a fixed-type whose units are seconds (**DURATION(1.0) = 1 second**).

A new task statement is the *delay* statement. We can put a task to sleep for a calculated amount of time by using the **delay** with an argument of type **DURATION**:

```
task Reactor_Watchdog;
task Reactor_Watchdog is
begin
    loop
        if <core overheating> then
            Run_Like_Hell;
        end if;
        delay 10.0;
    end loop
end Reactor_Watchdog;
```

This task could be declared in the main procedure of a program and remain executing in the background while other processes were in the foreground.

Using the **delay** statement we can suspend (put to sleep) our task for a minimum amount of time. In the example above, our task would be checking the core about every ten seconds. Because other tasks may be using the processor or other resources needed by this task, the delay may be more than ten seconds, but never less. Using the **delay** we aren't wasting the processor's time by leaving the task active when not needed.

Another Ada task construct is the *select* construct. A task may have several entries, any of which can occur in any order. The **select** structure has four possible variants. The basic structure is this:

```
select
    -- accept structure #1
or
    -- accept structure #2

-- possibly more "or" alternatives

end select;
```

Using the basic structure, when the task encounters the **select** structure it will wait for one or the other entries to be made. The first entry made will be serviced, and the select structure will exit at the bottom.

The next variant may have an **else** part:

```
select
     -- accept structure #1
or
     -- accept structure #2
else
     -- alternative actions
end select;
```

When this structure is encountered the task will check to see if any of the **accept** alternatives have a caller waiting. If no callers are waiting the **else** part of the **select** structure will be executed and the structure will exit at the bottom. This variant is called *select with an else*.

Another variant is when we wish to wait only a certain amount of time for any of the rendezvous to be made:

```
select
     -- accept structure #1
or
     -- accept structure #2
or
     delay 30.0;
     -- actions to take on time-out
end select;
```

When the above **select** is encountered, if neither accept #1 or accept #2 make a rendezvous within 30 seconds, the time-out actions execute, and after they have finished the structure exits at the bottom. This is called *select with a delay*. We can't use the **else** variant combined with this variant because the delay alternative would never be executed.

The fourth and last variant is when we want alternatives considered selectively, using (possibly) external criteria:

```
select
     when Daytime =>
          -- accept structure #1;
or
     when Nighttime =>
          -- accept structure #2;
end select;
```

The **when** selections use a Boolean expression to determine whether or not to consider an alternative for selection. If the Boolean is **FALSE**, it's as if the alternative doesn't even exist. The **when** construct is called a *guard*, and a select structure that includes them is called a *select with guards*.

Selects with guards may combine delays, simple selections, and/or elses in the same structure, with the restriction that an else and a delay may not appear in the same select:

```
select
    when Daytime =>
        accept Entry_1( Var : in out SOME_TYPE ) do
            Var := Var -1;
        end Entry_1;
or
    when Nighttime =>
        accept Entry_2;
or
    accept Entry_3( Var : in out SOME_TYPE) do
        Var := Var + 1;
    end Entry_3;
or
    delay 30.0;
    Do_Something_Else;
end select;
```

The guard expressions are evaluated on entry to the select structure, and in the case of a delay alternative are not reevaluated.

Task Termination

Since our tasks usually have a loop surrounding them they would never terminate by themselves by running off the end of the body, unless we took other actions. There are three possibilities for terminating tasks that run in infinite loops.

The first is a simple exit from the loop. We could combine this exit with an entry call, to allow the parent to terminate the task at any given point:

```
    --
    loop
        select
            accept Go_Away do
                exit;
            end Go_Away;
        or
            --
            --
    end loop;
end <task>;
```

The second way is to add a **terminate** alternative to the **select** structure:

```
select
     terminate;
or
     -- accept structure #1
or
     -- accept structure #2
end select;
```

The **terminate** alternative is selected, and the task terminates, only if the parent is ready to terminate, all other tasks dependent on the parent are terminated, or all other tasks are waiting at a select which includes a **terminate** alternative. In particular a task will not select the terminate while there are entry calls queued for *any* entry to the task, including entries not in the select structure that contains the terminate alternative.

The last way to terminate a task is done externally, by the parent. An **abort** is considered an abnormal termination. The general form of the **abort** is this:

```
abort <task_name>;

abort Reactor_Watchdog;
```

Since by implication a main program is a customer task we can use task statements within a main program. A graceful, yet foolproof, way of killing a task, and making sure that it is dead, is to *give the task its last wishes:*

```
select
     Reactor_Watchdog.Go_Away;
     delay 30;
     abort Reactor_Watchdog;
or
     delay 60;
     abort Reactor_Watchdog;
end select;
```

The select structure used here is shown in the next section, but is included here with other termination alternatives. This section of code basically says "wait 60 seconds to rendezvous with **Reactor__Watchdog**, but if he doesn't respond, blow him away. If he does respond, give him 30 seconds to clean up, then finish him off, just to make sure".

The implication that a main program is a task does not mean we can use task statements that are meaningless within the context we use them, however. For example, we couldn't use a **terminate** alternative to exit a main program because the **terminate** alternative must appear in a **select** strucutre, and a **select** structure must have at least one **accept** statement. Unless the main program were a task with at least one entry (an impossible alternative), we can't have an accept.

Timed Entry Calls

The *select with delay* allows a server task to wait only so long for a service request. We also can approach timing from the standpoint of the caller by using the *timed entry call*.

There are two forms of the timed entry, one which includes a delay time and one which gives the server one and only one shot at service. The last is called a *conditional entry call*. The forms look like this:

```
-- timed entry
select
     <task call>
     <other actions desired>
or
     delay <max waiting time>;
     <alternative action>
end select;

-- conditional entry call
select
     <task call>
     <other actions desired>
else
     <alternative action>
end select;
```

The syntactic difference between the two forms is the substitution of the else for the or. In the case of the timed entry call, if <max waiting time> is exceeded, <alternative action> is executed. In the case of the conditional entry call, if <task call> can't be made immediately, <alternative action> is executed, for example:

```
-- timed entry call
select
     Reactor_Watchdog.Go_Away;
or
     delay 30;
end select;
```

```
-- conditional entry call
select
     Reactor_Watchdog.Go_Away;
else
     abort Reactor_Watchdog;
end select;
```

We can think of all calls as timed calls. There was some discussion during the design of the Ada language of making all calls syntactically identical, with three types of arguments determining the waiting time:

```
time 0          = conditional call
time infinite   = unconditional (regular) call
time finite     = timed-entry call
```

Task Priorities

Task priority is used to arbitrate between tasks that are competing for the same resources. We can explicitly assign a priority to a task by using the priority pragma. The **priority** pragma is placed in the specification of a task, along with the **entry** declarations:

```
task Reactor_Watchdog is
     pragma priority( 10 );
     entry Go_Away;
end Reactor_Watchdog;
```

The **priority** is specified by a static integer expression, with a higher number being more urgent. The implementation can specify how many levels of priority are allowed. If you don't explicitly set a priority, the compiler will assign a priority.

The only place that the priority matters is when two or more tasks are waiting for a common resource (although the CPU is a resource). The higher priority task will get the resource. This doesn't mean that a low priority task can be "booted out" by a higher one (a recent interpretation of the language semantic rules says a low priority task *must* be booted when a higher priority task becomes computable. Check your implementation). It only means that if two tasks need something at the same time, the environment will give it to the higher priority task first.

The language rules state that resource allocation has to be "fair". A task won't be permitted to "starve", or wait forever while two other equal priority tasks exchange a needed resource.

Within a task the priority criterion for selecting between more than one open entry in a multiple choice select structure is arbitrary. Again the language rules state that selection has to be "fair", so one entry isn't favored over the other in a select loop with lots of entries queued up.

Tasks have three attribute functions available, aside from the representation attributes storage__size, size, and address. They are T'callable, T'terminated, and E'count, where T is a task name and E is a entry name.

T'callable returns a Boolean that is FALSE if the task T is terminated, completed, or is abnormal in some fashion. Otherwise callable returns TRUE.

T'terminated returns a Boolean which is TRUE if the task T has terminated or is FALSE if the task is not.

E'count returns a *universal__integer* which is the number of calls currently queued for entry E. This number should be used with caution, as timed entries can extract calls and new calls can add calls to the queue. This attribute is allowed only directly in the body of the task containing the entry.

Interrupts

Tasks may have entries attached directly to machine hardware interrupts. Hardware interrupts are asychronous calls to specific machine locations generated by hardware external to the CPU, such as the heartbeat interrupt used by many computers to control timing applications. We use a representation clause inside the task specification to vector the hardware interrupt to the task entry:

```
task Heartbeat_Interrupt is
     entry Rst7;
          for Rst7 use at 16#38#;
end Heartbeat_Interrupt;
```

The *Language Reference Manual* does not specifically state that registers are saved on entry; one would assume that to be the case, but a few tests are in order to find out for sure in a given implementation.

A hardware interrupt has priority over any other task. However, if the interrupt handler task is busy when an interrupt occurs, it is queued like any other entry call.

Only one interrupt entry may be attached to any one interrupt location.

You could extrapolate this function to any hardware vectoring. For example, in CP/M environments disk errors end up doing a *warm boot* by jumping to location 0. A text editor could patch an interrupt handler into location 0 to catch fatal disk errors to avoid loss of text, though a good compiler would already have done that and arranged for the raising of an exception instead.

The compiler environment specification or the computer's hardware manual will tell you exactly what interrupts are available and what they do.

Task applications can be divided into four categories:

- concurrent actions,
- routing messages,
- managing resources, and
- interrupt handling.

We saw interrupt handling in the last section. The other applications will be briefly elaborated below.

Concurrent actions

Independent actions that are parallel in nature can be expressed naturally as tasks. In a nuclear reactor we could use our task **Reactor__Watchdog** to monitor core coolant and have another concurrent task to monitor voltage output from the reactor generator. A host computer may have dual processors, in which case true concurrency is possible, or the host may be a single CPU system, like a ZX81, in which case time multiplexing will be needed. The "fairness doctrine" won't allow our core coolant task to sleep too long while the voltage monitor is hogging the processor.

Simple problems can also be expressed concurrently, for example solutions of simulaneous equations. A multiprocessor system would probably operate faster if all the CPUs were busy solving systems of equations in parallel, rather than a single processor doing serial computation.

Message routing

Tasks may be used to route messages in a system, while the parent task continues its business. A packet server could accept packet text from an customer and then build a packet and transmit and retransmit if necessary while the parent computed the next message. Several callers could hand messages to a packet-switching task. If the packet server became overloaded, the callers would wait until the messages cleared.

Print spoolers are another example of message routing, as well as our system log task we saw at the beginning of the chapter.

Controlling resources

Tasks may be used to control access to system resources—a logging printer, for example. If two tasks attempt to output a log message at the same time, the results would be unpredictable. We can coordinate our tasks by a scheduling task like the following:

```
task Printer is
     entry Seize;
     entry Release;
end Printer;

task body Printer is
begin
     loop
          accept Seize;
          accept Release;
     end loop;
end Printer;
procedure Seize renames Printer.Seize;
procedure Release renames Printer.Release;
```

When a task needed the printer it could call **Seize**, print the line, and then call **Release**. While one task has called **Seize**, **Printer** will wait for **Release**. Another task calling **Seize** will have to wait for the first task to call **Release** before the new **Seize** call can be accepted.

The task could be generalized to allow the same body to be used for different devices using the *task type* declaration:

```
task type DEVICE_MANAGER is
     entry Seize;
     entry Release;
end DEVICE_MANAGER;

task body DEVICE_MANAGER is
begin
     loop
          accept Seize;
          accept Release;
     end loop;
end DEVICE_MANAGER;
```

We then can use the task type **Device__Manager** to declare management tasks for any device:

```
Printer : DEVICE_MANAGER;
Disk_A  : DEVICE_MANAGER;
Disk_B  : DEVICE_MANAGER;
Modem   : DEVICE_MANAGER;
```

Tasks have an enormous potential for microcomputer use. Since programs are tasks, an Ada environment will provide automatic multitasking abilities, with good communication paths between programs. Concurrent applications will be far easier to write, and as more computers include multiple CPUs and coprocessors, the potential for really powerful software will increase dramatically.

14
Conclusions

In this final chapter we will take a look a standard programming support environment, which integrates the Ada compiler with a library manager and other facilities. We also will discuss some uses of Ada that have not yet become apparent this early in the cycle of compiler development; and we will make suggestions for further reading.

Let's look first at the state of the art today for mainframes and for microcomputers.

After living only in theory and imagination for so many years, mainframe Ada compilers are starting to come out of the woodwork. In the time this book was being written, at least 15 of them had received validation certificates. The VAX seems to be the preferred host, and there are four or five of them available now for that machine. Perhaps if you have access to a university computer system you can persuade the administration to purchase Ada for the VAX that universities always seem to have somewhere.

DEC's own VAX/VMS Ada compiler is said to compile about 1000 lines a minute, and produces code that's nearly as fast as DEC Pascal's. It's unclear whether or not the DEC system includes an Ada environment. Most likely the DEC compiler will use the standard DEC tools and produce standard DEC object files for the VAX. As far as we know the DEC system will not be retargeted for other processors.

The most complete Ada compiler implementation for microcomputers is the TeleSoft subset for the IBM-PC XT running under TeleSoft's ROS operating system (meaning it is not compatible with the standard PC operating systems). At a cost of approximately $5000, it is also beyond the financial reach of most of us.

The next most complete system is the R&R Software subset compiler, Janus/Ada Version 1.5.0. This system runs under CP/M-80 and CP/M-86, and MS-DOS version 1.x and 2.x. It is the subset used for developing programs for most of this book. The word from R&R is that this version will be around for a while, frozen with its present capabilities. R&R is working on a full Ada compiler for 16-bit MS-DOS computers, and has predicted validation for the fourth quarter of 1985. This compiler, when validated, may be out of the financial range of individuals. Probably there will be a middle ground compiler from R&R, that is, one that can recognize full Ada grammar but cannot implement all of it.

Several other full compilers for 8088/PC-DOS have been announced or rumored; they probably will be out by 1986, and probably will cost about $1000.

SuperSoft's A compiler rounds out the Ada compilers for microcomputers. This compiler is more limited than Janus/Ada's CP/M version, but is also truer to the Ada language.

By the time this book is in your hands, of course, things will be different, and you'll probably be chuckling to yourself about the quaint ideas we had back in the "olden" days. Fortunately for the authors, the Ada environment is still in its infancy, and so we have an opportunity to make predictions with a fair assurance that by the time they are proven wrong, nobody will remember them.

The Ada Environment

The programs Ada was especially designed to do—large, complex, long-lived programs requiring continuous maintenance—pose problems that go far beyond a compiler's sphere and involve the entire environment where programs are developed, executed, and maintained. What exactly do we mean by "environment"? An environment was recommended for Ada at the same time the language specifications were laid down.

The word "environment" has a number of different meanings, even in the restricted context of computer software. When we talk about the environment of a programming language, three separate environments spring to the mind of a knowledgeable user: the user interface, the programming environment, and the program execution environment.

It is only the second of these—the programming environment—that concerns us in this book. Ada's programming support environment is much more comprehensive than anything of its kind developed before. In theory it includes the editor used to write source text, a compiler or interpreter to translate source text into executable code, perhaps a linker to combine library and run time support modules with the translated code, a debugger, and the basic operations that control these environmental components—the operating system of the programming environment.

In the programming environment the programmer prepares a source text, repeatedly compiles and corrects it until all the syntax is correct, then tests the program for proper operation, after which he or she debugs it and analyzes data and program flow.

During the Ada design process a concept for a support environment was developed along with the compiler. This environment concept is known as the Ada Programming Support Environment (APSE). A full APSE should include all the tools you could ever want to get a program up and running.

These are two satellite environment concepts: the KAPSE (Kernel APSE) is the interface to the underlying system used for program development, and the MAPSE (Minimal APSE) is the minimum system required to write the source text and get it translated to executable code.

The KAPSE is a portable interface to the underlining operating system on the machine the programmer will be using. It is possible to have a KAPSE without another operating system interfacing to the machine (running on the "bare metal"), although most often the KAPSE will interface to some sort of operating system. At a minimum, a KAPSE should provide support for all of the primitive operations needed by a programmer. For example, a programmer shouldn't have to drop out of the APSE to delete a file from the operating system. The KAPSE also must provide a data base manager for the various program text files and files of compiled code, because many functions required for Ada are not features of most operating systems (the enforcement of compilation order, as one example).

The Minimal APSE

The MAPSE is just what is absolutely required to get your program running. Specifically, in addition to the KAPSE you need an Ada compiler to translate your program from its source form into some form where it will be executable.

An Ada linker also will be required in most cases because system linkers tend to be written early in the evolution of an operating system, and are usually limited (CP/M-80's LOAD is a classic example of a primitive linker). A linker can do wonderful things in theory, and very good linkers do exist in some operating systems (for CP/M, L80 by Microsoft or LINK80 by Digital Research are not bad, despite bit-stream file formats that make Ada designers, who have enough problems already, want to throw up). The minimal APSE usually will provide an Ada linker, for use only with Ada programs.

There also must be a "sufficient" editor in the minimal APSE—that is, one that can take input from the terminal and read and write files to the *underlying KAPSE data base*. An ordinary editor such as WordStar may not fill the bill because its interface is to the operating system file system rather than the KAPSE data base.

Aside from the requirement to work with an underlying data base, the minimal APSE can get by without fancy features such as "language modes" (e.g., the ones in EMACS) or editors that can help you put together source code, checking syntax and structure, indenting and finding keywords. Even a line editor like **ED** or **EDLIN** could be used in a MAPSE. It's fairly certain that someone will write a full-featured screen editor in Ada, and port it to all APSEs.

The minimal APSE must contain a documentation facility—something to write documentation with. This doesn't have to be fancy, just usable enough to write the documentation to ship with the program. Again, just like the editor, some day the documentation facility will be written in Ada and standardized. However, in a minimal APSE it will probably be a text formatter brought over from the native operating system and the program editor will be used to generate source documents for it, the way the UCSD Pascal program editor is used as a text editor.

Additionally there must be a command parser ("shell") capable of handling the commands that are passed to the other tools in the minimal APSE and to all tools that will be in the APSE. This may be written in the native language of the underlying hardware, and operating systems language like C, or it may be written in Ada.

Last of all, the minimal APSE requires a library manager to provide the proper interface to the data base managed by the KAPSE. Ada's separate compilation requires a library manager able to make the proper dependency relationships between specifications, bodies, and other program units. The library manager completes what is required in the minimal APSE.

The APSE

The full APSE includes all the features of the KAPSE and MAPSE, and a host of other goodies. As Ada matures as a language in actual use, even more interesting items will no doubt be suggested and adopted. For now let's look at the six items most likely to be found in a good APSE.

The first is a *symbolic debugger*, different than the symbolic debuggers for most programming languages because most programming languages are weakly typed.

The problems that occur in strongly typed languages are varied. For example you can give a data item any bit pattern (storage format) you want in a weakly typed language. But is this correct in a strongly typed language? Certainly not in the program text—but how about in the debugger? And what happens if a variable somehow does produce a constraint error? How does the debugger handle those kinds of occurrances? With an enumeration type it's hard to spot these errors, due to its internal numeric representation. With an arithmetic type it may be easy, but still different from a weakly typed language. In addition, things like exceptions, tasks, and generics all create interesting questions of implementation for the designer of a symbolic debugger for Ada.

The second tool we are likely to find in a full APSE is an importer/exporter. Not all software used in the Ada environment will be written in Ada even 10 years from now; certainly, for the present, not all software will be written in Ada. The importer provides a means to bring into the APSE source files, object files, load modules, or run units that may have been prepared outside the APSE. The exporter provides a means of taking Ada object files and run units/bound units out of the APSE, perhaps to some embedded target system where they will be executed, or some place where they will be burned into a PROM.

A third tool that one is likely to find in an APSE is a data or control flow analyzer. Many compilers and language systems have had data and control flow analyzers. However, due to the separate compilation requirements in Ada, the compiler is provided information on what kind of data and control flows between modules to a degree not required before in other languages.

In a full APSE you are also likely to have a proof of correctness checker; this could tell you if the program will do what you think it will. (Some say this is beyond the state-of-the-art, this may be true.)

A fifth tool one might find in a full APSE would be a performance profiler. This would be a program that would indicate after the execution of a particular Ada program or set of Ada programs how execution proceeded through that program set. It would identify those parts of the program that were most heavily executed and thus should be most considered for redesign and/or efficiency changes.

Timing is essential in the environment of embedded systems. We should expect to see in the future a timing analyzer, a program which analyzes your Ada program and indicates how much CPU and/ or clock time will actually be required. It would be very good if these were integrated with things like the data and control flow analyzer so that worst- and best-case, as well as average, execution time can be provided for programs.

Ada Programming Methodology

An Ada programming support environment alone is not enough, just as a language alone is not enough and an execution environment is not enough. We also need a set of methodological principles enabling us to write Ada programs.

The methodology includes things like how to organize, how to put together certain parts of programs, and how to design. Take, for example, asynchronous routines in an aircraft radar system. What is the task? Is it an aircraft? Is it a radar? Is it a radar signal blip? These are the kinds of questions we don't know and until we understand the real world our program lives in, we won't be able to design good Ada programs (or good programs in any language).

Methodology is information having to do with reusability—how to understand the problem in such a way that you can organize it to be reused, often in contexts you didn't think about when you first did the design.

Another item is modifiability. Once you've written the program and you discover it isn't perfect (we know—the odds are against you writing imperfect code, but bear with us), you have to be able to modify it with minimal effect on the existing hardware and software environment. More important, your code should stand up to modification by somebody else five years from now.

Another methodological question has to do with reliability—how we design programs so that when one part of them fails, other parts still continue to run. This is the something hardware designers have been looking for for years now; they are beginning to find some solutions. We need similar solutions for software.

Where are we, the DoD community and the Ada community, now? We have a good language defined; reasonable compilers for Ada are beginning to appear; our environments are starting to come along—yet our methods are still unclear and they need work. Where do we go from here? Let's examine this question in the context of four different kinds of users.

In *computer science departments* that have previously taught the standard languages FORTRAN and COBOL (and maybe done a little teaching in Pascal for data structures) there will be a major change. The computer science department will have a language that does most of the things that good professional programmers have wanted for years.

As it is very hard to be educated in algebra and calculus if you have not first learned to add, subtract, multiply, and divide, it is hard to teach abstraction, object-orientated design, modifiability, and maintainability when you have a language that fights you at every turn. Generally available lanaguages such as FORTRAN and Pascal are examples of languages that fight you.

Languages that provide the functions necessary to give students practice using advanced concepts are few and far between. Usually they are research languages with cheesy compilers and are locked up behind passwords by the grad students who designed them.

Ada will give computer science departments a modern language for their students to practice the principles of modern programming, which until now have been taught "hands-off" for lack of a complier that supports them. An immediate benefit is that software engineering will be better taught. The integrated features of the APSE will *force* software engineering to be taught at the same time that it *allows* software engineering to be taught.

It has been said that the theory of psychology is the theory of the psychology of the college freshman, because they are the subjects of all experimentation. It has also been said that computer science is the 50-line FORTRAN program—perhaps a valid accusation in many places. Ada, by allowing us to build and integrate large pieces of software, will enable computer science departments to teach the kind off curriculum that they have always wished to teach, and that the real-world employer wants the new employee to have.

Microcomputer users have to keep in mind that Ada was not designed to be easily compiled, or to have a fast or small compiler, but one which produces extremely efficient object code. So, on a micro, a compiler for Ada is likely to be big and slow compared to one for another programming language which is less functional. We may never see full Ada compilers for 64K, 8-bit micros running floppies, but we probably will see Ada compilers on 16-bit or 32-bit micros which produce not only native code but also cross-compile for their 8-bit counterparts.

The large-scale user has always been interested in such things as configuration control, tracking, changes, baselines, and maintainability. Because of the separate compilation facility and because of the library manager required by Ada, the APSE will be built in such a way to give the large-scale user building large systems those kinds of capabilities. The tracking that will appear in the APSE will be so natural five years from now that we'll forget that there were good operating systems such as Multics that did it five years ago. Even now, most DoD projects use Ada as PDL (Program Design Language) for programs written in other languages, because of the transportability of the program descriptions.

As we continue researching programming languages, methods, and environments, it becomes more and more clear that not only the language we write things in but the way in which we connect them is of importance. The success of LISP as a programming language has been due in a large measure to the fact that you can dynamically define routines and call them into execution in the middle of a program or change them when you discover that you really haven't solved the problem.

While Ada was a language designed for easy static binding of program modules in a research environment, in a rapid development environment or in a rapid prototyping environment, it will be necessary to provide some method of replacing Ada modules—some means of doing the equivalent of Multics dynamic linking, or some means of doing the equivalent of the transfer vector changes found in some programming languages and operating systems.

At this point we don't know how well Ada adapts itself to this kind of change. There are those in the Ada community who believe that this kind of dynamic linking is wrong. There are those in the community who believe that it is not only right but it is the kind of thing that must be done in order to make Ada programs useful in the long run.

This is not the only research issue in Ada. There are questions of verification, of reliability, and of portability (both numeric and nonnumeric) to be handled by the research community.

Software Engineering

Ada is a language that is going to allow us to do software engineering. If we think about what happens with ordinary engineering, we have a designer or architect who designs what we do—this translates to the Ada specification. Then we have a builder who builds something to that specification—this translates to the Ada body.

Other languages do not allow this separation of specification, or design, and body, or construction. This feature of Ada is what allows "software engineering", the design of programs in a top-down fashion, with programmer interchangability.

Software Components

It is in the area of standard packages that Ada provides a great hope: We now have the packages `Standard`, `Calendar`, `Text_IO`, and the other two `IO` packages, `System`, and some others. *Everybody* has these, so code written in terms of these standard packages will be extremely portable. Other packages will be developed, standardized, and made available to Ada users.

We expect a much wider library of software components as people learn how to use Ada generics and tasks, enumeration types, proper techniques for separating package specifications from bodies, packaging data, types and procedures separately, and multiple-level interface design. Ada then will be able to reach its true potential.

Jean Ichbiah, the designer of Ada, firmly believes that Ada will enable the growth of a software components industry. He feels that the textual separation of the specification and body, coupled with the enforcement of specification restrictions in all code that utilizes the specification and linker enforcement of specification/body matching makes software components a likelihood.

Previously the best-written software component could be compromised due to tinkering with the portions of its interface, or items reachable through the interface, that needed to be made public for the component to perform its function. And even if the user did not try to tinker, there wasn't any way for the designer of a component to be sure that his or her component implementation could not be compromised due to inadvertant slips, such as name-clashes, by the users of the component.

In Ada we expect that components, families of components for one purpose, and libraries of components will become available.

We can expect the emergence of companies specialized in designing, developing, and verifying the necessary operations of software components of a particular type. They will publish this specification, in Ada. They then will implement the body, and distribute the body as machine code only, probably in a library under access controls. This will decrease the probability of theft or misuse of these components.

We also can expect families of components implementing a single specification. Here the "function" of all bodies conforming to a single specification is the same; they differ in performance, capacity, modifiability, recovery, etc. Users here will code to a single specification for their particular application. They then will select a body from the family of bodies; this particular member will meet the "semantic" needs for the particular packaging of the application for a particular target (e.g., CP/M with 64K and two 800K-byte disks).

Associated with the family of components will be some part of the APSE so that users will be able to specify things such as "When linking this program, choose the particular family members that give large capacity at the expense of increased disk space."

We also expect libraries of components, such as the equivalent of the NAG or IMSL mathematical libraries, the CORE graphics package, or a set-of-terminal drivers. These most likely will come from highly specialized producers of software utilities. It is likely that they will be available as families as well as single components.

So what will prevent Ada software from becoming a reality? Managers won't wish to be dependent on some other firm, preferring poor software they know they can maintain/enhance to good software in which they don't have access to the source code. This will be met by source-code escrow, and by source-licensing agreements on secure-systems (e.g., Multics with its multilevel access controls and B2 rating) that will protect the owner's investment while allowing controlled sharing.

Managers may distrust the quality of code they cannot white-box test themselves. This will be met by independent test/validate organizations that will provide a seal of approval somewhat like the UL (Underwriters Laboratories) seal for electrical equipment.

Managers may reject components because they do not meet their needs—they are either not complete enough or take too many resources (memory, disk, etc). This will be met by the families of components discussed earlier.

Designers and programmers may reject components because they were not invented here. This is an attitude problem, and may be the hardest to solve.

Designers and programmers may reject components because it's more work to find one that meets their needs than to implement one themselves. This argument is rejected since we know the ease of finding components today on well-organized systems like Multics (although the components are limited to a single, powerful target environment). We expect the Ada software repositories to have powerful indexing and browsing capabilities and to be networked for increased availability and variety of components.

The above argument also is rejected because we expect the software components to be more reliable (read "bug-free") than implemented-once code. (For example, each Multics developer is responsible for the maintenance of 100,000 lines of PL/1-based software components, which he/she does well. This is counter to the industry belief that 50,000 lines of code is the maximum maintainable by a single programmer.)

Managers may reject components because of the liability questions upon component malfunction that affects a larger area. This question is inadequately asked today; answers will be hard. Firms may choose not to develop and sell components in light of product-liability decisions that have made producing firms responsible for consequences of their product, even when misused.

In light of the potential problems, why will software components succeed? Assuming they do become available, they'll succeed because their availability will make it possible to create programs in much less elapsed time. One of this textbook's authors completed a program in five weeks part-time using available LISP and PL/1 components. He estimates it would take three years full-time to do the same job on a system where those components are not available in any language. (Both systems run on the same hardware—but have different operating systems and component interaction conventions.) This presumes our author can find out how the components work well enough when reimplementing them.

Further Reading

As you get involved in Ada programming you probably will want to expand your library on the subject. We recommend the following books:

Reference Manual for the Ada Programming Language (ANSI/MIL-STD-1815A-1983) Available in bookstores. When you get over the shock of a 300-page tome using a frequently unfamiliar terminology, you appreciate how well-designed, thorough, and, in fact, well-written the Ada Manual (a.k.a. the Language Reference Manual—(LRM) really is. It includes an excellent index, listings for all system library packages (we include only **Standard**, **Text_IO**, **Direct_IO**, and **Sequential_IO** in the appendices to this book), a syntax summary in Backus-Naur Form (BNF), and enough details about the language to serve as specifications for a compiler.

You don't need the Ada Manual to write programs in Ada, but it is a reference you probably will want at hand as the last word on how Ada should operate. A silver-colored edition published by Springer-Verlag is at many bookstores, and a green-bound copy is available from the American National Standards Institute (ANSI).

Programming in Ada, Second Edition, by J.G.P. Barnes (Reading, MA: Addison-Wesley, 1984) J.G.P. Barnes, a member of the Ada design team, has long been an enthusiastic proponent of the language. His book is notable for its complete treatment of Ada's syntax, illustrated with short, extremely lucid examples.

Software Engineering with Ada, by Grady Booch (Menlo Park, CA: Benjamin-Cummings, 1983) Grady Booch has taught courses in the Ada programming language at the Air Force Academy for a number of years. His book is a standard introduction to the "big picture" in using Ada for constructing large-scale systems. After a general description of the language he offers a series of design problems and formal specifications for their solution, including operations on a binary tree, data base inquiry, process control, and a generic set package.

Ada: An Advanced Introduction, by Narain Gehani (Englewood Cliffs, NJ: Prentice-Hall, 1983) Bell Laboratories' Narain Gehani summarizes Ada's basic syntax in the first third of this book, then moves on to thorough discussions of data types, packages, tasking, generics, and implementation dependencies.

Ada for Experienced Programmers, by Nico Habermann and Dewayne Perry (Reading, MA: Addison-Wesley, 1983) Nico Habermann and Dewayne Perry, both of Carnegie-Mellon University, give a complete presentation of Ada in parallel with Pascal. That is to say, they describe classic programming problems, then give examples of their solution first in Pascal and then in Ada. The result is an overview of the differences in good coding style between the two languages.

APPENDIX A

Notes and References

This appendix contains notes on implementation specific information and general notes.

Many (but not all) of the nonstandard features and omissions of Janus and SuperSoft are noted. The other microcomputer Ada compiler, by TeleSoft, is close enough to validation that no notes are required.

While there are more notes pertaining to Janus, in the opinion of at least one of the authors, Janus is superior to SuperSoft for production programming—SuperSoft implements less of the language, and therefore only a single note is required for some chapters: "Not implemented in SuperSoft". Improved and more standard versions of Janus Ada were being announced for MS-DOS at the time of this writing.

Typographical Conventions

The standard typographical conventions for Ada are to place keywords in lowercase boldfaced type, and everything else in normal weight, uppercase type. We chose to deviate from this standard because it can't be duplicated by any practical means with a micro.

We chose to place reserved words in lowercase type, program unit, object, and subprogram names with the first letter of each member word capitalized (except acronyms like I/O in all caps), and type names, named numbers, enumeration literals, and labels in uppercase.

Preface

1. Most of the example programs in this book were run on the CP/M version of R. R. Software's Janus Ada, available from Workman & Associates, 112 Marion Avenue, Suite 3B,

Pasadana, CA 91106. A number of other versions of Janus, including a PC-DOS subset compiler for under $100, is available from R. R. Software, P. O. Box 1512, Madison, WI 53701.

1. The program **Greet__World** is slightly different for SuperSoft "A", and significantly different in Janus/Ada. The SuperSoft version looks like this:

```
-- SuperSoft A version of Hello World

procedure Greet_World is
begin
        Put( "Hello, world" );
        New_Line;
end Greet_World;

-- Filename:     GRTWRLD.ADA
-- Compile:      A>A GRTWRLD
-- Link:         A>L
--               *INIT
--               *GRTWRLD
--               *ADALIB/S
--               *GREET/N/E
-- Run:          A>GREET
```

The difference is in the *context clause* for this program; in Ada we need to include a standard I/O package **Text__IO**; this is mostly built-in in SuperSoft "A". We have included the compile, link, and execution information as comments at the end.

The Janus version has more differences, mostly due to Janus' requirement that a unit submitted for compilation be either a package specification or a package body—if there is executable code then the unit must be a package body. In Janus it is possible to have a package body without a matching specification, which is not legal in Ada (a unit of this sort would be a procedure instead). The Janus version of **Greet__World** looks like this:

```
-- Janus version of Hello World

package body J1x17 is

        procedure Greet_World is
        begin
```

```
            Put( "Hello, world" );
            New_Line;
      end Greet_World;

begin
      Greet_World;      -- This invokes the procedure --
end J1x17;

-- Filename:    J1X17.PKG
-- Compile:     A>JANUS J1X17
-- Link:        A>JLINK J1X17
-- Run:         A>J1X17
```

Again, the I/O routines are built-in, and no context clause is required.

2. Janus has most of the routines from **Text_IO**, but they are spread between the compiler and two packages, **IO** and **Util**. SuperSoft includes most of the common routines of **Text_IO** in five files, **TEXTIO.ADA**, the specification of the package, **TEXTBODY.ADA**, the body of the package, **TEXTBODY.REL**, the compiled body, **TEXTIO.REL**, the compiled specification, and **TEXT_IO.SYM**, a symbol table created by the compiler to use when compiling dependent units. In general both in SuperSoft and Janus you need **.SYM** files on the source or compiler disk when compiling, and the **.REL** (SuperSoft) or **.JRL** (Janus) files on the linker or source disk when linking. The **.ADA** (SuperSoft) and **.PKG** and **.LIB** (Janus) files supplied with your compiler need not be present in the system after you first compile them.

3. The SuperSoft command line for compilation would be:

```
A>A B:MYFILE
```

The linker commands for SuperSoft are more complicated and require the explicit linkage by the programmer of all dependent packages in a specific order. Assuming **Myfile** needed the package **Text_IO**, a linkage session with SuperSoft would look like this:

```
A>L                    -- invoke the SuperSoft linker
*INIT                  -- Link run-time initialization code
*TEXTBODY,TEXTIO       -- Link text_io body and spec.
*MYFILE                -- Link your code
*ADALIB/S              -- Search run-time library
*MYFILE/N/E            -- name .COM file "MYFILE.COM"
```

Supersoft "A" is available from SuperSoft, P. O. Box 1628, Champaign, IL 61820.

---

Chapter 2

1. Illegal identifiers:

First-Index   Can't have a hyphen
__Buffer   Can't start/end with underbar
23A   First character must be a letter
Last Line   Can't have spaces
Marker∧   No punctuation legal except for underbar
A$ No punctuation legal except for underbar

2. Janus Ada keeps all letters significant in identifiers; SuperSoft keeps only the first ten letters. Janus requires that package names be the same as the system filename, and doesn't allow compilation of anything but packages (bodies or specifications). SuperSoft uses only package specifications as system file names. The use of the underline character in package names should be avoided in both Janus and SuperSoft because the underline is not a legal operating system character in CP/M and many versions of MS-DOS.

3. Embedding reserved words in identifiers—it is common practice to append reserved words to the *ends* of identifiers: **OUTER__LOOP**, **Word__Array**, etc.

4. **Put("begin")** outputs   **begin**

5. Janus does not support based real numbers.

6. SuperSoft does not allow named numbers.

7. Janus' type **CHARACTER** is not an enumeration type, as it is in full Ada.

8. SuperSoft does not support the attribute functions **first** and **last**.

Chapter 3

1. Janus doesn't allow constants, Boolean result operators, memberships, or the ABS operator in static expressions.

2. **procedure A__char**—Janus and SuperSoft don't need either the context clause (**with Text__IO**) or the dot notation in the calls to **Put**. SuperSoft will reject the dot notation (it's not allowed in SuperSoft and Janus will choke on the reference to **Text__IO**, which is not a Janus package.

3. **procedure Print__Circle__Area**: See above note.

4. Both Janus and SuperSoft have restrictions on the use of enumeration types—for example, neither compiler allows for the input of enumeration types. Janus 1.5.0 has a bug regarding enumeration types defined in a package specification—the type isn't properly exported. Use trial and error a while before committing to a large project using enumeration types.

5. Janus does not allow overloaded enumeration literals. Since Janus characters are not enumeration literals, both Janus and SuperSoft do not allow a character literal in an enumeration.

6. The subtype **NATURAL** is an *unsigned integer*. Janus predefines this type, but not **POSITIVE**. SuperSoft doesn't predefine either **NATURAL** or **POSITIVE**.

7. Check your compiler reference manual to determine which pragmas are implemented and whether they do anything or not.

8. **Count1**. Janus and SuperSoft depart somewhat from standard Ada. Listings are provided below:

```
-- Janus version of count1


package body JCNT1 is

    procedure Count1 is
        Input_Char : CHARACTER;
        Counter    : INTEGER := 0;
        Control_Z  : constant CHARACTER := CHARACTER'val( 26 );
    begin
    <<START>>
        Get( Input_Char );
        if Input_Char in ' '..'~' then
            Counter := Counter + 1;
        end if;
        if Input_Char /= Control_Z then
            goto START;
        end if;
        Put( Counter );
    end Count1;


begin
    Count1;
end JCNT1;
```

```
-- Filename:     JCNT1.PKG
-- Compile:      A>JANUS JCNT1
-- Link:         A>JLINK JCNT1
-- Run:          A>JCNT1
```

The Janus version has no instantiation for integer I/O, no context clause, and is embedded in a package body.

```
-- SuperSoft version of count1

procedure Count1 is
    Input_Char : CHARACTER;
    Counter    : INTEGER := 0;
    Control_Z  : constant CHARACTER := CHARACTER'val( 26 );
begin
<<START>>
    Get( Input_Char );
    if Input_Char in ' '..'~' then
        Counter := Counter + 1;
    end if;
    if Input_Char /= Control_Z then
        goto START;
    end if;
    Put( Counter );
end Count1;
```

```
-- Filename:     A3X39.ADA
-- Compile:      A>A A3X39
-- Link:         A>L
--               *INIT
--               *A3X39
--               *ADALIB/S
--               *COUNT1/N/E
-- Run:          A>COUNT1
```

The SuperSoft version turned up a new bug in SuperSoft; the **goto** missed the target label **START** and hits the beginning of the procedure. The declaration is reelaborated each time through the loop. You can test this by inserting debugging statements to print the value of **Counter** after each line, and by inserting a **Put** statement just before the target label. Somebody at SuperSoft missed this one, probably because the **goto** is almost never used in Ada.

Chapter 4

1. Figure 4-4—version for Janus.

```
-- Janus version of factorial front-end

package body Facfend is

    procedure Factorial is
        Number, Result : INTEGER;
    begin
    <<TOP>>
        Put( "Type a number from 1 to 7: " );
        Get( Number );
        if Number < 1 then
            Put( "The number is too small - " );
            goto TOP;
        elsif Number > 7 then
            Put( "The number is too large - " );
            goto TOP;
        else
            Put( "The number is acceptable." );
        end if;

        -- compute factorial and print result.
    end Factorial;

begin
    Factorial;
end Facfend;
        -- Filename:    FACFEND.PKG
        -- Compile:     A>JANUS FACFEND
        -- Link:        A>JLINK FACFEND
        -- Run:         A>FACFEND
```

The Janus version has no instantiation of integer I/O, no context clause, and is embedded in a package body. This program fragment can be compiled and run.

The SuperSoft version blows up on the same **goto** bug listed in the notes for the last chapter.

2. Figure 4-12—versions for Janus and SuperSoft.

```
-- Janus version of Figure 4-12

package body Jfactor is

    procedure Factorial is
        Max_Number : constant INTEGER := 7;
        Min_Number : constant INTEGER := 1;
        Result, N  : INTEGER := 1;
    begin
        loop
            Put( "Type a number between 1 and 7: " );
            Get( N );
            exit when N <= Max_Number and N >= Min_Number;
            Put( "That number is not acceptable - " );
        end loop;
        New_Line;
        for Index in 2..N loop
            Result := Result * Index;
        end loop;
        Put( "The factorial of " );
        Put( N );
        Put( " is " );
        Put( Result );
        New_Line;
    end Factorial;

begin
        Factorial;
end Jfactor;

-- Filename:    JFACTOR.PKG
-- Compile:     A>JANUS JFACTOR
-- Link:        A>JLINK JFACTOR
-- Run:         A>JFACTOR
```

As usual we don't have the instantiation of integer I/O, no context clause, and the procedure is embedded in a package body.

```
-- SuperSoft version of Figure 4-12

procedure Factorial is
    Max_Number : constant INTEGER := 7;
    Min_Number : constant INTEGER := 1;
    Result, N  : INTEGER := 1;
```

```
begin
    loop
        Put( "Type a number between 1 and 7: " );
        Get( N );
        exit when N <= Max_Number and N >= Min_Number;
        Put( "That number is not acceptable - " );
    end loop;
    New_Line;
    for Index in 2..N loop
        Result := Result * Index;
    end loop;
    Put( "The factorial of " );
    Put( N );
    Put( " is " );
    put( Result );
    New_Line;
end Factorial;

-- Filename:    AFACTOR.ADA
-- Compile:     A>A AFACTOR
-- Link:        A>L
--              *INIT
--              *AFACTOR
--              *ADALIB/S
--              *AFACTOR/N/E
-- Run:         A>AFACTOR
```

The SuperSoft version is also missing the instantiation of integer I/O and the context clause.

3. Figure 4-15—Janus and SuperSoft versions.

```
-- Janus version of Figure 4-15

package body Wc4 is
    subtype VISIBLE_CHARACTERS is CHARACTER range '!'..'~';
    Input_Char              : CHARACTER;
    Word_Count, Char_Count  : INTEGER := 0;
    Control_Z               : CHARACTER := CHARACTER'val( 26 );
    In_A_Word               : BOOLEAN := FALSE;
begin
    Put( "Enter text, end with ^Z: " );
    loop
        Get( Input_Char );
```

```
                exit when Input_Char = Control_Z;
                Char_Count := Char_Count + 1;
                if
                        not In_A_Word and Input_Char in VISIBLE_CHARACTERS
                then
                        In_A_Word := TRUE;
                        Word_Count := Word_Count + 1;
                elsif
                        In_A_Word and Input_Char not in VISIBLE_CHARACTERS
                then
                        In_A_Word := FALSE;
                end if;
        end loop;
        New_Line;
        Put( "Words counted: " ); Put( word_count ); New_Line;
        Put( "Chars counted: " ); Put( char_count ); New_Line;
end Wc4;


--  Filename:    WC4.PKG
--  Compile:     A>JANUS WC4
--  Link:        A>JLINK WC4
--  Run:         A>WC4
```

This follows the same modifications made to other programs—no context clause, no instantiation, embedded in a package body.

```
--  SuperSoft version of Figure 4-15

procedure Wc4 is
    Input_Char              : CHARACTER;
    Word_Count, Char_Count  : INTEGER := 0;
    Control_Z               : CHARACTER := CHARACTER'val( 26 );
    In_A_Word               : BOOLEAN := FALSE;
begin
    Put( "Enter text, end with ^Z: " );
    loop
        Get( Input_Char );
        exit when Input_Char = Control_Z;
        Char_Count := Char_Count + 1;
        if
                not In_A_Word and Input_Char in '!'..'~'
        then
                In_A_Word := TRUE;
```

```
                Word_Count := Word_Count + 1;
            elsif
                In_A_Word and Input_Char not in '!'..'~'
            then
                In_A_Word := FALSE;
            end if;
        end loop;
        New_Line;
        Put( "Words counted: " ); Put( word_count ); New_Line;
        Put( "Chars counted: " ); Put( char_count ); New_Line;
    end Wc4;

    -- Filename:    WC4.ADA
    -- Compile:     A>A WC4
    -- Link:        A>L
    --                *INIT
    --                *WC4
    --                *ADALIB/S
    --                *WCT4
    -- Run:         A>WCT4
```

The SuperSoft version has no context clause, no instantiation, and shows an omission—the membership operators in and not in aren't defined to operate on subtypes—in fact, we couldn't find any reference to these operators at all in the syntax summary of the SuperSoft manual, although they do work for discrete ranges, as you can see.

Chapter 5

1. Neither SuperSoft nor Janus allows named parameter passing.

2. Neither SuperSoft nor Janus allows default parameters.

3. The examples in Figures 5-5 and 5-6 are in full Ada syntax. In Ada, a package body cannot be compiled before its specification is compiled.

4. In Janus a subprogram body may appear in any part of a declaration. In Ada no other declarative item may appear after the first subprogram body in a declaration part. This is to reduce the chances of an obscure logical error.

5. Janus does not allow nesting of packages.

6. Supersoft does not support named component (dot) notation; therefore any withed package must also be used to maintain portability.

7. Janus does not allow dot notation to reference variables in other subprograms or blocks. SuperSoft does not allow dot notation at all.

8. Neither Janus or SuperSoft supports renaming declarations.

9. Neither Janus or SuperSoft allows the overloading of operators. Janus does not allow the overloading of function return types.

10. Janus does not allow separate compilation.

11. Janus considers a main program to be the initialization code of a package body. The package body with the highest degree of dependency (the one which **with**s other packages but is not itself **with**ed) to is the main program.

In SuperSoft the main program is the procedure which is linked just before **ADALIB** in the linkage list.

Chapter 6

1. Specifically the I/O packages most microcomputer users won't need are the formatted I/O programs at the end of the chapter. Almost all of the others are very useful.

2. Janus and SuperSoft relax their type checking for file streams somewhat.

3. Janus has a nonstandard format for **Open** in versions 1.5.0 and below, as well as nonstandard type names for **FILE__TYPE** and **FILE__MODE**. Janus also does not allow the use of the **Form** parameter.

4. As noted earlier, both Janus and SuperSoft have part of **Text__IO** built into the compiler, rather than package **Text__IO**. Janus does not have a package **Text__IO** and distributes the implemented parts of the Ada standard **Text__IO** in the packages **IO** and **Util**.

5. Janus file objects are of type **FILE**, rather than of type **FILE__TYPE**. New versions of Janus are moving toward the standard **Text__IO** type names and functions.

6. Since neither Janus or SuperSoft support generics, instantiation is not needed for numeric I/O. However, since generics are not available, this means that only the types defined in the I/O packages are able to be output. Janus version 1.5.0 has a fake generic **Direct__IO** package **Randio**, which in their own words is "clumsy".

7. Janus does not support exceptions at all, and so I/O errors have to be tested for after each I/O attempt, in the manner of C. SuperSoft has no predefined exceptions but allows user-defined exception. The I/O packages with SuperSoft define many of the exceptions we will see in Chapter 6. Unfortunately SuperSoft has a subtle bug in exception handling which we were unable to trace exactly, so be careful when using exceptions in SuperSoft.

8. Neither Janus or SuperSoft has a `Form` parameter, and consequently neither has the `Form` function. Janus' file management differs from `Standard` in number, type, and position of arguments. SuperSoft's file management should be gone over by someone familiar with the CP/M BDOS calls and have the right error checking and CP/M procedures installed. Given the default form parameters in standard Ada, code written for SuperSoft should be very portable in the file management area. For both compilers be sure to check your current implementation to see what subprograms are currently included and the type, position, and number of parameters, and return value types for functions.

9. Janus implements the default file subprograms in package `Util`. SuperSoft does not allow redirection of the default files and therefore does not have these subprograms.

10. Both Janus and SuperSoft will return line terminators as characters (`ASCII.CR` characters, to be precise), instead of skipping them as would be expected from the Ada specification. `Skip_Line` still works, though.

11. The Janus `Get` procedures for strings and characters are done through the operating system string-input calls, and so system editing characters and aborts will work—you also have to press `RETURN` before interpretation of the input begins. Some of the Janus `Get` subprograms are *functions* rather than procedures—in particular, `Get_Line`. SuperSoft uses the CP/M console-input function (character-at-a-time) for both character and string input, which allows for single-key response by your program. SuperSoft's `Get_Line` and string `Get` do not interpret editing characters—for example, a backspace is echoed to the screen all right, but it is explicitly entered in the string as a backspace. Some validated mainframe compilers (e.g., TeleSoft Ada 2.1 for the VAX) also act this way—it may be correct but it's damned inconvenient. You need to either rewrite the `Get` procedures or parse the input in your program.

12. Since Janus has a nonstandard string type it is not necessary to use a slice of an input to open a file, as in procedure `Whatever`. SuperSoft has a standard string type but not slices (see Chapter 7;), so you're on your own as far as figuring out how to slice the parameters in situations such as that in procedure `Whatever`. We weren't able to find an elegant way to do this, but listed below is what we did find. While we're on the subject, SuperSoft also doesn't automatically convert filenames to uppercase—sound familiar, MBASIC fans?

```
-- A slice function for SuperSoft (or other subsets that
-- don't support slices)

    function Slice( In_Str : STRING;
                    Lo, Hi : INTEGER ) return STRING is
        Slice_Valu : STRING( 1..(Hi - Lo + 1) );
    begin
        for Index in 1..Slice_Valu'last loop
            Slice_Valu( Index ) := In_Str( Index + Lo - 1 );
```

```
              end loop;
              return Slice_Valu;
          end Slice;

  -- Test fixture for slice function:
      begin -- Test
          Put( Slice( "Hello", 2, 4 ) );
          Put( Slice( "Goodbye", 1, 5 ) );
          Put( Slice( "1234567890", 1, 10 ) );
      end; -- Test;
```

13.   Janus supports FLOATs, LONG__FLOATs, and LONG__INTEGERs with separate I/O packages, which must be **with**ed before these types may be I/O'ed. SuperSoft has FLOAT I/O in **Text__IO**, but only in a limited sense—no formatting parameters are included.

14.   SuperSoft has no I/O for enumeration types. Janus has output for enumerations but a bug prevents proper output unless the type declaration is in the same physical file as the I/O statement—you can't output an enumeration type declared in a package specification. Janus does not support input of enumeration types.

15.   SuperSoft doesn't have direct or sequential I/O. Janus has these functions spread out in several files.

16.   Due to the lack of enumeration type input in both SuperSoft and Janus, procedure **Dialogue** doesn't fly on either.

17.   Since SuperSoft does not allow default file redirection, package CMD does not work in SuperSoft.

```
  -- Test fixture for CMD and SDF
  -- For Janus Ada Version 1.5.0

with SDF, CMD, UTIL, IO, Sfloatop, SfloatIO;
package body Testsdf is
    use SDF, CMD, Sfloatop;

Response, Int : INTEGER;
Flt           : FLOAT;
```

```
begin
        -- Test command line argument function
    if Argc /= 0 then
        Put( "Command line arguments are:" );
        New_Line;
        for Index in 1..Argc loop
            Put( Argv( Index ) );
            New_Line;
        end loop;
    else
        Put( "No command line arguments specified." );
    end if;
    New_Line;
        -- Test SDF, ask whether integer or floats are desired
    Put( Util.Standard_Output(),
      "Enter 1 for integer read, 2 for float read: " );
    Get( Util.Standard_Input(),Response );
    if Response = 1 then
        -- Test the integer function "get_int"
        while not IO.End_Of_File( Util.Current_Input() ) loop
            Get_Int( Util.Current_Input(), Int );
            Put( Int );
            New_Line;
        end loop;
    else
        -- Test the float function "get_float"
        while not IO.End_Of_File( Util.Current_Input() ) loop
            Get_Float( Util.Current_Input(), Flt );
            SfloatIO.Put( Flt );
            New_Line;
        end loop;
    end if;
end Testsdf;

---------JANUS-----------------
-- Filename:    TESTSDF.PKG
-- Compile:     A>JANUS TESTSDF
-- Link:        A>JLINK TESTSDF
-- Run:         A>TESTSDF
```

Chapter 7

1. Janus does not implement multidimensional arrays.

2. Janus requires that arrays be declared with static bounds. Unconstrained arrays are still allowed as subprogram parameters.

3. Janus does not allow operators for Boolean arrays, but Janus does allow bitwise manipulation of integers, which is a nonstandard way to achieve the same effect.

4. The operators $<$, $<=$, $>$, $>=$ are not implemented for arrays in Janus. The nonstandard Janus string has these operators defined, however, and strings are where these operators are used most (in reference to arrays).

5. Janus does not implement most of the array attribute functions.

6. Neither Janus or SuperSoft implements aggregates.

7. Neither Janus or SuperSoft implements slices.

8. Some record attributes are missing from both Janus and SuperSoft.

9. SuperSoft does not implement either discriminants or variant records. Janus has a nonstandard way of implementing variant records and discriminants.

Chapter 8

1. Janus has a nonstandard BCD fixed type, which is fine for decimal operations but which falls down with oddball values for **delta**. SuperSoft does not implement fixed point numbers at all.

2. Janus has a double-precision **FLOAT** in a set of separate packages.

3. SuperSoft doesn't implement the floating point constraint.

4. SuperSoft does not implement access types.

5. Janus does not allow initialization of allocators.

6. SuperSoft does not implement incomplete type declarations.

Chapter 9

1. The procedures and functions in this chapter are written in as general a way as possible, using as few nonstandard or advanced features of Ada as possible, to fit the largest number of subsets and full Ada compilers.

2. The Value function can be rewritten for SuperSoft using the Slice function given in the notes for Chapter 6.

Chapter 10

1. SuperSoft does not support deferred constants or private types.

2. Neither SuperSoft nor Janus supports generics.

Chapter 11

1. Neither Janus nor SuperSoft supports representation specifications.

2. Janus uses a nonstandard procedure in place of Unchecked_Deallocation.

Chapter 13

1. Neither Janus nor SuperSoft supports multitasking.

APPENDIX B
Glossary

Accept statement—See *entry*.

Access parameter—A value of an *access type* (an *access value*) is either a null value, or a value that *designates* an *object* created by an *allocator*. The designated object can be read and updated via the access value. The definition of an access type specifies the type of objects designated by values of the access type. See also *collection*.

Actual parameter—See *parameter*.

Aggregate—the *evaluation* of an aggregate yields a value of a *composite type*. The value is specified by giving the value of each *component*. Either *positional association* or *named association* may be used to indicate which value is associated with which component.

Allocator—The evaluation of an *allocator* creates an *object* and returns a new *access value* which *designates* the object.

Array type—A value of an array type consists of *components* which are all of the same *sub-type* (and hence, of the same type). Each component is uniquely distinguished by an *index* (for a one-dimensional array) or by a sequence of indices (for a multidimensional array). Each *index* must be a value of a *discrete type* and must lie in the correct index *range*.

Assignment—Assignment is the *operation* that replaces the current value of a *variable* by a new value. An *assignment statement* specifies a variable on the left, and on the right, an *expression* whose value is to be the new value of the variable.

Attribute—The evaluation of an attribute yields a predefined characteristic of a named entity; some attributes are *functions*.

Block statement—a block statement is a single statement that may contain a sequence of statements. It may also include a *declarative part*, and *exception handlers*; their effects are local to the block statement.

Body—A body defines the execution of a *subprogram, package,* or *task*. A *body stub* is a form of body that indicates that this execution is defined in a separate compiled *sub-unit*.

Collection—a collection is the entire set of *objects* created by evaluation of *allocators* for an *access type*.

Compilation unit—A compilation unit is the *declaration* or the *body* of a *program unit*, presented for compilation as an independent text. It is optionally preceded by a *context* *clause*, naming other compilation units upon which it depends by means of one or more *with* clauses.

Component—A component is a value that is part of a larger value, or an *object* that is part of a larger object.

Composite type—A composite type is one whose values have *components*. There are two kinds of composite types: *array types* and *record types*.

Constant—See *object*.

Constraint—A constraint determines a subset of the values of a *type*. A value in that subset *satisfies* the constraint.

Context clause—See *compilation unit*.

Declaration—A declaration associates an *identifier* (or some other notation) with an entity. This association is in effect within a region of text called the *scope* of the declaration. Within the scope of the declaration, there are places where it is possible to use the identifier to refer to the associated declared entity. At such places the identifier is said to be a *simple name* of the entity; the *name* is said to *denote* the associated entity.

Declarative part—A declarative part is a sequence of *declarations*. It may also contain related information such as *subprogram bodies* and *representation clauses*.

Denote—See *declaration*.

Derived type—A derived type is a *type* whose operations and values are replicas of those of an existing type. The existing type is called the *parent type* of the derived type.

Designate—See *access type, task*.

Direct visibility—See *visibility*.

Discrete type—A discrete type is a *type* which has an ordered set of distinct values. The discrete types are the *enumeration* and *integer types*. Discrete types are used for indexing and iteration, and for choices in case statements and record *variants*.

Discriminant—A discriminant is a distinguished *component* of an *object* or value of a *record type*. The *subtypes* of other components, or even their presence or absence, may depend on the value of the discriminant.

Discriminant constraint—A discriminant constraint on a *record type* or *private type* specifies a value for each *discriminant* of the *type*.

Elaboration—The elaboration of a *declaration* is the process by which the declaration achieves its effect (such as creating an *object*); this process occurs during program execution.

Entry—An entry is used for communication between *tasks*. Externally, an entry is called just as a *subprogram* is called; its internal behavior is specified by one or more *accept statements* specifying the actions to be performed when the entry is called.

Enumeration type—An enumeration type is a *discrete type* whose values are represented by enumeration literals which are given explicitly in the *type declaration*. These enumeration literals are either *identifiers* or *character literals*.

Evaluation—The evaluation of an *expression* is the process by which the value of the *expression* is computed. This process occurs during program execution.

Exception—An exception is an error situation which may arise during program execution. To *raise* an exception is to abandon normal program execution so as to signal that the error has taken place. An *exception handler* is a portion of program text specifying a

---

response to the exception. Execution of such a program text is called *handling* the exception.

Expanded name—An expanded name *denotes* an entity which is *declared* immediately within some construct. An *expanded name* has the form of a *selected component*: the *prefix* denotes the construct (a *program unit*; or a *block*, loop, or *accept statement*); the *selector* is the *simple name* of the entity.

Expression—An expression defines the computation of a value.

Fixed-point type—See *real type*.

Floating-point type— See *real type*.

Formal parameter—See *parameter*.

Function—See *subprogram*.

Generic unit—A generic unit is a template either for a set of *subprograms* or for a set of *packages*. A subprogram or package created using the template is called an *instance* of the generic unit. A *generic instantiation* is the kind of *declaration* that creates an instance. A generic unit is written as a subprogram or package but with the *specification* prefixed by a *generic formal part* which may declare *generic formal parameters*. A generic formal parameter is either a *type*, a *subprogram*, or an *object*. A *generic unit* is one of the kinds of *program unit*.

Handler—See *exception*.

Index—See *array type*.

Index constraint—An index constraint for an *array type* specifies the lower and upper bounds for each index *range* of the array type.

Indexed component—An indexed component *denotes* a *component* in an *array*. It is a form of *name* containing expressions which specify the value of the *indices* of the array component. An indexed component may also denote an *entry* in a family of entries.

Instance—See *generic unit*.

Integer type—An integer type is a *discrete type* whose values represent all integer numbers within a specific *range*.

Lexical element—A lexical element is an identifier, a *literal*, a delimiter, or a comment.

Limited type—A limited type is a *type* for which neither *assignment* nor the predefined comparison for equality is implicitly declared. All *task* types are limited. A *private type* can be defined to be limited. An equality operator can be explicitly declared for a limited type.

Literal—A literal represents a value literally, that is, by means of letters and other characters. A literal is either a numeric literal, an enumeration literal, a character literal, or a string literal.

Mode—See *parameter*.

Model number—A model number is an exactly representable value of a *real type*. *Operations* of a real type are defined in terms of operations on the model numbers of the type. The properties of the model numbers and of the operations are the minimal properties preserved by all implementations of the real type.

Name—A name is construct that stands for an entity: it is said that the name *denotes* the entity, and that the entity is the meaning of the name. See also *declaration prefix*.

Named association—A named association specifies the association of an item with one or more positions in a list, by naming the positions.

Object—An object contains a value. A program creates an object either by *elaborating* an *object declaration* or by *evaluating* an *allocator*. The declaration or allocator specifies a *type* for the object; the object can only contain values of that type.

Operation—An operation is an elementary action associated with one or more *types*. It is either implicitly declared by the *declaration* of the type, or it is a *subprogram* that has a *parameter* or *result* of the type.

Operator—An operator is an operation which has one or two operands. A unary operator is written before an operand; a binary operator is written between two operands. This notation is a special kind of *function call*. An operator can be declared as a function. Many operators are implicitly declared by the *declaration* of a *type* (for example, most type declarations imply the declaration of the equality operator for values of the type).

Overloading—An identifier can have several alternative meanings at a given point in the program text: this property is called *overloading*. For example, an overloaded enumeration literal can be an *identifier* that appears in the definitions of two or more *enumeration types*. The effective meaning of an *overloaded identifier* is determined by the context. *Subprograms, aggregates, allocators*, and string *literals* can also be *overloaded*.

Package—A package specifies a group of logically related entities, such as *types, objects* of those types, and *subprograms* with *parameters* of those types. It is written as a *package declaration* and a *package body*. The package declaration has a *visible part*, containing the *declarations* of entities that can be explicitly used outside the package. It may also have a *private part* containing structural details that complete the specification of the visible entities, but which are irrelevant to the user of the package. The *package body* contains implementations of *subprograms* (and possibly *tasks* as other packages) that have been specified in the package declaration. A package is one of the kinds of *program unit*.

Parameter—A parameter is one of the named entities associated with a *subprogram, entry,* or *generic unit*, and used to communicate with the corresponding subprogram body, *accept statement* or generic body. A *formal parameter* is an identifier used to denote the name entity within the body. An *actual parameter* is the particular entity associated with the corresponding formal parameter by a *subprogram call, entry call,* or *generic instantiation*. The *mode* of a formal parameter specifies whether the associated actual parameter supplies a value for the formal parameter, or the formal parameter supplies a value for the actual parameter, or both. The association of actual parameters with formal parameters can be specified by *named associations*, by *positional associations*, or by a combination of these.

Parent type—See *derived type*.

Positional association—a positional association specifies the association of an item with a position in a list, by using the position in the text to specify the item.

Pragma—A pragma conveys information to the compiler.

Prefix—A prefix is used as the first part of certain kinds of *name*. A *prefix* is either a *function call* or a *name*.

Private part—See *package*.

Private type—A private type is a *type* whose structure and set of values are clearly defined, but not directly available to the user of the type. A private type is known only by its *discriminants* (if any) and by the set of *operations* defined for it. A private type and its applicable operations are defined in the *visible part* of a *package*, or in a *generic formal part*. *Assignment*, equality, and inequality are also defined for *private types*, unless the private type is limited.

Procedure—See *subprogram*.

Program—A program is composed of a number of *compilation units*, one of which is a *subprogram* called the *main program*. Execution of the program consists of execution of the main program, which may invoke subprograms declared in the other compilation units of the program.

Program unit—A program unit is any one of a *generic unit*, *package*, *subprogram*, or *task unit*.

Qualified expression—A qualified expression is an *expression* preceded by an indication of its *type* or *subtype*. Such qualification is used when, in its absence, the expression might be ambiguous (for example as a consequence of *overloading*).

Raising an exception—See *exception*.

Range—A range is a contiguous set of values of a *scalar type*. A range is specified by giving the lower and upper bounds for the values. A value in the range is said to *belong* to the range.

Real type—A real type is a *type* whose values represent approximations to the real numbers. There are two kinds of real types: *fixed point types* are specified by an absolute error bound; *floating point types* are specified by a relative error bound expressed as a number of significant decimal digits.

Record type—A value of a record type consists of *components* which are usually of different *types* or *subtypes*. For each component of a record value or record *object*, the definition of the record specifies an identifier that uniquely determines the component with the record.

Renaming declaration—A renaming declaration declares another *name* for an entity.

Rendezvous—A rendezvous is the interaction that occurs between two parallel *tasks* when one task has called an *entry* to the other task, and a corresponding *accept statement* is being executed by the other task on behalf of the calling task.

Representation clause—A representation clause directs the compiler in the selection of the mapping of a *type*, an *object*, or a *task* onto features of the underlying machine that executes a program. In some cases, representation clauses completely specify the mapping; in other cases, they provide criteria for choosing a mapping.

Satisfy—See *constraint, subtype*.

Scalar type—An *object* or value of a scalar *type* does not have *components*. A *scalar type* is either a *discrete type* or a *real type*. The values of a *scalar type* are ordered.

Scope—See *declaration*.

Selected component—A selected component is a *name* consisting of a *prefix* and of an identifier called the *selector*. Selected components are used to denote record components, *entries*, and *objects* designated by access values; they are also used as *expanded names*.

Selector—See *selected component*.

Simple name—See *declaration, name*.

Statement—A statement specifies one or more actions to be performed during the execution of a program.

Subcomponent—A subcomponent is either a *component* or a component of another subcomponent.

Subprogram—A subprogram is either a *procedure* or a *function*. A procedure specifies a sequence of actions and is invoked by a *procedure call* statement. A *function* specifies a sequence of actions and also returns a value called the *result*, and so a *function call* is an *expression*. A subprogram is written as a *subprogram declaration*, which specifies its *name*, *formal parameters*, and (for a function) its result; and a *subprogram body* which specifies the sequence of actions. The subprogram call specifies the *actual parameters* that are to be associated with the formal parameters. A subprogram is one of the kinds of *program units*.

Subtype—A subtype of a *type* characterizes a subset of the values of the type. The subset is determined by a *constraint* on the type. Each value in the set of values of a subtype *belongs* to the subtype and *satisfies* the constraint determining the subtype.

Subunit—See *body*.

Task—A task operates in parallel with other parts of the program. It is written as a *task specification* (which specifies the *name* of the task and the names and *formal parameters* of its entries), and a *task body* which defines its execution. A *task unit* is one of the kinds of *program units*. A *task type* is a *type* that permits the subsequent declaration of any number of similar tasks of the type. A value of a task type is said to *designate* a task.

Type—A type characterizes both a set of values, and a set of *operations* applicable to those values. A *type definition* is a language construct that defines a type. A particular type is either an *access type*, an *array type*, a *private type*, a *record type*, a *scalar type*, or a *task type*.

Use clause—A use clause achieves *direct visibility* of *declarations* that appear in the *visible* parts of named *packages*.

Variable—See *object*.

Variant part—A variant part of a *record* specifies alternative record *components*, depending on a *discriminant* of the record. Each value of the discriminant establishes a particular alternative of the variant part.

Visibility—At a given point in a program text, the *declaration* of an entity with a certain identifier is said to be *visible* if the entity is an acceptable meaning for an occurrence at that point of the identifier. The declaration is *visible* by *selection* at the place of the *selector* in a *selected component* or at the place of the name in a *named association*. Otherwise, the declaration is *directly visible*, that is, if the identifier alone has that meaning.

Visible part—See *package*.

With clause—See *compilation unit*.

NOTE: This glossary is reproduced in its entirety from the *Language Reference Manual*.

APPENDIX C
Compiling with Janus and SuperSoft

This appendix contains hints, tips, and feature comparisons of the Janus/Ada compiler, available from R&R Software, and the Maranatha "A" compiler, available from SuperSoft. While this material will be dated, perhaps it will give you a feel for the things to look for in a compiler, and if you already own one of these compilers, maybe it will give you some help.

Both compiler manuals have a listing of the features of Ada that are not implemented, and you should consult your manual for Truth as represented by your implementation.

We are using Janus version 1.5.0 and SuperSoft version 3.00 for this book, the latest available at the time of this writing.

In general terms, SuperSoft seems to have the best match to Ada syntax. Strings in particular are very standard in SuperSoft. Unfortunately Ada is a complex and delicately balanced language, and the omission of just one feature sends ripples of inconvenience through the rest of the language. Slices, in particular, come to mind here. Ada strings are unwieldy at best, and without slices the strings in SuperSoft are agony to work with. A package like our variant string handler in Chapter 9 is a must for any program doing string work.

The Janus folks opted to use a nonstandard string type in Janus/Ada. Their string type is strongly modeled after the Pascal MT$^+$ string type, undoubtably because the Janus/Ada compiler was orginally written in MT$^+$ and "bootstrapped" into Ada from there. This makes the Janus string as easy to use as BASIC strings, but very nonportable. In addition it takes the pressure off the development of the array attribute functions crucial to string work. They aren't needed for strings, so they aren't available for any array types. Again, the variant strings presented in Chapter 9 can solve most of the portability problems.

In general Janus version 1.5.0 seems to be a better compiler than the SuperSoft "A" 3.00. Janus is evolving steadily (at least the 16-bit version) and is fairly bug-free. SuperSoft seems to be fixed at the stage it is at, and the I/O library has some nasty and subtle bugs. It needs to be reworked by someone familiar with both Ada and the operating system.

The lack of exceptions in Janus 1.5.0 makes the I/O fairly nonportable. I/O in Ada depends heavily on exceptions to determine the results of opens and disk writes. The I/O is a cross between Ada and C, with the least desirable features of both included.

Quirks exist in both complier's console I/O. Janus (at least in CP/M) uses the BDOS "get string" function, which means that it will work with submit files and XSUB, but also means that the operating system editing characters are in effect and can't be passed to the program. It also leaves the Control-C abort active for all inputs and means that RETURN must be pressed before characters are passed even to a character **get**.

SuperSoft, conversely, uses the "get character" BDOS call and stuffs whatever comes in into your parameter. When using the **Get_Line** procedure, for example, everything but carriage returns are returned in the string, including backspaces.

Other bugs exist in both compilers, which presumably will be fixed by the time you read this. For example an enumeration type can't be declared in a Janus package specification and then be output in the body—the compiler doesn't generate an error, but garbage comes out when you try to **Put** the type. SuperSoft has a bizarre and nasty bug in the exception handler for I/O.

When actually compiling, Janus wins for ease of use. A side effect of this ease of use is that constants can't be declared in a specification. The SuperSoft linkage procedure is critical and time-consuming.

The manuals for both compilers are pretty good, but both lack a few bits of essential information, or bury it where it's not easy to find. Here are our tips for using the compilers.

Janus

Set up the compiler and linker disks as per the manual and carry out the instructions as they are. What they don't come right out and say is this:

1. The compilation unit in Janus is the package. The main program in Janus is the intialization section of a package body. The main program won't have a specification. Janus does quite well at linking, so after all subordinate packages and their specifications have been compiled you can compile the main program package body. The compiled specifications of all **with**ed packages must be on either the source disk (the disk where the main program is) or on the default disk while compiling. When linking the main program, the compiled bodies of all **with**ed packages must be on either the default or source disks.

2. Each pass of the compiler can only handle one compilation unit at a time, either a package specification or a package body. A separate file is required for each, as is a separate compilation. The specification must be compiled first.

3. The file names of specifications and bodies must match the package names. The extensions are as follows:

```
.LIB       a package specification
.PKG       a package body
.SYM       a compiled specification
.JRL       a compiled body
```

The compiler assumes, unless told otherwise, that you are compiling a package body, and will supply a default extension of .PKG to a bare filename on the command line.

SuperSoft

Follow the disk set-up and compiling direction as per the manual. Then:

1. Package names have no relationship to their filenames. For example, the package **text__io** is supplied in source form as **TEXTIO.ADA**, the specification, and **TEXTBODY.ADA**, the body.
2. The compiler will generate a file with the extension **.SYM** for each specification compiled. **text__io** will have a file called **TEXT__IO.SYM** generated. Note that the underbar (underline) character is an illegal system name character, and these files will be very hard to erase. An ambiguous file specification will be needed.
3. Both the specification and the body produce linkable code for the object program. These files have the extension **.REL**, and have the same main name as the source file.
4. Both the specification and the body **.REL** must be explicitly linked when linking the object program. The order is critical, so be sure you read and understand the manual. The explanation is pretty good, except for forgetting to mention that both spec and body have to be linked.

APPENDIX D
Predefined Library
Units

The package **Standard** contains all predefined identifiers in Ada. This is a listing of **Standard**'s specifications. **Standard**'s body is implementation defined.

Typically, it is embedded in the compiler. The initial versions of Janus and SuperSoft have standard packages that are incomplete for one reason or another.

In microcomputer compilers without generics, the package ASCII embedded in **Standard** is separate and it might not be used at all since it adds 4K to the size of the program using it.

UNIVERSAL REAL is an anonymous type.

```
package Standard is

-- first is the type BOOLEAN and its operators

type BOOLEAN is (FALSE, TRUE);

-- the predefined relational operators for boolean types are:

function "="    (Left, Right : BOOLEAN) return BOOLEAN;
function "/="   (Left, Right : BOOLEAN) return BOOLEAN;
function "<"    (Left, Right : BOOLEAN) return BOOLEAN;
function "<="   (Left, Right : BOOLEAN) return BOOLEAN;
function ">"    (Left, Right : BOOLEAN) return BOOLEAN;
function ">="   (Left, Right : BOOLEAN) return BOOLEAN;

-- the predefined logical operators for boolean types are

function "and"  (Left, Right : BOOLEAN) return BOOLEAN;
```

```
function "or"    (Left, Right : BOOLEAN) return BOOLEAN;
function "xor"   (Left, Right : BOOLEAN) return BOOLEAN;

-- the predefined logical negation operator for boolean types is:

function "not"  (Left, Right : BOOLEAN) return BOOLEAN;


-- Universal type UNIVERSAL_INTEGER is predefined.

type INTEGER is implementation_defined;

-- the predefined relational operators for integer types are

function "="     (Left, Right : INTEGER) return BOOLEAN;
function "/="    (Left, Right : INTEGER) return BOOLEAN;
function "<"     (Left, Right : INTEGER) return BOOLEAN;
function "<="    (Left, Right : INTEGER) return BOOLEAN;
function ">"     (Left, Right : INTEGER) return BOOLEAN;
function ">="    (Left, Right : INTEGER) return BOOLEAN;

-- predefined arithmetic types

function "+"     (Right : INTEGER) return INTEGER;
function "-"     (Right : INTEGER) return INTEGER;
function "abs"   (Right : INTEGER) return INTEGER;

function "+"     (Left, Right : INTEGER) return INTEGER;
function "-"     (Left, Right : INTEGER) return INTEGER;
function "*"     (Left, Right : INTEGER) return INTEGER;
function "/"     (Left, Right : INTEGER) return INTEGER;
function "rem"   (Left, Right : INTEGER) return INTEGER;
function "mod"   (Left, Right : INTEGER) return INTEGER;

function "**"    (Left : INTEGER; Right : INTEGER) return INTEGER;


-- the universal type UNIVERSAL_REAL is predefined.

type FLOAT is implementation_defined;

function "="     (Left, Right : FLOAT) return BOOLEAN;
```

```
function "/="   (Left, Right : FLOAT) return BOOLEAN;
function "<"    (Left, Right : FLOAT) return BOOLEAN;
function "<="   (Left, Right : FLOAT) return BOOLEAN;
function ">"    (Left, Right : FLOAT) return BOOLEAN;
function ">="   (Left, Right : FLOAT) return BOOLEAN;

function "+"    (Right : FLOAT) return FLOAT;
function "-"    (Right : FLOAT) return FLOAT;
function "abs"  (Right : FLOAT) return FLOAT;

function "+"    (Left, Right : FLOAT) return FLOAT;
function "-"    (Left, Right : FLOAT) return FLOAT;
function "*"    (Left, Right : FLOAT) return FLOAT;
function "/"    (Left, Right : FLOAT) return FLOAT;

function "**"   (Left : FLOAT; Right : INTEGER) return FLOAT;

-- The following characters form the standard ASCII set.
-- Character literals corresponding to control characters are
-- not identifiers; they are indicated in italics.

type CHARACTER is                    [underscoring of characters indicates italics]

( nul,   soh,   stx,   etx,    eot,   enq,   ack,   bel,
  bs,    ht,    lf,    vt,     ff,    cr,    so,    si,
  dle,   dc1,   dc2,   dc3,    dc4,   nak,   syn,   etb,
  can,   em,    sub,   esc,    fs,    gs,    rs,    us,

  ' ',   '!',   '"',   '#',    '$',   '%',   '&',   ''',
  '(',   ')',   '*',   '+',    ',',   '-',   '.',   '/',
  '0',   '1',   '2',   '3',    '4',   '5',   '6',   '7',
  '8',   '9',   ':',   ';',    '<',   '=',   '>',   '?',

  '@',   'A',   'B',   'C',    'D',   'E',   'F',   'G',
  'H',   'I',   'J',   'K',    'L',   'M',   'N',   'O',
  'P',   'Q',   'R',   'S',    'T',   'U',   'V',   'W',
  'X',   'Y',   'Z',   '[',    '\',   ']',   '^',   '_',

  '`',   'a',   'b',   'c',    'd',   'e',   'f',   'g',
  'h',   'i',   'j',   'k',    'l',   'm',   'n',   'o',
  'p',   'q',   'r',   's',    't',   'u',   'v',   'w',
  'x',   'y',   'z',   '{',    '|',   '}',   '~',   del  );
```

```
for CHARACTER use

-- The 128 member ASCII character set without holes
-- (0,1,2,3,4,5,6, ..., 124, 125, 126, 127);


-- The predefined operators for character type are the same as as
-- for any enumeration type; e. g., the relational operators [ <,
-- <=, =, >, >=, /= ] for comparisons and the ampersand [ & ]  for
-- concatenations.
package ASCII is

-- control characters                    [underscoring of characters indicates italics]

NUL        : constant CHARACTER := nul;
SOH        : constant CHARACTER := soh;
STX        : constant CHARACTER := stx;
ETX        : constant CHARACTER := etx;
EOT        : constant CHARACTER := eot;
ENQ        : constant CHARACTER := enq;
ACK        : constant CHARACTER := ack;
BEL        : constant CHARACTER := bel;
BS         : constant CHARACTER := bs;
HT         : constant CHARACTER := ht;
LF         : constant CHARACTER := lf;
VT         : constant CHARACTER := vt;
FF         : constant CHARACTER := ff;
CR         : constant CHARACTER := cr;
SO         : constant CHARACTER := so;
SI         : constant CHARACTER := si;
DLE        : constant CHARACTER := dle;
DC1        : constant CHARACTER := dc1;
DC2        : constant CHARACTER := dc2;
DC3        : constant CHARACTER := dc3;
DC4        : constant CHARACTER := dc4;
NAK        : constant CHARACTER := nak;
SYN        : constant CHARACTER := syn;
ETB        : constant CHARACTER := etb;
CAN        : constant CHARACTER := can;
EM         : constant CHARACTER := em;
SUB        : constant CHARACTER := sub;
ESC        : constant CHARACTER := esc;
FS         : constant CHARACTER := fs;
```

```
GS          : constant CHARACTER := gs;
RS          : constant CHARACTER := rs;
US          : constant CHARACTER := us;
DEL         : constant CHARACTER := del;


-- Other characters

EXCLAM      : constant CHARACTER := '!';
SHARP       : constant CHARACTER := '#';
PERCENT     : constant CHARACTER := '%';
COLON       : constant CHARACTER := ':';
QUERY       : constant CHARACTER := '?';
L_BRACKET   : constant CHARACTER := '[';
R_BRACKET   : constant CHARACTER := ']';
UNDERLINE   : constant CHARACTER := '_';
L_BRACE     : constant CHARACTER := '{';
R_BRACE     : constant CHARACTER := '}';

-- lowercase letters:

LC_A        : constant CHARACTER := 'a';
...
LC_Z        : constant CHARACTER := 'z';

END ASCII;

-- predefined subtypes:

subtype NATURAL  is INTEGER range 0..INTEGER'last;
subtype POSITIVE is INTEGER range 1..INTEGER'last;

-- predefined string type:

type STRING is array (POSITIVE range <>) OF CHARACTER;
pragma pack(STRING);

-- predefined operators for string types are as follows:

-- comparisons

function "="    (Left, Right : STRING) return BOOLEAN;
function "/="   (Left, Right : STRING) return BOOLEAN;
function "<"    (Left, Right : STRING) return BOOLEAN;
function "<="   (Left, Right : STRING) return BOOLEAN;
```

```
function ">"     (Left, Right : STRING) return BOOLEAN;
function ">="    (Left, Right : STRING) return BOOLEAN;

-- concatenation of strings and characters

function "&"     (Left : STRING;     Right: STRING)     RETURN STRING;
function "&"     (Left : CHARACTER;  Right: STRING)     RETURN STRING;
function "&"     (Left : STRING;     Right: CHARACTER)  RETURN STRING;
function "&"     (Left : CHARACTER;  Right: CHARACTER)  RETURN STRING;

type DURATION is delta implementation_defined
                range implementation_defined;

-- The predefined operations for the type
-- duration are the same as for any
-- fixed-point type.

-- The predefined exceptions:

CONSTRAINT_ERROR : exception;
NUMERIC_ERROR    : exception;
PROGRAM_ERROR    : exception;
STORAGE_ERROR    : exception;
TASKING_ERROR    : exception;

end Standard; -- package specifications
package body Standard is

     -- implementation defined

end Standard; -- package body
```

Ada has no intrinsic I/O routines. The following predefined package specifications are required for all Ada compilers, however. The bodies of these packages are implementation dependent and come with the compilers as precompiled library modules. These listings are drawn from the Ada Reference Manual, Chapter 14.

(*Note:* It is feasible to trim down these specifications to what is actually needed in a given program.)

```
-- Specification of the Package Sequential_IO
---------------------------------------------

with IO_Exceptions;
generic
   type ELEMENT_TYPE is private;
package Sequential_IO is

   type FILE_TYPE is limited private;

   type FILE_MODE is (IN_FILE, OUT_FILE);


   --File Management

   procedure Create (File : in out FILE_TYPE;
                     Mode : in FILE_MODE := OUTFILE
                     Name : in STRING :="";
                     Form : in STRING := "");

   procedure Open    (File : in out FILE_TYPE;
                     Mode : in FILE_MODE;
                     Name : in STRING;
                     Form : in STRING := "");

   procedure Close  (File : in out FILE_TYPE);
   procedure Delete (File : in out FILE_TYPE);
   procedure Reset  (File : in out FILE_TYPE; in FILE_MODE);
   procedure Reset  (File : in out FILE_TYPE);

   function Mode    (File : in FILE_TYPE) return FILE_MODE;
   function Name    (File : in FILE_TYPE) return STRING;
   function Form    (File : in FILE_TYPE) return STRING;

   function Is_Open (File : in FILE_TYPE) return BOOLEAN;

   -- Input and Output operations

   procedure Read  (File : in FILE_TYPE; Item : out ELEMENT_TYPE);
   procedure Write (File : in FILE_TYPE; Item : in  ELEMENT_TYPE);

   function End_Of_File(File : in FILE_TYPE) return BOOLEAN;
```

```
   -- Exceptions

   STATUS_ERROR          : exception renames IO_Exceptions.STATUS_ERROR;
   MODE_ERROR            : exception renames IO_Exceptions.MODE_ERROR;
   NAME_ERROR            : exception renames IO_Exceptions.NAME_ERROR;
   USE_ERROR             : exception renames IO_Exceptions.USE_ERROR;
   DEVICE_ERROR          : exception renames IO_Exceptions.DEVICE_ERROR;
   END_ERROR             : exception renames IO_Exceptions.END_ERROR;
   DATA_ERROR            : exception renames IO_Exceptions.DATE_ERROR;

private
   -- implementation-depedent
end Sequential_IO;




-- Specifications of the Package Direct_IO
--------------------------------------------

with IO_Exceptions;
generic
   type ELEMENT_TYPE is private;
package Direct_IO is

   type FILE_TYPE is limited private;

   type    FILE_MODE is (IN_FILE, INOUT_FILE, OUT_FILE);
   type    COUNT      is range ( -- implemanentation_defined);
   subtype POSITIVE_COUNT is COUNT range 1..COUNT'last;


   --File Management

   procedure Create (File : in out FILE_TYPE;
                     Mode : in FILE_MODE :=INOUT_FILE;
                     Name : in STRING := "";
                     Form : in STRING := "");

   procedure Open    (File : in out FILE_TYPE;
                     Mode : in FILE_MODE;
                     Name : in STRING;
                     Form : in STRING :="");
```

```
procedure Close  (File : in out FILE_TYPE);
procedure Delete (File : in out FILE_TYPE);
procedure Reset  (File : in out FILE_TYPE; Mode : in FILE_MODE);
procedure Reset  (File : in out FILE_TYPE);

function Mode    (File : in FILE_TYPE) return FILE_MODE;
function Name    (File : in FILE_TYPE) return STRING;
function Form    (File : in FILE_TYPE) return STRING;

function Is_Open (File : in FILE_TYPE) return BOOLEAN;

--Input and output operations

procedure Read (File : FILE_TYPE;
                Item : out ELEMENT_TYPE;
                From : POSITIVE_COUNT);
procedure Read (File : FILE_TYPE; Item : out ELEMENT_TYPE);

procedure Write(File : FILE_TYPE;
                Item : in ELEMENT_TYPE;
                To   : POSITIVE_COUNT);
procedure Write(File : FILE_TYPE; Item : in ELEMENT_TYPE);

procedure Set_Index(File : in FILE_TYPE; To : in POSITIVE_COUNT);

function Index(File : in FILE_TYPE; return POSITIVE_COUNT;
function Size (File : in FILE_TYPE; return COUNT;

function End_Of_File (File : in FILE_TYPE) return BOOLEAN;

--Exceptions

STATUS_ERROR  : exception renames IO_Exceptions.STATUS_ERROR;
MODE_ERROR    : exception renames IO_Exceptions.MODE_ERROR;
NAME_ERROR    : exception renames IO_Exceptions.NAME_ERROR;
USE_ERROR     : exception renames IO_Exceptions.USE_ERROR;
DEVICE_ERROR  : exception renames IO_Exceptions.DEVICE_ERROR;
END_ERROR     : exception renames IO_Exceptions.END_ERROR;
DATA_ERROR    : exception renames IO_Exceptions.DATE_ERROR;
private
   -- implementation-dependent
end Direct_IO;
```

```
-- Specifications of the Package Text_IO
-----------------------------------------

with IO_Exceptions
package Text_IO is

    type FILE_TYPE is limited private;

    type FILE_MODE is (IN_FILE, OUT_FILE);

    type COUNT is range 0 .. Implementation_defined;
    subtype POSITIVE_COUNT is COUNT range 1 .. COUNT'last;
    UNBOUNDED : constant COUNT := 0; -- line and page length

    subtype FIELD        is INTEGER range 0 .. implementation_defined;
    subtype NUMBER_BASE is INTEGER range 2 .. 16;

    type TYPE_SET is (LOWER_CASE, UPPER_CASE);


    --File Management

    procedure Create (File : in out FILE_TYPE;
                      Mode : in FILE_MODE := OUTFILE
                      Name : in STRING :="";
                      Form : in STRING := "");

    procedure Open   (File : in out FILE_TYPE;
                      Mode : in FILE_MODE;
                      Name : in STRING;
                      Form : in STRING := "");

    procedure Close  (File : in out FILE_TYPE);
    procedure Delete (File : in out FILE_TYPE);
    procedure Reset  (File : in out FILE_TYPE; Mode : in FILE_MODE);
    procedure Reset  (File : in out FILE_TYPE);

    function Mode    (File : in FILE_TYPE) return FILE_MODE;
    function Name    (File : in FILE_TYPE) return STRING;
    function Form    (File : in FILE_TYPE) return STRING;

    function Is_Open (File : in FILE_TYPE) return BOOLEAN;

    -- Control of default input and out files
```

```
procedure Set_Input  (File : in FILE_TYPE);
procedure Set_Output (File : in FILE_TYPE);

function Standard_Input  (File : in FILE_TYPE);
function Standard_Output (File : in FILE_TYPE);

function Current_Input  (File : in FILE_TYPE);
function Current_Output (File : in FILE_TYPE);

-- Specification of line and page lengths

procedure Set_Line_Length  (File : in FILE_TYPE; To : in COUNT);
procedure Set_Line_Length  (To : in COUNT);

procedure Set_Page_Length  (File : in FILE_TYPE; To : in COUNT);
procedure Set_Page_Length  (To : in COUNT);

function Line_Length (File : in FILE_TYPE) return COUNT;
function Line_Length return COUNT;

function Page_Length (File : in FILE_TYPE) return COUNT;
function Page_Length return COUNT;

-- Column, Line, and Page Control

procedure New_Line  (File : FILE_TYPE;
                     Spacing : in POSITIVE_COUNT := 1);

procedure New_Line  (Spacing : in POSITIVE_COUNT := 1);

procedure Skip_Line  (File : FILE_TYPE;
                      Spacing : in POSITIVE_COUNT := 1);

procedure Skip_Line  (Spacing : in POSITIVE_COUNT := 1);

function End_Of_Line (File : in FILE_TYPE) return BOOLEAN;
function End_Of_Line  return BOOLEAN;

procedure New_Page  (File : in FILE_TYPE);
procedure New_Page;

procedure Skip_Page  (File : in FILE_TYPE);
procedure Skip_Page;
```

```
function End_Of_Page (File : in FILE_TYPE) return BOOLEAN;
function End_Of_Page return BOOLEAN;

function End_Of_File (File : in FILE_TYPE) return BOOLEAN;
function End_Of_File return BOOLEAN;

procedure Set_Col  (File : in FILE_TYPE; To : in POSITIVE_COUNT);
procedure Set_Col  (To   : in POSITIVE_COUNT);

procedure Set_Line (File : in FILE_TYPE; To : in POSITIVE_COUNT);
procedure Set_Line (To   : in POSITIVE_COUNT);

function Col  (FILE: in FILE_TYPE) return POSITIVE_COUNT;
function Col   return POSITIVE_COUNT;

function Line (FILE: in FILE_TYPE) return POSITIVE_COUNT;
function Line  return POSITIVE_COUNT;

function Page (FILE: in FILE_TYPE) return POSITIVE_COUNT;
function Page  return POSITIVE_COUNT;

-- Character Input-Output

procedure Get(File : in FILE_TYPE; Item : out CHARACTER);
procedure Get(File : out CHARACTER);
procedure Put(File : in FILE_TYPE; Item : in CHARACTER);
procedure Put(Item : in CHARACTER);

-- String Input-Output

procedure Get(File : in FILE_TYPE; Item : out STRING);
procedure Get(File : out STRING);
procedure Put(File : in FILE_TYPE; Item : in STRING);
procedure Put(Item : in STRING);

procedure Get_Line(File : in FILE_TYPE;
                   Item : out STRING; Last : out NATURAL);
procedure Get_Line(File : out STRING; Last : out NATURAL);
procedure Put_Line(File : in FILE_TYPE; Item : in STRING);
procedure Put_Line(Item : in STRING);

-- Generic package for Input-Output of Integer Types
```

```
generic
   type NUM is range <>;
package Integer_IO is

   Default_Width : FIELD := NUM'Width;
   Default_Base  : NUMBER_BASE := 10;

   procedure Get(File : in FILE_TYPE;
                 Item : out NUM; Width : in FIELD :=0);
   procedure Get(ITME : out NUM; Width : in FIELD :=0);

   procedure Put(File  : in FILE_TYPE;
                 Item  : in NUM;
                 Width : in FIELD := Default_Base);
                 Base  : in NUMBER_BASE :=Default_Base);
   procedure Put(Item  : in NUM;
                 Width : in FIELD := Default_Width;
                 Base  : in NUMBER_BASE := Default_Base);

   procedure Get(From : in  STRING;
                 Item : out NUM; Last : out POSITIVE);

   procedure Put(To   : out STRING;
                 Item : in NUM;
                 Base : in NUMBER_BASE := Default_Base);

end Integer_IO;


-- Generic packages for Input-Output of Real Types

generic
   type NUM is digits <>;
package Float_IO is

   Default_Fore : FIELD := 2;
   Default_Aft  : FIELD := NUM'digits-1;
   Default_Exp  : FIELD := 3;

   procedure Get(File : in FILE_TYPE;
                 Item : out NUM; Width : in FIELD :=0);
   procedure Get(Item : out NUM; Width : in FIELD := 0);
```

```
            procedure Put(File : in FILE_TYPE;
                          Item : NUM;
                          Fore : in FIELD := Default_Fore;
                          Aft  : in FIELD := Default_Aft;
                          Exp  : in FIELD := Default_Exp);
            procedure Put(Item : NUM;
                          Fore : in FIELD := Default_Fore;
                          Aft  : in FIELD := Default_Aft;
                          Exp  : in FIELD := Default_Exp);

            procedure Get(From : in STRING; Item : out NUM;
                          Last : out POSITIVE);
            procedure Put(To   : out STRING;
                          Item : NUM;
                          Aft  : in FIELD := Default_Aft;
                          Exp  : in FIELD := Default_Exp);
        end Float_IO
```

```
        generic
          type NUM is delta <>;
        package Fixed_IO is

          Default_Fore : FIELD := NUM'Fore;
          Default_Aft  : FIELD := NUM'Aft;
          Default_Exp  : FIELD :=0;

          procedure Get(File : in FILE_TYPE;
                        Item : out NUM; Width : in FIELD :=0);
          procedure Get(Item : out NUM; Width : in FIELD := 0);

          procedure Put(File : in FILE_TYPE;
                        Item : NUM;
                        Fore : in FIELD := Default_Fore;
                        Aft  : in FIELD := Default_Aft;
                        Exp  : in FIELD := Default_Exp);

          procedure Put(Item : NUM;
                        Fore : in FIELD := Default_Fore;
                        Aft  : in FIELD := Default_Aft;
                        Exp  : in FIELD := Default_Exp);

          procedure Get(From : in STRING;
                        Item : out NUM; Last : out POSITIVE);
```

```
       procedure Put(To   : out STRING;
                      Item : NUM;
                      Aft  : in FIELD := Default_Aft;
                      Exp  : in FIELD := Default_Exp);
    end Fixed_IO;


    -- Generic package for Input-Output of Enumeration Types

    generic
       type ENUM is (<>);
    package Enumeration_IO is

       Default_Width   : FIELD := 0;
       Default_Setting : TYPE_SET := UPPER_CASE;

       procedure Get(File : in FILE_TYPE;
                     Item : out ENUM);

       procedure Put(File  : FILE_TYPE;
                     Item  : ENUM;
                     Width : in FIELD    := Default_Width;
                     Set   : in TYPE_SET := Default_Setting);
       procedure Put(Item  : ENUM;
                     Width : in FIELD    := Default_Width;
                     Set   : in TYPE_SET := Default_Setting);

       procedure Get(From : in STRING;
                     Item : out ENUM; Last : out POSITIVE);
       procedure Put(To   : out STRING;
                     Item : in ENUM;
                     Set  : in TYPE_SET := Default_Setting);
    end Enumeration_IO


    -- Exceptions

       STATUS_ERROR : exception renames IO_Exceptions.STATUS_ERROR;
       MODE_ERROR   : exception renames IO_Exceptions.MODE_ERROR;
       NAME_ERROR   : exception renames IO_Exceptions.NAME_ERROR;
       USE_ERROR    : exception renames IO_Exceptions.USE_ERROR;
       DEVICE_ERROR : exception renames IO_Exceptions.DEVICE_ERROR;
       END_ERROR    : exception renames IO_Exceptions.END_ERROR;
```

```
   DATA_ERROR     : exception renames IO_Exceptions.DATE_ERROR
   LAYOUT_ERROR   : exception renames IO_Exceptions.LAYOUT_ERROR;

private
  -- implementation-dependent
end TEXT_IO;
```

NOTE: The packages in Appendix D are taken from the *Language Reference Manual*.

APPENDIX E
Syntax Graphs and Quick Reference

The syntax diagrams and other material in this appendix are drawn from David A. Smith's *ANSI Standard Ada—Quick Reference Sheet*, which was created for in-house training at Hughes Aircraft's Denver Engineering Laboratories. We have found them to be a helpful reference for both the novice Ada programmer and the experienced user who needs to look up specific language features.

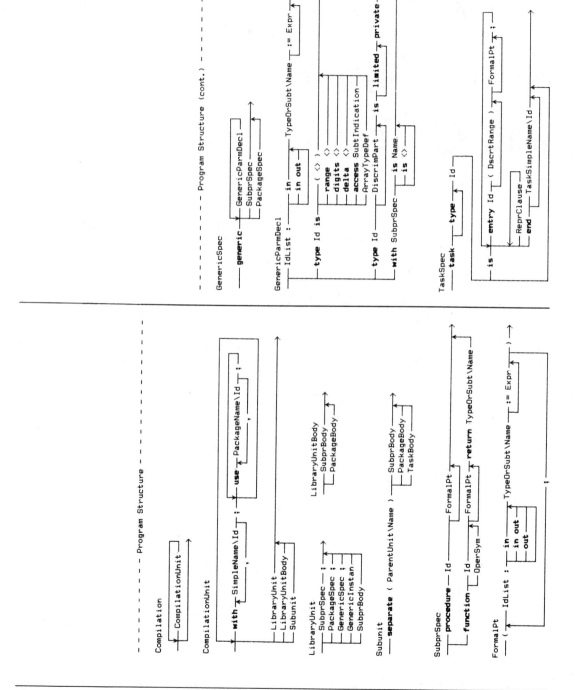

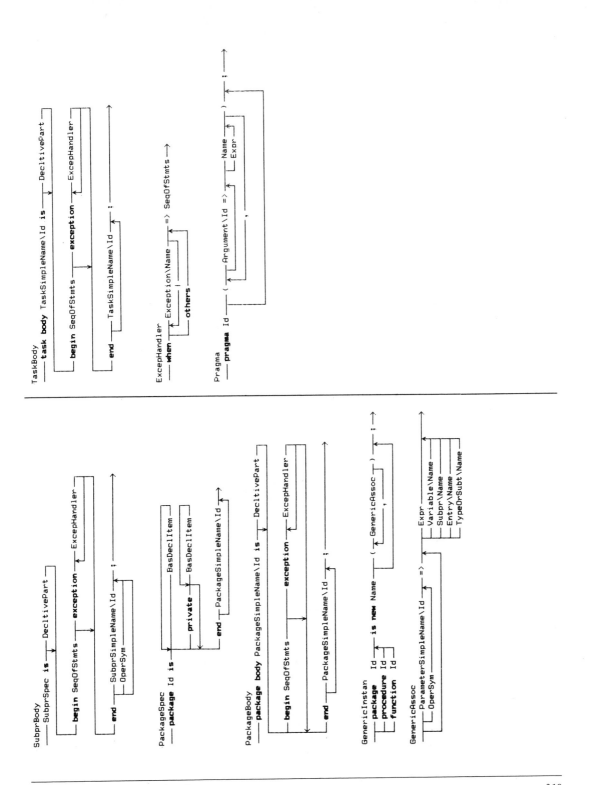

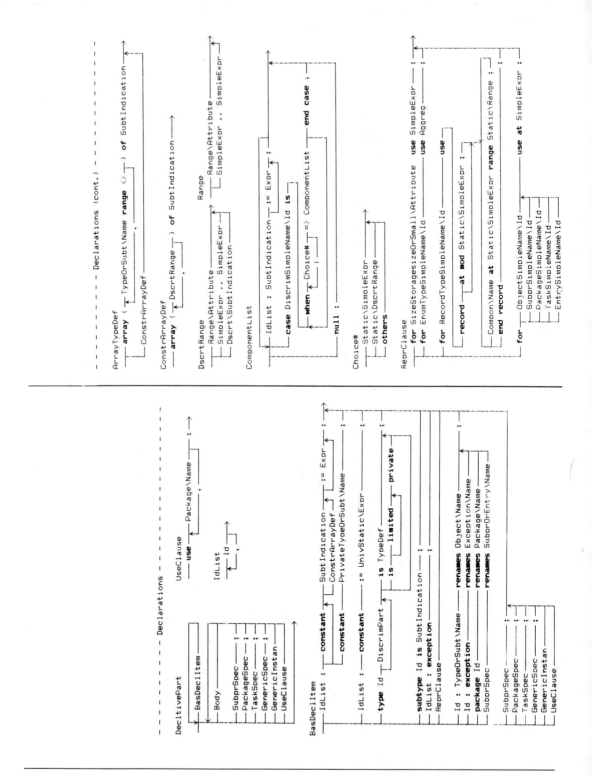

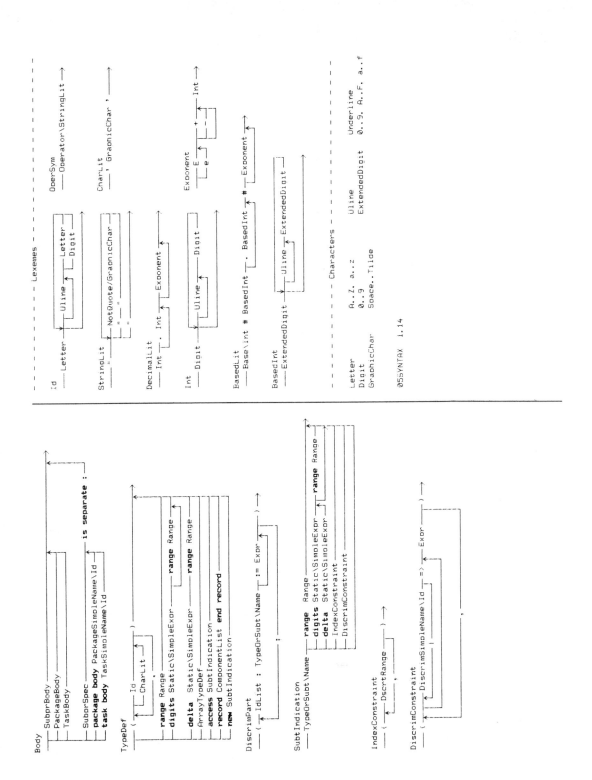

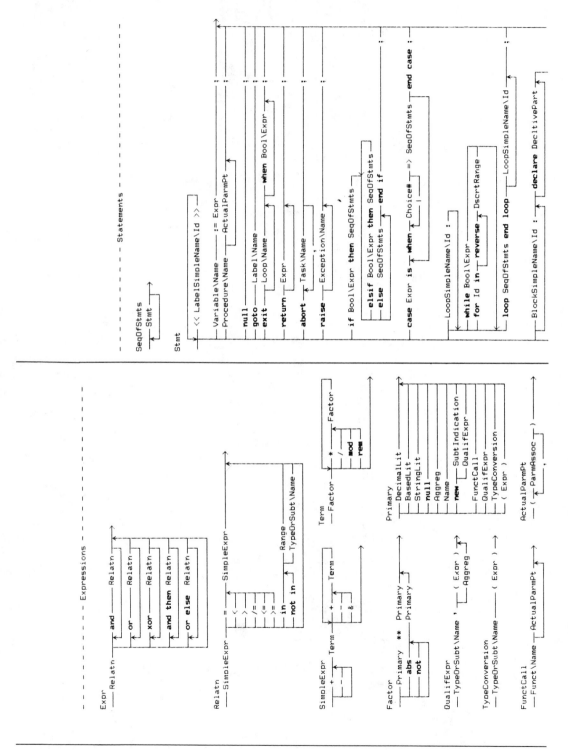

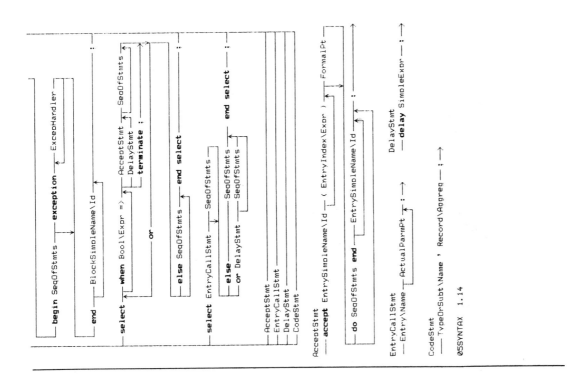

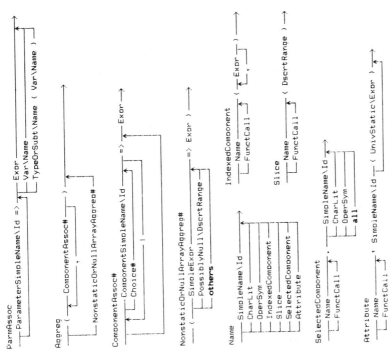

Ø5SYNTAX 1.14

```
package System is  -------------------------------- System ------
type    Address  is [ImplDef];
type    Name     is [ImplDefEnumType];
subtype Priority is Integer range [ImplDefined];
System_Name  : constant Name := [ImplDef];
Storage_Unit : constant := [ImplDef]; --Bits Per Storage Unit
Memory_Size  : constant := [ImplDef]; --Mem Size In Storage Units
Min_Int      : constant := [ImplDef]; --MostNeg Val Of Any IntType
Max_Int      : constant := [ImplDef]; --Largest Val Of Any IntType
Max_Digits   : constant := [ImplDef]; --Largest Possible "digits"
Max_Mantissa : constant := [ImplDef]; --Max Bits For Fixed Pt Type
Fine_Delta   : constant := [ImplDef]; --Min Delta For -1.0 .. 1.0
Tick         : constant := [ImplDef]; --Clock Period In Seconds
end System;


with IO_Exceptions;
package Text_IO is  -------------------------------- Text_IO ------
type    File_Type is limited private;
type    File_Mode is (In_File, Out_File);
type    Count     is range 0 .. [ImplDefined];
subtype Positive_Count is Count range 1 Count'Last;
Unbounded: constant Count := 0

subtype Field       is Integer range 0 .. [ImplDefined];
subtype Number_Base is Integer range 2 .. 16;
type    Type_set    is (Lower_Case, Upper_Case);

procedure Create(File: in out File_Type; Mode: File_Mode:=Out_File;
                 Name: String:="";       Form: String:="" );
procedure Open  (File: in out File_Type; Mode: File_Mode;
                 Name: String;           Form: String:="" );
procedure Close (File: in out File_Type);
procedure Delete(File: in out File_Type);
procedure Reset (File: in out File_Type; Mode: File_Mode);
procedure Reset (File: in out File_Type);

function Mode    (File: File_Type) return File_Mode;
function Name    (File: File_Type) return String;
function Form    (File: File_Type) return String;
function Is_Open (File: File_Type) return Boolean;

procedure Set_Input  (File: File_Type);
procedure Set_Output (File: File_Type);
function Standard_Input   return File_Type;
function Standard_Output  return File_Type;
function Current_Input    return File_type;
function Current_Output   return File_Type;
```

Reserved Words

abort	body	elsif	if	of	range	task
abs	case	end	in	or	record	terminate
accept	constant	entry	is	others	rem	then
access	declare	exception	limited	out	renames	type
all	delay	exit	loop	package	return	use
and	delta	for	mod	pragma	reverse	when
array	digits	function	new	private	select	while
at	do	generic	not	procedure	separate	with
begin	else	goto	null	raise	subtype	xor

Predefined Packages

```
package Standard is  -------------------------- Standard ------
type    Boolean   is (False, True);
type    Integer   is range [ImplDef];
type    Float     is digits [ImplDef];
type    Character is [EnumerationTypeOfAsciiCharSet];
subtype Natural   is Integer range 0 .. Integer'Last;
subtype Positive  is Integer range 1 .. Integer'Last;
type    String    is array (Positive range <>) of Character;
type    Duration  is delta [ImplDef] range [ImplDef] .. 126, 127];
   for Character use (0, 1, 2, ..., 126, 127);
   pragma Pack(String);

package Ascii is                                ----- Ascii -----
-- Nul Soh Stx Etx Eot Enq Ack Bel Bs  Ht  Lf  Vt  Ff  Cr  So  Si
-- Dle Dc1 Dc2 Dc3 Dc4 Nak Syn Etb Can Em  Sub Esc Fs  Gs  Rs  Us  Del
-- ! Exclam     & Ampersand  [ L_Bracket   ` Grave        a Lc_A
-- " Quotation  : Colon       \ Back_Slash  { L_Brace      : :
-- # Sharp      ; Semicolon   ] R_Bracket   | Bar          z Lc_Z
-- $ Dollar     ? Query       ^ Circumflex  } R_Brace
-- % Percent    @ At_Sign     _ Underline   ~ Tilde
end Ascii;

Constraint_Error, Numeric_Error, Program_Error : exception;
Storage_Error,    Tasking_Error                : exception;

end Standard;
```

```
--An underlined parameter denotes two subprograms, one with a file
--parameter and one using the current default inout or output file.

procedure Set_Line_Length (File: File_Type;  To: Count);
procedure Set_Page_Length (File: File_Type;  To: Count);
function  Line_Length     (File: File-type)  return Count;
function  Page_Length     (File: File-type)  return Count;

procedure New_Line    (File: File_Type; Spacing: Positive_Count:=1);
procedure Skip_Line   (File: File_Type; Spacing: Positive_Count:=1);
function  End_Of_Line (File: File_Type)  return Boolean;
procedure New_Page    (File: File_Type);
procedure Skip_Page   (File: File_Type);
function  End_Of_Page (File: File_Type)  return Boolean;
function  End_Of_File (File: File_Type)  return Boolean;
procedure Set_Col  (File: File_Type; To: Positive_Count);
procedure Set_Line (File: File_Type; To: Positive_Count);
function  Col  (File: File_Type)  return Positive_Count;
function  Line (File: File_Type)  return Positive_Count;
function  Page (File: File_Type)  return Positive_Count;

procedure Get      (File: File_Type; Item: out Character);
procedure Put      (File: File_Type; Item: in  Character);
procedure Get      (File: File_Type; Item: out String);
procedure Put      (File: File_Type; Item: in  String);
procedure Get_Line (File: File_Type; Item: out String;
                    Last: out Natural );
procedure Put_Line (File: File_Type; Item: in  String);


                                               ----- Integer_IO -----
generic type Num is range <>;
package Integer_IO is
   Default_Width : Field       := Num'Width;
   Default_Base  : Number_Base := 10;
   procedure Get (File : File_Type; Item: out Num;  Width: Field:=0);
   procedure Put (File: File_Type; Item: in  Num;
                  Width: Field    :=Default_Width;
                  Base : Number_Base :=Default_Base );
   procedure Get (From: in  String; Item: out Num;
                  Last: out Positive );
   procedure Put (To : out String; Item: in  Num;
                  Base: Number_Base:=Default_Base );
end Integer_IO;


                                               ----- Float_IO -----
generic type Num is digits <>;
package Float_IO is
   Default_Fore : Field := 2;
   Default_Aft  : Field := Num'Digits-1;
   Default_Exp  : Field := 3;
   procedure Get(File: File_Type; Item: out Num; Width: Field:=0);
   procedure Put(File: File-type; Item: in  Num;
                 Fore: Field:=Default_Fore;
                 Aft : Field:=Default_Aft;
                 Exp : Field:=Default_Exp );
   procedure Get(From: in  String; Item: out Num;
                 Last: out Positive );
   procedure Put(To  : out String; Item: in  Num;   -- Fore fills string
                 Aft : Field:=Default_Aft;
                 Exp : Field:=Default_Exp );
end Float_IO;


                                               ----- Fixed_IO -----
generic type Num is delta <>;
package Fixed_IO is
   Default_Fore : Field := Num'Fore;
   Default_Aft  : Field := Num'Aft;
   Default_Exp  : Field := 0;
   -- Same subprogram definitions as in "Float_IO"
end Fixed_IO;


                                               ----- Enumeration_IO -----
generic type Enum is (<>);
package Enumeration_IO is
   Default_Width   : Field     := 0;
   Default_Setting : Type_Set := Upper_Case;
   procedure Get (File : File_Type; Item: out Enum );
   procedure Put (File : File_Type; Item: in  Enum;
                  Width: Field    :=Default_Width;
                  Set  : Type_Set :=Default_Setting );
   procedure Get (From: in  String; Item: out Enum );
                  Last: out Positive );
   procedure Put (To : out String; Item: in  Enum;
                  Set : Type_Set:=Default_Setting );
end Enumeration_IO;

--IO_Exceptions renamed here: Status_Error, Mode_Error, Name_Error,
-- Use_Error, Device_Error, End_Error, Data_Error, Layout_Error

private
   -- implementation dependent
end Text_IO;

Q6HELPS  3.4
```

Predefined Language Attributes

PREFIX P	ATTRIBUTE	RESULT TYPE	MEANING
[1]	P'Address	System.Address	Address of item
TySb:X	P'Aft	UInt	# chars after .
TySb:Any	P'Base'...	<BT>	Base type of type p
Objt:AppTsk	P'Callable	Bool	Task is callable
Objt:W/Dscr	P'Constrained	Bool	Obj is constrained
TySb:Privat	P'Constrained	Bool	Subt is constrained
Entry	P'Count	UInt	# waiting calls
TySb:X	P'Delta	UReal	Spec'd delta
TySb:L	P'Digits	UInt	Spec'd digits
TySb:L	P'Emax	UInt	Max exponent in Mn
TySb:L	P'Epsilon	UReal	(next Mn>1.0) - 1.0
TySb:IELX	P'First	<BT> [2]	First val in subtype
ObSb:Array	P'First	<IxTy>	Lo bound of 1st indx
ObSb:Array	P'First(N)	<IxTy>	Lo bound of Nth indx
Objt:RecCmp	P'First_Bit	UInt	Bit dspl from 1st Su
TySb:X	P'Fore	UInt	# chars before .
TySb:IE	P'Image(...)	<BT> -> Str	Printed form of ...
TySb:L	P'Large	UReal	Maximum Mn
TySb:IELX	P'Last	<BT> [2]	Last val in subtype
ObSb:Array	P'Last	<IxTy>	Hi bound of 1st indx
ObSb:Array	P'Last(N)	<IxTy>	Hi bound of Nth indx
Objt:RecCmp	P'Last_Bit	UInt	Bit dspl from 1st Su
ObSb:Array	P'Length	UInt	# values of 1st indx
ObSb:Array	P'Length(N)	UInt	# values of Nth indx
TySb:L	P'Machine_Emax	UInt	Max exponent in Mr
TySb:L	P'Machine_Emin	UInt	Most neg exp in Mr
TySb:L	P'Machine_Mantissa	UInt	# radix dgts in Mr
TySb:LX	P'Machine_Overflows	Bool	Exception if o/flo
TySb:L	P'Machine_Radix	UInt	Radix used in Mr
TySb:L	P'Machine_Rounds	Bool	Ops exact or rounded
TySb:LX	P'Mantissa	UInt	# bits in Mn ("B")
TySb:IE	P'Pos(...)	<BT> -> UInt	Position num of ...
Objt:RecCmp	P'Position	UInt	Dspl of field (Su's)
TySb:IE	P'Pred(...)	<BT> -> <BT>	Predecessor of ...
ObSb:Array	P'Range	<IxTy>..<IxTy>	Range of 1st index
ObSb:Array	P'Range(N)	<IxTy>..<IxTy>	Range of Nth index
TySb:L	P'Safe_Emax	UInt	Max exponent in Sn
TySb:LX	P'Safe_Large	UReal	Maximum Sn
TySb:LX	P'Safe_Small	UReal	Minimum Sn > 0
ObTy:Any	P'Size	UInt	Size of obj (bits)
TySb:LX	P'Small	UReal	Minimum Mn > 0
TySb:Access	P'Storage_Size	UInt	Space for objs(Su's)
ObTy:Task	P'Storage_Size	UInt	ActivationSize(Su's)
TySb:IE	P'Succ(...)	<BT> -> <BT>	Successor of ...
Objt:AppTsk	P'Terminated	Bool	Task is terminated
TySb:IE	P'Val(...)	AnyInt -> <BT>	Inverse of "Pos"
TySb:IE	P'Value(...)	Str -> <BT>	Inverse of "Image"
TySb:IE	P'Width	UInt	Max of "Image(...)"

Predefined Language Pragmas

— **pragma** Controlled (AccessTypeSimpleName\Id) ; →

After the type declaration and in the same DeclitivePart or PackageSpec. (Not allowed for a derived type.) Suppresses garbage collection.

— **pragma** Elaborate (⎡ LibraryUnitSimpleName\Id ⎤) ; →

Between a context clause and the subsequent LibraryUnit, LibraryUnitBody, or SubUnit. Each name must be mentioned in the context clause.
Requires prior elaboration of each named LibraryUnit\Body.

— **pragma** Inline (⎡ SubprOrGenericSubpr\Name ⎤) ; →

1) After the declaration(s) of the named subprogram and in the same DeclitivePart or PackageSpec, or
2) After the named LibraryUnit (1 name only).
This pragma may be ignored, on a per-call basis.

— **pragma** Interface (Language\Name , Subpr\Name) ; →

1) After the named SubprSpec in the same DeclitivePart or PackageSpec, or
2) After the named LibraryUnit.

— **pragma** List (⎡ **On** / **Off** ⎤) ; →

Anywhere a pragma is allowed. Turns compiler listing on/off.

— **pragma** Memory_Size (NumericLiteral) ; →

Before the 1st CompilationUnit. Sets "System.Memory-Size".

— **pragma** Optimize (⎡ **Time** / **Space** ⎤) ; →

In a DeclitivePart. Applies to the associated body or block.

— **pragma** Pack (RecordOrArrayTypeSimpleName\Id) ; →

Same places as a ReprClause, and before use of a representation attribute of the packed entity.
Storage minimization is preferred for the data type.

— **pragma** Page ; →

Anywhere a pragma is allowed. Ejects page in compiler listing.

— **pragma** Priority (Static\Expression) ; →

1) In a TaskSpec, or 2) In the DeclitivePart of a main subpr. Value must be in integer subtype "System.Priority"; larger value means greater urgency. Don't use for synchronization.

```
— pragma Shared ( VariableSimpleName\Id )  —→
    After the variable declaration and in the same DeclivePart or
    PackageSpec and before any other use of the variable name
    (except Address ReprClause).  Variable type must be access
    or scalar with indivisible machine operations.
    Causes all reads\writes of the variable to be done to memory.

— pragma Storage-Unit ( NumericLiteral )  —→
    Before 1st CompilationUnit.  Sets "System.Storage-Unit".

— pragma Suppress (  —— Check\Id  ——[ , On => ┌← Name ←┐ ] )  —→

  1) With or without the name, in a DeclivePart; or
  2) With the name, in the PackageSpec where the name is declared.
     Suppresses checking for the specified exception from this point
     on.  If name is given, checking is only suppressed for the
     named entity.  (This pragma need not have any effect.)

  CheckId               Exception         Name denotes (if present):
  Discriminant-Check,   Constraint-Error  Object,Type
  Access-Check,
  Index-Check,
  Length-Check,
  Range-Check
  Division-Check,       Numeric-Error     NumericType
  Overflow-Check
  Elaboration-Check     Program-Error     TaskUnit,GenericUnit,Subpr
  Storage-Check         Storage-Error     AccessType,TaskUnit,Subpr

— pragma System-Name ( ┌─ EnumerationLiteral\Id ─────┐ )  —→
                       └─ EnumerationLiteral\Char\Id ─┘
    Before 1st CompilationUnit.  Sets "System.System-Name".

- - - - - - - - - - - - - - - - - - - - - - - - - - - - - - - - -
  1) A pragma may only appear after a semicolon delimiter (but not
     in a formal part or discriminant part).
  2) If a pragma name is undefined or pragma argument is incorrect,
     then the program is still legal but the pragma is ignored.
  3) These  predefined  pragmas  must  be  provided  in  every
     implementation, but not all are required to have an effect.
```

NATURE OF PREFIX
```
[1]  Object, Program Unit (subpr,package,task), Label, or Entry.
       (Function name refers to function itself, not call.)
TySb: Type or subtype, including the following abbreviations,
       I=Integer type or subt        L=Floating-pt type or subt
       E=Enumeration type or subt    X=Fixed-point type or subt
Objt: Object.
       "Objt:RecCmp" = Component of a record object.
ObSb: Object or constrained subtype
       "ObSb:Array" = AppArrayObject, or ConstrainedArraySubtype
ObTy: Object, type, or subtype.
       "ObTy:Any"  = AnyObject,        or AnyTypeOrSubtype
       "ObTy:Task" = TaskObject,       or TaskType
Note--"AppXxx" means "appropriate to type Xxx" -- ie, the prefix is
       an object of type Xxx or a pointer object to type Xxx.
```

RESULT TYPE
```
<BT>   : Base type of prefix
<IxTy> : Base type of array index position
[2]    : P'First and P'Last for a floating point (sub) type need
         not yield model or safe numbers.
```

ABBREVIATIONS
```
   Mn=ModelNumber, Sn=SafeNumber, Mr=MachineRepr, Su=StorageUnit
```

RELATIONSHIPS AMONG FLOATING-POINT ATTRIBUTES
```
P'Digits  = D           P'Mantissa = B = Ceil(D*log(10)/log(2)+1)
P'Emax    = 4*B         P'Small    = 2 ** (-4*B - 1)
P'Epsilon = 2 ** (1-B)  P'Large    = 2 ** (4*B) *  (1 - 2**(-P))
     B = 5  8 11 15 18 21 25 28 31 35 38 41 45 48 51 55 58 61 65 68
     D = 1  2  3  4  5  6  7  8  9 10 11 12 13 14 15 16 17 18 19 20
-- Safe numbers have the same (binary) mantissa as model numbers but
-- possibly larger expon.  The machine rep may have more precision.
```

RELATIONSHIPS AMONG FIXED-POINT ATTRIBUTES
```
P'Delta = D             P'Mantissa = B
P'Small = the largest power of 2 <= D (or is given in a ReprClause)
P'Large = (2**B-1) * S   --- for an unconstrained type
-- Safe numbers may be more precise or have larger range than
-- model numbers -- they are the model numbers of the base type.
```

APPENDIX F

ASCII Symbols

decimal	octal	hex	symbol
0	0	0	NUL
1	1	1	SOH
2	2	2	STX
3	3	3	ETX
4	4	4	EOT
5	5	5	ENQ
6	6	6	ACU
7	7	7	BEL
8	10	8	ES
9	11	9	HT
10	12	A	LF
11	13	B	VT
12	14	C	FF
13	15	D	CR
14	16	E	SO
15	17	F	SI
16	20	10	DLE
17	21	11	DC1
18	22	12	DC2
19	23	13	DC3
20	24	14	DC4
21	25	15	NAK
22	26	16	SYU
23	27	17	ETB
24	30	18	CAN
25	31	19	EM

decimal	octal	hex	symbol
64	100	40	@
65	101	41	A
66	102	42	B
67	103	43	C
68	104	44	D
69	105	45	E
70	106	46	F
71	107	47	G
72	110	48	H
73	111	49	I
74	112	4A	J
75	113	4B	K
76	114	4C	L
77	115	4D	M
78	116	4E	N
79	117	4F	O
80	120	50	P
81	121	51	Q
82	122	52	R
83	123	53	S
84	124	54	T
85	125	55	U
86	126	56	V
87	127	57	W
88	130	58	X
89	131	59	Y

Char	Hex	Octal	Dec
Z	5A	132	90
[	5B	133	91
\	5C	134	92
]	5D	135	93
^	5E	136	94
_	5F	137	95
`	60	140	96
a	61	141	97
b	62	142	98
c	63	143	99
d	64	144	100
e	65	145	101
f	66	146	102
g	67	147	103
h	68	150	104
i	69	151	105
j	6A	152	106
k	6B	153	107
l	6C	154	108
m	6D	155	109
n	6E	156	110
o	6F	157	111
p	70	160	112
q	71	161	113
r	72	162	114
s	73	163	115
t	74	164	116
u	75	165	117
v	76	166	118
w	77	167	119
x	78	170	120
y	79	171	121
z	7A	172	122
{	7B	173	123
		7C	174	124
}	7D	175	125
~	7E	176	126
DEL	7F	177	127

Char	Hex	Octal	Dec
SUB	1A	32	26
ESC	1B	33	27
FS	1C	34	28
GS	1D	35	29
RS	1E	36	30
VS	1F	37	31
SP	20	40	32
!	21	41	33
"	22	42	34
#	23	43	35
$	24	44	36
%	25	45	37
&	26	46	38
'	27	47	39
(	28	50	40
)	29	51	41
*	2A	52	42
+	2B	53	43
,	2C	54	44
-	2D	55	45
.	2E	56	46
/	2F	57	47
0	30	60	48
1	31	61	49
2	32	62	50
3	33	63	51
4	34	64	52
5	35	65	53
6	36	66	54
7	37	67	55
8	38	70	56
9	39	71	57
:	3A	72	58
;	3B	73	59
<	3C	74	60
=	3D	75	61
>	3E	76	62
?	3F	77	63

APPENDIX G
Attribute Functions and Pragmas

This appendix reproduces the sections of the *Language Reference Manual* summarizing attribute functions and pragmas. References to numbered paragraphs refer to appropriate sections of the *LRM*.

Attribute Functions

This annex summarizes the definitions given elsewhere of the predefined language attributes.

P'ADDRESS—For a prefix P that denotes an object, a program unit, a label, or an entry:

Yields the address of the first of the storage units allocated to P. For a subprogram, package, task unit, or label this value refers to the machine code associated with the corresponding body or statement. For an entry for which an address clause has been given, the value refers to the corresponding hardware interrupt. The value of this attribute is of the type **ADDRESS** defined in the package **SYSTEM**. (See 13.7.2)

P'AFT—For a prefix P that denotes a fixed-point subtype:

Yields the number of decimal digits needed after the point to accommodate the precision of the subtype P, unless the delta of the subtype P is greater than 0.1, in which case the attribute yields the value one. (**P'AFT** is the smallest positive integer N for which $(10**N)*P'DELTA$ is greater than or equal to one.) The value of this attribute is of the type universal_integer. (See 3.5.10.)

P'BASE—For prefix P that denotes a type or subtype:

This attribute denotes the base type of P. It is only allowed as the prefix of the name of another attribute: for example, **P'BASE'FIRST**. (See 3.3.3)

P'CALLABLE—For a prefix P that is appropriate for a task type:

Yields the value **FALSE** when the execution of the task P is either completed or terminated, or when the task is abnormal; yields the value **TRUE** otherwise. The value of this attribute is of the predefined type **BOOLEAN**. (See 9.9.)

P'CONSTRAINED—For a prefix P that denotes an object of a type with discriminants:

Yields the value **TRUE** if a discriminant constraint applies to the object P, or if the object is a constant (including a formal parameter or generic or generic formal parameter of mode in); yields the value **FALSE** otherwise. If P is a generic formal parameter of mode in out, or if P is a formal parameter of mode in out or out and the type mark given in the corresponding parameter specification denotes an unconstrained type with discriminants, then the value of this attribute is obtained from that of the corresponding actual parameter. The value of this attribute is of the predefined type **BOOLEAN**. (See 3.7.4.)

P'CONSTRAINED—For a prefix P that denotes a private type or subtype:

Yields the value **FALSE** if P denotes an unconstrained nonformal private type with discriminants; also yields the value **FALSE** if P denotes a generic formal private type and the associated actual subtype is either an unconstrained type with discriminants or an unconstrained array type; yields the value **TRUE** otherwise. The value of this attribute is of the predefined type **BOOLEAN**. (See 7.4.2.)

P'COUNT—For a prefix P that denotes an entry of a task unit:

Yields the number of entry calls presently queued on the entry (if the attribute is evaluated within an accept statement for the entry P, the count does not include the calling task). The value of this attribute is of the type `universal_interger`. (See 9.9.)

P'DELTA—For a prefix P that denotes a fixed point subtype:

Yields the value of the delta specified in the fixed accuracy definition for the subtype P. The value of this attribute is of the type `universal_real`. (See 3.5.10.)

P'DIGITS—For a prefix P that denotes a floating-point subtype:

Yields the number of decimal digits in the decimal mantissa of model numbers of the subtype P.

(This attribute yields the number D of section 3.5.7.) The value of this attribute is of the type universal_integer. (See 3.5.8.)

P'EMAX—For a prefix P that denotes a floating-point subtype:

Yields the largest exponent value in the binary canonical form of model numbers of the subtype P. (This attribute yields the product 4*B of section 3.5.7.) The value of this attribute is of the type universal_integer. (See 3.5.8.)

P'EPSILON—For a prefix P that denotes a floating-point subtype:

Yields the absolute value of the different between the model number 1.0 and the next model number above, for the subtype P. The value of this attribute is of the type universal_real. (See 3.5.8.)

P'FIRST—For a prefix P that denotes a scalar type, or a subtype of a scalar type:

Yields the bound of P. The value of this attribute has the same type as P. (See 3.5.)

P'FIRST—For a prefix P that is appropriate for an array type, or that denotes a constrained array subtype:

Yields the lower bound of the first index range. The value of this attribute has the same type as this lower bound. (See 3.6.2 and 3.8.2.)

P'FIRST(N)—For a prefix P that is appropriate for an array type, or that denotes a constrained array subtype:

Yields the lowers bound of the Nth index range. The value of this attribute has the same type as this lower bound. The argument N must be a static expression of type universal_integer. The value of N must be positive (nonzero) and no greater than the dimensionality of the array. (See 3.6.2 and 3.8.2.)

P'FIRST_BIT—For a prefix P that denotes a component of a record object:

Yields the offset, from the start of the first of the storage units occupied by the component, of the first bit occupied by the component. This offset is measured in bits. The value of this attribute is of the type universal_integer. (See 13.7.2.)

P'FORE—For a prefix P that denotes a fixed point subtype:

Yields the minimum number of characters needed for the integer part of the decimal representation of any value of the subtype P, assuming that the representation does not include an exponent, but includes a one-character prefix that is either a minus sign or a space. (This minimum number does not include superfluous zeros or underlines, and is at least two.) The value of this attribute is of the type universal__integer. (See 3.5.10.)

P'IMAGE—For a prefix P that denotes a discrete type or subtype:

This attribute is a function with a single parameter. The actual parameter X must be a value of the base type of P. The result type is the predefined type STRING. The result is the image of the value of X, that is, a sequence of characters representing the value in display form. The image of an integer value is the corresponding decimal literal, without underlines, leading zeros, exponent, or trailing spaces, but with a one-character prefix that is either a minus sign or a space.

The image of an enumeration value is either the corresponding identifier in uppercase or the corresponding character literal (including the two apostrophes); neither leading nor trailing spaces are included. The image of a character other than a graphic character is implementation-defined. (See 3.5.5.)

P'LARGE—For a prefix P that denotes a real subtype:

The attribute yields the largest positive model number of the subtype P. The value of this attribute is of the type universal__real. (See 3.5.8. and 3.5.10.)

P'LAST—For a prefix P that denotes a scalar type, or a subtype of a scalar type:

Yields the upper bound of P. The value this attribute has the same type as P. (See 3.5.)

P'LAST—For a prefix P that is appropriate for an array type, or that denotes a constrained array subtype:

Yields the upper bound of the first index range. The value of this attribute has the same type as this upper bound. (See 3.6.2. and 3.8.2.)

P'LAST(N)—For a prefix P that is appropriate for an array type, or that denotes a constrained array subtype:

Yields the upper bound of the Nth index range. The value of this attribute has the same type as this upper bound. The argument N must be a static expression of type universal__integer. The value of N must be positive (nonzero) and no greater than the dimensionality of the array. (See 3.6.2 and 3.8.2.)

P'LAST_BIT—For a prefix P that denotes a component of a record object:

Yields the offset, from the start of the first of the storage units occupied by the component, of the last bit occupied by the component. This offset is measured in bits. The value of this attribute is of the type universal_integer. (See 13.7.2)

P'LENGTH—For a prefix P that is appropriate for an array type, or that denotes a constrained array subtype:

Yields the number of values of the first index range (zero for a null range). The value of this attribute is the type universal_integer. (See 3.6.2.)

P'LENGTH(N)—For the prefix P that is appropriate for an array type, or that denotes a constrained array subtype:

Yields the number of values of the Nth index range (zero for a null range). The value of this attribute is of the type universal_integer. The argument N must be a static expression of the type universal_integer. The value of N must be positive (nonzero) and greater than the dimensionality of the array. (See 3.6.2 and 3.8.2.)

P'MACHINE_EMAX—For a prefix P that denotes a floating point type or subtype:

Yields the largest value of exponent for the machine representation of the base type of P. The value of this attribute is of the type universal_integer. (See 13.7.3.)

P'MACHINE_EMIN—For a prefix P that denotes a floating point type or subtype:

Yields the smallest (most negative) value of exponent for the machine representation of the base type of P. The value of this attribute is the type universal_integer. (See 13.7.3.)

P'MACHINE_MANTISSA—For a prefix P that denotes a floating point type or subtype:

Yields the number of digits in the mantissa for the machine representation of the base type of P (the digits are extended digits in the range) to **P'MACHINE_RADIX** - 1). The value of this attribute is of the type universal_integer. (See 13.7.3.)

P'MACHINE_OVERFLOWS—For a prefix P that denotes a floating point type or subtype:

Yields the value **TRUE** if every predefined operation on values of the base type of P either provides a correct result, or raises the exception **NUMERIC_ERROR** in overflow situation; yields the value **FALSE** otherwise. The value of this attribute is of the predefined type .BOOLEAN. (See 13.7.3.)

P'MACHINE_RADIX—For a prefix P that denotes a floating point type or subtype:

Yields the value of the radix used by the machine representation of the base type of P. The value of this attribute is of the type **universal_integer**. (13.7.3)

P'MACHINE_ROUNDS—For a prefix P that denotes a real type or subtype:

Yields the value **TRUE** if every predefined arithmetic operation on values of the base type of P either returns an exact result or performs rounding; yields the value **FALSE** otherwise. The value of this attribute is of the predefined type **BOOLEAN**. (See 13.7.3.)

P'MANTISSA—For a prefix P that denotes a real subtype:

Yields the number of binary digits in the binary mantissa of model numbers of the subtype P. (This attribute yields the number B of section 3.5.7 for a floating point type, or of section 3.5.9 for a fixed point type.) The value of this attribute is of the type **universal_integer**. (See 3.5.8 and 3.5.10)

P'POS—For a prefix P that denotes a discrete type or subtype:

This attribute is a function with a single parameter. The actual parameter X must be a value of the base type of P. The result type is the type **universal_integer**. The result is the position number of the value of the actual parameter. (See 3.5.5.)

P'POSITION—For a prefix P that denotes a component of a record object:

Yields the offset, from the start of the first storage unit occupied by the component. This offset is measured in storage units. The value of this attribute is of the type **universal_integer**. (See 13.7.2.)

P'PRED—For a prefix P that denotes a discrete type or subtype:

This attribute, a function with a single parameter X, must be a value of the base type of P. The result type is the base type of P. The result is the value whose position number is one less than that of X. The exception **CONSTRAINT_ERROR** is raised if X equals **P'BASE'FIRST**. (See 3.5.5.)

P'RANGE—For a prefix P that is appropriate for an array type, or that denotes a constrained array subtype:

Yields the first index range of P, that is, the **P'FIRST**.

P'RANGE(N)—For a prefix P that is appropriate for an array type, or that denotes a constrained array subtype:

Yields the Nth index range of P, that is the range P'FIRST(N) ..P'LAST(N). (See 3.6.2.)

P'SAFE__EMAX—For a prefix P that denotes a floating-point type or subtype:

Yields the largest exponent value in the conanical form of safe numbers of the base type of P. (This attribute yields the number E of section 3.5.7.) The value of this attribute is of the type universal__integer. (See 3.5.8.)

P'SAFE__LARGE—For a prefix P that denotes a real type or subtype:

Yields the largest positive safe number of the base type of P. The value of this attribute is of the type universal__real. (See 3.5.8 and 3.5.10.)

P'SAFE__SMALL—For a prefix P that denotes a real type or subtype:

Yields the smallest positive (nonzero) safe number of the base type of P. The value of this attribute is of the type of universal__real. (See 3.5.8 and 3.5.10.)

P'SIZE—For a prefix P that denotes an object:

Yields the number of bits allocated to hold the object. The value of this attribute is of the universal__integer. (See 13.7.2.)

P'SIZE—For a prefix P that denotes any type of subtype:

Yields the minimum number of bits that is needed by the implementation to hold any possible object of the type or subtype P. The value of this attribute is of the type universal__integer. (See 13.7.2.)

P'SMALL—For a prefix P that denotes a real subtype:

Yields the smallest positive (nonzero) model number of the subtype P. The value of this attribute is of the type universal__real. (See 3.5.8 and 3.5.10.)

P'STORAGE__SIZE—For a prefix P that denotes an access type or subtype:

Yields the total number of storage units reserved for the collection associated with the base type of P. The value of this attribute is of the type universal__integer. (See 13.7.2.)

P'STORAGE_SIZE—For a prefix P that denotes a task type or a task object:

Yields the number of storage units reserved for each activation of a task of the type P or for the activation of the task object P. The value of this attribute is of the type universal_integer. (See 13.7.2.)

P'SUCC—For a prefix P that denotes a discrete type or subtype:

This attribute is a function with a single parameter. The actual parameter X must be a value of the base type of P. The result type is the base type of P. The result is the value whose position number is one greater than that of X. The exception CONSTRAINT_ERROR is raised if X equals P'BASE'LAST. (See 3.5.5.)

P'TERMINATED—For a prefix P that is appropriate for a task type:

Yields the value TRUE if task P is terminated; yields the value FALSE otherwise. The value of this attribute is of the predefined type BOOLEAN. (See 9.9.)

P'VAL—For a prefix P that denotes a discrete type or subtype:

This attribute is a special function with a single parameter X which can be of any integer type. The result is the base type of P. The result is the value whose position number is the universal_integer value corresponding to X. The exception CONSTRAINT_ERROR is raised if the universal_integer value corresponding to X is not in the range P'POS(P'BASE'FIRST)..P'POS(P'BASE'LAST). (See 3.5.5.)

P'VALUE—For a prefix P that denotes a discrete type or subtype:

This attribute is a function with a single parameter. The actual parameter X must be a value of the predefined type STRING. The result type is the base type of P. Any leading and any trailing spaces of the sequences of characters that correspond to X are ignored.

For an enumeration type, if the sequence of characters has the syntax of an enumeration literal and this literal exists for the base type of P, the result is the corresponding enumeration value. For an integer type, if the sequence of characters has the syntax of an integer, with an optional single leading character that is a plus or minus sign, and if there is a corresponding value in the base type of P, the result is this value. In any other case, the exception CONSTRAINT_ERROR is raised. (See 3.5.5.)

P'WIDTH—For a prefix P that denotes a discrete subtype:

Yields the maximum image length over all values of the subtype P (the image is the sequence of characters returned by the attribute IMAGE). The value of this attribute is of the type universal_integer. (See 3.5.5.)

CONTROLLED—Takes the simple name of an access type as the single argument. This pragma is only allowed immediately within the declarative part or package specification that contains the declaration of the access type; the declaration must occur before the pragma. This pragma is not allowed for a derived type. This pragma specifies that automatic storage reclamation must not be performed for objects designated by values of the access type, except upon leaving the innermost block statement, subprogram body, or task body that encloses the access type declaration, or after leaving the main program (see 4.8).

ELABORATE—Takes one or more simple names denoting library units as arguments. This pragma is only allowed immediately after the context clause of a compilation unit (before the subsequent library unit or secondary unit). Each argument must be the simple name of a library unit mentioned by the context clause. This pragma specifies that the corresponding library unit body must be elaborated before the given compilation unit. If the given compilation unit is a subunit, the library unit body must be elaborated before the body of the ancestor library unit of the subunit (see 10.5).

INLINE—Takes one or more names as arguments; each name is either the name of a subprogram or the name of a generic subprogram. This program is only allowed at the place of a declarative item in a declarative part or package specification, or after a library unit in a compilation but before any subsequent compilation unit. This pragma specifies that the subprogram bodies should be expanded inline at each call whenever possible; in the case of a generic subprogram, the pragma applies to calls of its instantiations (see 6.3.2).

INTERFACE—Takes a language name and a subprogram name as arguments. This pragma is allowed at the place of a declarative item and must apply in this case to a subprogram declared by an earlier declarative item of the same declarative part or package specification. This pragma is also allowed for a library unit; in this case the pragma must appear after the subprogram declaration, and before any subsequent compilation unit. This pragma specifies the other language (and thereby the calling conventions) and informs the compiler that an object module will be supplied for the corresponding subprogram (see 13.9).

LIST—Takes one of the identifiers **ON** or **OFF** as the single argument. This pragma is allowed anywhere a pragma is allowed. It specifies that listing of the compilation is to be continued or suspended until a **LIST** pragma with the opposite argument is given within the same compilation. The pragma itself is always listed if the compiler is producing a listing.

MEMORY_SIZE—Takes a numeric literal as the single argument. This pragma is only allowed at the start of a compilation, before the first compilation unit (if any) of the compilation. The effect of this pragma is to use the value of the specified numeric literal for the definition of the named number **MEMORY_SIZE** (see 13.7).

OPTIMIZE—Takes one of the identifiers **TIME** or **SPACE** as the single argument. This pragma is only allowed within a declarative part and it applies to the block or body enclosing the declarative part. It specifies whether time or space is the primary optimization criterion.

PACK—Takes the simple name of a record or array type as the single argument. The allowed positions for this pragma, and the restrictions on the named type, are governed by the same rules as for a representation clause. The pragma specifies that storage minimization should be the main criterion when selecting the representation of the given type (see 13.1).

PAGE—This pragma has no argument, and is allowed anywhere a pragma is allowed. It specifies that the program text that follows the pragma should start on a new page (if the compiler is currently producing a listing).

PRIORITY—Takes a static expression of the predefined integer subtype **PRIORITY** as the single argument. This pragma is only allowed within the specification of a task unit or immediately within the outermost declarative part of a main program (see 9.8).

SHARED—Takes the simple name of a variable as the single argument. This pragma is allowed only for a variable declared by an object declaration and whose type is a scalar or access type; the variable declaration and the pragma must both occur (in this order) immediately within the same declarative part or package specification. This pragma specifies that every read or update of the variable is a sychronization point for that variable. An implementation must restrict the objects for which this pragma is allowed to objects for which each of direct reading and direct updating is implemented as an indivisible operation (see 9.11).

STORAGE_UNIT—Takes a numeric literal as the single argument. This pragma is only allowed at the start of a compilation, before the first compilation unit (if any) of the compilation. The effect of this pragma is to use the value of the specified numeric literal for the definition of the named number **STORAGE_UNIT** (see 13.7).

SUPPRESS—Takes as arguments the identifier of a check and optionally also the name of either an object, a type or subtype, a subprogram, a task unit, or a generic unit. This pragma is only allowed either immediately within a declarative part or immediately within a package specification. The permission to omit the given check extends from the place of the pragma to the end of the declarative region associated with the innermost enclosing block statement or program unit. For a pragma given in a package specification, the permission extends to the end of the scope of the named entity.

If the pragma includes a name, the permission to omit the given check is further restricted: It is given only for operations on the named object or on all objects of the base type of a named type or subtype; for calls of a named subprogram; for activations of tasks of the named task type; or for instantiations of the given generic unit (see 11.7).

SYSTEM_NAME—Takes an enumeration literal as the single argument. This pragma is only allowed at the start of a compilation, before the first compilation unit (if any) of the compilation. The effect of this pragma is to use the enumeration literal with the specified identifier for the definition of the constant SYSTEM_NAME. This pragma is only allowed if the specified identifier corresponds to one of the literals of the type NAME declared in the package System (see 13.7).

APPENDIX H
A Comparison of Ada, C, and Pascal

This comparison is not intended as a good versus bad, nor is it intended to show the advantages of one language over another. It is intended to be used as a reference for programmers familiar with C or Pascal to use to gain access to Ada's way of doing things.

Identifier names

Ada identifiers are very similar to C and Pascal identifiers. The exceptions are that Pascal does not allow the *underbar* or *underline* character in an identifer, and C allows the underbar to appear as the first or last character of an identifier.

Data types and sizes

The major difference between C and Ada data types is that the C character type may contain any 8-bit numeric value, while the Ada character is an enumeration type. Thus C-style arithmetic is not allowed directly on characters in Ada. The Ada form is similar to Pascal's. Ada provides a real type with fixed accuracy, while Pascal and C do not. C does not provide an equivalent to the Ada and Pascal enumeration types. Thus Boolean values in C are represented as zero/not zero.

Constants

Ada constants are different than C's and Pascal's. In C a constant is implemented by preprocessor macros. In Pascal a constant is always the given value. In Ada a constant is only constant during a given call to a subprogram. The next call, the expression defining the constant, is reevaluated and may produce a different result (as when a global variable is used in an expression defining a constant). The Ada *named number* is closer to the C and Pascal versions of constants.

Initialization

Any variable may be initialized when declared in Ada or C. Pascal does not allow for initialization.

Declarations

Ada and Pascal variables are declared in the `<object>`-colon-`<type>` form. C variables are declared `<type>` `<object>` form. All three languages require that a variable be declared before it is used. A C program may have function calls before the function is defined, while Ada and Pascal require that a function or procedure be defined before use. In Pascal this is done with a *forward* reference. Ada uses a similar form but requires that the parameter list and return type be repeated in the complete definition of the subprogram; Pascal does not have the same requirements.

Arithmetic operators

Basic arithmetic operations are the same for the three languages, with the precedence being different (see *Precedence*, below). C does not have exponentiation operators; Pascal and Ada do. C lacks the unary-plus operator.

Relational operators

The six relational operators are duplicated in the three languages. Boolean results are returned. Symbol equivalencies are shown below:

Ada	Pascal	C	Name
=	=	==	equals
/=	<>	!=	not equal
>	>	>	greater-than
>=	>=	>=	greater-than/equal
<	<	<	less-than
<=	<=	<=	less-than/equal

Logical operators

Logical operators are similar in the three languages. Pascal does not have an **xor** operator. Precedence varies greatly between the three languages; check the precedence tables when translating. The symbol equivalencies are:

Ada	Pascal	C	Name
and	and	&&	logical and
or	or	::	logical or
xor			logical exclusive-or
not	not	!	logical not

Another source of difficulty is the order of evaluation of logical operators in Ada versus C (see *Precedence*, below).

Prefix and postfix operators

Ada and Pascal don't use the prefix and postfix unary increment and decrement operators of C. Ada was designed to be heavily optimized and therefore these types of operation were omitted for the sake of human readers. The same reasoning is used for the omission from Ada of the += types of assignment operators found in C.

Conditional expressions

Niether Ada nor Pascal allows conditional expressions like C's ? : ternary expression.

Precedence and order of evaluation

The rules of precedence are significantly different between the languages and are a possible source of insidious error. A major difference in precedence between C and Ada is that the Ada unary operators are lower in precedence than the multiplying binary operators.

While C has automatic short-circuit form evaluation of logical **and** or **or**, Ada requires the short-circuit form be explicitly specified. Short circuiting is the bypassing of unnecessary evaluations once the outcome of a logical expression can be determined. Therefore in C we can depend on logical terms being evaluated from left to right, while in Ada no ordering of logical term evaluation is specified, except when the short-circuit forms are applied.

Type conversions

Ada and Pascal require explicit type conversion functions between objects of different types. C will promote terms of an expression as needed to perform an evaluation, and automatically convert to the destination type. In cases where an ambiguity may appear, the C *cast* takes the place of the type conversion functions of Ada of Pascal.

Control statements

Ada, C, and Pascal have similar control structures implemented. The differences lie in defining compound statements under the control of the statements.

In Ada compound statements are delimited by the reserved words composing the control structure (e.g., *loop*) and the *end* statement associated with all Ada control structures.

Pascal uses a *begin* and *end* combination to delimit compound statements. C uses curly braces to enclose compound statements.

Loops

C, Ada, and Pascal all have the basic *while* loop, with similar properties. All three have a *for* loop construct, with several differences.

In Ada a *for* loop implicitly declares an index variable that is local to the loop and which hides a variable of the same name declared external to the loop. A Pascal index variable must be explicitly declared. Both Ada and Pascal do not allow assignment to the index variable inside the loop, and leave the index variable undefined upon exit from the loop. The C *for* need not even have an index variable, and if it does it must be declared explicitly. Ada and Pascal initial and terminal expressions are evaluated once, on entry to the loop. C initializing expressions are evaluated on entry, but the terminal expression is evaluated at the end of each iteration and need not even concern the index variable, if one exists. Ada and Pascal do not allow the alteration of index increment size, while C does.

Ada has no *do—while* structure as C and Pascal do. However, Ada has a simple *loop-end loop* which has a positionable exit statement. The Ada simple loop can be written to look like a *do-until* loop, a *do-while* loop, or something in between.

Ada also allows named loops and breaking out of nested loops by referring to a loop name when exiting.

Case

All three languages have a *case* structure, referred to as a *switch* in C. The constructions and limitations are fairly similar. However, Pascal requires that all possibilities are explicitly exhausted, while C has a *default* option and Ada has an *others* option. Ada and Pascal don't allow choices to "fall through," while C choices do fall through unless a *break* statement is placed in each choice.

Goto

All three languages have the *goto* statement available. Ada and C use identifiers as target labels for *goto*, while Pascal uses a number-colon arrangement. Pascal has the most restricted form: a goto label must be declared at the start of a block. Ada gotos may not jump into a loop, case, or compound statement. In C, as usual, you can pretty much do as you like with gotos. In all three languages a goto statement and matching label must be within a subprogram, although most C libraries have an interfunction goto and target called *setjmp()* and *longjmp()*.

Break/continue

There is no equivalent in Ada or Pascal for the *break* or *continue* statements of C. However, the Ada simple loop with the positionable exit makes these constructions pretty much unnecessary.

Labels

Ada has two forms of labels: The goto target, which is an identifier with arrows on each end (`<<target>>`), and names for loops and blocks, which are identifiers followed by a colon. C and Pascal have only goto target labels.

Functions and procedures

Ada and Pascal both have two categories of subprograms—*procedures* and *functions*. C has only *functions*, which can be used as either. The basic difference between a procedure and a function is that functions return values and may only be used as parts of expressions in Ada and Pascal, while procedures are used as statements and may not be used in expressions.

Return values

In Ada and Pascal only functions return values. Ada and Pascal may return any type of data, while C can only return scalar types and pointers. A C return type need not be declared and is assumed to be *integer*, while Ada and Pascal return types must be declared.

Parameter values

In Ada and Pascal any data type may be passed to a subprogram, and values passed must be type-compatible with the declared formal parameters. In C, only scalar values and pointers may be passed, and the number and type of parameters need not match the formal parameters.

Additional considerations are parameter modes. C passes parameters by value only, and modification of actual parameters can only be done by using pointers.

Ada and Pascal have a value mode, called *in* in Ada and *value* in Pascal. Ada and Pascal also have a mode whereby a value may be passed and returned in an actual parameter in Ada called *in out* and in Pascal *variable*. Ada has a third mode, where values may be returned in the actual parameter but not passed to the subprogram, called *out* parameter mode.

External values

Ada has no provision for accessing external values, as in the case of *extern* storage class in C. The packaging concept eliminates the need for this sort of storage class, however, while keeping Ada's strong typing. Pascal does not use external values.

Scope

The rules for scope are almost identical for all three languages.

Static variables

Ada and Pascal have no *static* storage class as C does, but the same effect is realized in Ada by embedding a package containing declarations global to the package inside other packages. Thus a variable can be stored static inside the inner package, and used by one or more procedures inside the package.

Recursion

All three languages have similar recursive capabilities.

Conditional compilation

Ada and Pascal don't have built-in conditional compilation. In Ada conditional compilation under the language is done by writing a case statement with a constant as a switch value and hoping that the compiler will optimise the unreachable code out of existence. The Ada designers did envision condition compilation as part of the Ada support environment. Nothing says that you can't write a preprocessor for Ada, or even that you can't use a C preprocessor on the front end of Ada code.

Pointers

C has by far the most extensive array of pointers and operations, and the fewest restrictions on their uses. This is sometimes good and sometimes bad. Most of the good reasons for C's pointers are taken care of by other Ada features, such as being able to pass strings and pointers as parameters to subprograms. Ada's pointers are called "access types". The reason for this, it would appear chiefly, is because the DoD said that Ada couldn't have pointers. Ada pointers are used very much like Pascal's, with similar binding. Ada provides no pointer arithmetic, but pointer math can be faked using *size* attribute calls and unchecked conversion, at least to a system-dependent degree.

Strings

Ada strings are arrays of characters. The length of Ada strings is an integral part of the array, so no "end mark" is required, such as the commonly used *null* terminating C strings. This means that unlike C you can't trash areas beyond the ends of strings by accident. Some restricted string manipulation is possible in Ada by using slices and sliding. Variant strings may be implemented in the same way C does, by writing subprograms to manipulated strings. Ada allows unconstrained array passing to subprograms, similar to the conformant strings found in nonstandard Pascal. Standard Pascal has strings similar to Ada's but the lack of conformant array passing makes them almost unusable.

Subprogram pointers

Ada and Pascal have no equivalent to C's function pointers, so subprograms can't be passed as parameters to other subprograms. Ada subprograms can be passed as parameters at the instantiation of generic packages.

Data structures

Ada and Pascal have similar data structures, the two varieties being arrays and records. C also has arrays, and *structures* are the equivalent to Ada's nonvariant record type. Ada's variant records are similar to *unions* in C, except that Ada keeps track of the current composition of the record, while C does not.

I/O

Ada and C both used I/O written in the host language as functions or procedures. Pascal has I/O statements that are part of the language. Ada's I/O is more standardized than C's. The principal differences between the three languages are that Pascal allows relaxed type checking by the use of the I/O statements, which is convenient but restricts the user to the I/O provided by the language. C allows any number or type of parameters in calls, even if the called functions formal parameters don't match, and only scalar and pointer values, which makes possible functions like *printf*. Ada uses overloading and generics to provide bomb-proof type checking and the flexibility needed for I/O.

Memory management

As might be expected, because of C's liberal use of pointers C has a complete memory management system available for the programmer. In C you ask for a chunk of memory and you do what you want with it.

In Ada and Pascal you can have memory dynamically allocated, but it's only convenient to get it in a size that corresponds to a given data type, and the address is typed such that you can't easily ask for a character to be allocated and then assign the address to an integer pointer.

If desired, procedures or functions can be written in Ada to allocate and free up any sized piece of memory, and to convert the addresses to any desired type. It is easier to do this in Ada than in C, as the Ada memory manager will do the dirty work for you. Note however, that this sort of practice is not good Ada programming style.

Based literals

Numbers of other than base 10 are represented differently in Ada, C, and Pascal. Ada uses a notation where the sharp sign indicates a based literal to represent numbers in any base from 2 to 16:

```
<base(in decimal)> # <number> # { E <exponent> # }
```

2#1001# is 9 decimal. 16#FF# is 255 decimal.

C uses:

```
0x<number>           for hex notation, and
0<number>            for octal (a leading zero)
```

Pascal uses no based constants.

Comments

All three languages are stream-oriented languages where (theoretically) carriage returns are meaningless. However, Ada uses the carriage return to terminate a comment. All three languages allow a comment anywhere a space may occur, but if comments are embedded in Ada the program must continue on to the next line. Equivalent symbols are:

```
Ada        Pascal        C        name
--         (*            /*       start comment
{c/r}      *)            */       end comment
```

Context clauses

Ada's **with** and **use** clauses are similar to C's #include preprocessor directive except that in Ada the **with**'ed package does not have to be recompiled each time. Pascal doesn't have an equivalent form.

Additional features of Ada

Generics, Tasking, Pragmas, Derived Types, Packaging, Aggregates, Default Parameters, Named Parameters, Overloading, Private Types, Exceptions, Representation Specifications, and most Attribute Functions are concepts in Ada that have no close analog in Pascal or C. Translating these to C or Pascal will require a complete rethinking of the program structure.

Index

character type, 24, 25
choose symbol, 64, 83
Chop__Tree procedure, 248
Close, 114–115
COBOL, 270
column positioning, 133, 134
command parser, 268
comments, 18–19, 348
Compare function, 192–194
compilation, 4, 9
    conditional, 345–346
    separate, 98–100
compilation order, 100
compilation units, 100
compiler(s), 265–266
compiler directives, 50
compile-time errors, 9
compiling:
    with Janus, 298–300
    with SuperSoft, 298, 299, 300
composite types, 23, 24, 27, 148–172
    See also names of specific composite types
compound delimiters, 12
compound statement, 59
computer science departments, 270
Concatenate procedure, 194, 195
concatenation operator, 154
concurrent actions, 262
condition(s), 68–69
conditional compilation, 345–346
conditional entry call, 259
conditional expressions, 342
conformable types, 227
constants, 39, 41–43, 340–341
    deferred, 215
constrained arrays, 151
constrained record, 165
constraint, 46–47
constructs, structured, 3
context clause, 52, 92, 276, 277, 278, 348
context specification, 92
control flow analyzer, 268
control structures, 56–75, 343
conversion, 47–48, 343
    unchecked, 233
Copy procedure, 189–191
Countl procedure, 279–280
Count__Tree function, 245, 246
CP/M, 9–10, 249, 261, 265
C programming language, 340–348
C Programming Language, The (Kernighan and
    Ritchie), 241

Create, 114
customer task, 250
custom packages, 101

dashes, 14, 18–19
data abstraction, 3
data encapsulation, 4
DATA__ERROR, 113
data flow analyzer, 268
data literal, 19
data structures, 346
data types, 23–28, 340
    access, 23, 24, 179–182, 222
    arrays, 148–160, 222–223
    Boolean, 24, 26
    character, 24, 25
    conformable, 227
    custom, 27–28, 44–47
    designated, 179
    discrete, 24–26, 28, 221, 222
    encapsulation of, 213
    enumeration, 25–26, 27–28, 44–46, 48–50,
        127–129, 222, 279, 288
    fixed point, 173, 175–176, 221
    floating point, 173, 174–175, 221
    as generic formal parameters, 220–223
    integer, 25, 221, 222
    limited private, 105, 119, 216–217
    numeric type conversion and, 47–48
    parent, 178
    predefined scalar, 24
    private, 23, 24, 105, 119, 213–217, 221–222, 252
    real numeric, 173–176
    records, 148, 160–170, 223
    scalar, 23–26, 148
    string, 27, 187–212
    task, 23, 24, 250, 251, 252, 263
    universal real, 174
    user-defined enumeration, 25, 27–28, 44–46
    variant, 188–189
data typing, 3, 21–23
deallocation, unchecked, 234
decimal point, 20
declaration, 341
    access types, 180–181
    array types, 149–151
    constant, 41
    entry, 250
    generic, 218–219
    incomplete type, 182, 241
    subprogram, 52, 79–81
    subtype, 47

FORTRAN, 270
functions, 7, 78–79, 80, 344
   attribute, 49, 330–337

Gehani, Narain, 274
generic declarations, 218–219
generic formal parameters, 219–224
   objects as, 219–220
   subprograms as, 223–224
   types as, 220–223
generic objects, 219–220
generic program units, 4, 77, 107, 218–225
generic specification, 218–219
Get, 119, 121–123, 124–125, 287
Getchar procedure, 147
Get__Float, 147
Get__Int, 147
global variables, 81, 94
goto, 67–68, 93, 280, 344
graphs, syntax, 317–327
"greater than-equal to" symbol, 14
guard bits, 229
guard expressions, 256–257

Habermann, Nico, 274
hardware control, 239–240
High-Order Language Working Group (HOLWG), 2

IBM-PC, 249, 265
Ichbiah, Jean, 2, 272
identifiers, 15–16, 278, 340
if statements, 58–65
image attribute, 108
implicit conversion, 47
importer/exporter, 268
incomplete type declaration, 182, 241
index, 129
Index function, 131
index range, 14
information hiding, 90
initialization, 40–41, 181, 341
initialization code, 91–92
in-line assembler code, 232–233
in out parameters, 81, 82, 219
in parameter, 81, 219
input/output (I/O), 103–147, 347
   concept of, 104–106
   direct, 129–132
   enumeration, 127–129
   errors, 108–113
   functions, 7
   packages, 106, 137–146

page formatting, 132–133
   positioning, 133–136
   for real types, 126–127
   sample packages, 137–146
   sample procedure, 136–137
   sequential, 129–132
   text, 115–125, 132–133
instance, 218
instantiation, 44, 53, 106–108, 218, 224
integer(s), 20, 22, 23, 24, 221, 222
   text I/O for, 124–125
   unsigned, 279
integer operators, 32–35
integer type, 25
Intel Component Data Catalog, 240
interface pragma, 233
inter-language interface, 233
intermediate code, 9
interrupts, 261, 262
I/O errors, 108–113
I/O functions, 7
I/O packages, 106, 137–146
is, 90

Janus, 275–289
   compiling with, 298–300

KAPSE (kernal APSE), 267
keywords, 17–18

label, 14, 93, 344
languages, 270–271
last bit, 156, 163
LAYOUT__ERROR, 113, 135–136
length, 156
length clause, 229
Length function, 191–192
"less than-equal to" symbol, 14
library, 4
   standard I/O, 7
   subprograms in, 78
library unit, 100
   predefined, 301–316
limited private type, 105, 119, 221, 252
line length, 132, 133
line terminator, 119–120, 123, 287
linked lists, 182–184
linker, 267
linker commands, 277
literals, 97
   based, 347
   data, 19

waiting task, sleeping, 254
warm boot, 261
when statement, 66
while loop, 72–73, 3 ;

Width, 124, 125
with clause, 92–93, 96, 100
WordStar, 237, 267
Write, 130